Lesbian Lives

Identity and Auto/Biography in the Twentieth Century

Nicky Hallett

Pluto Press

LONDON • STERLING, VIRGINIA

First published 1999 by Pluto Press
345 Archway Road, London N6 5AA
and 22883 Quicksilver Drive, Sterling, VA 20166–2012, USA

British Library Cataloguing in Publication Data
A catalogue record for this book is available from the British Library

ISBN 0 7453 1132 6 hbk

Library of Congress Cataloging-in-Publication Data
A catalog record for this book is available from the Library of Congress

Designed and produced for Pluto Press by
Chase Production Services, Chadlington, OX7 3LN
Typeset from disk by Gawcott Typesetting, Buckingham
Printed in the EC by T.J. International, Padstow

For Lucy, my mum, who died at Chapter 4,
and for Rosie, who helped me through both.

Acknowledgements

I should like to thank Anne Beech, Editorial Director of Pluto Press, for her encouragement and clear advice in the early stages of this book's development; Robert Webb for his work in the later stages of production; and Helen Skelton for her patient and careful copy-editing.

I am grateful to the staff of the Fawcett Library, London Guildhall University, and of Sheffield City Archives for their help in identifying and retrieving archive material. Where the material is identifiable by author it is listed in the bibliography; otherwise it is referenced in the text: FL indicates the Fawcett Library and CC indicates the Carpenter Collection at Sheffield City Archives.

Nicky Hallett
April 1999

Contents

Cow Lick[1]

that day my hair was parted by a herd of heifers
summoned by my baton to the fence
gathering with eager faces as I talked
taptapped my ash twig on the wood
then one of them began to lick my hand
a strategy of seduction I later saw in lovers, to make me miss
    my thread
and another found my chin
so before long several simultaneously sucked
and salivated my face skin
with pink fronded tongues
foamed peagreen with masticated grass
the ecstasy was unspeakable
for them and for me
and shattered only by my mother
as I dripped saliva from my eyes lids
screaming ringworm

Preface

The purpose of this book is to explore lesbian lives. It takes snapshots of two periods within the twentieth century, the 1920s and 1930s, and the 1980s and 1990s. These are chosen, not necessarily because of assumptions that they can be contrasted as well as compared, but because it is possible to ask if there has been any change in the nature of lesbian (self-) representation over the course of a century. We might expect, for example, that the late nineteenth- and early twentieth-century sexological construction and depiction of lesbians might have been challenged or amended, even by non-lesbians, almost one hundred years later. We might expect to see new modes of lesbian self-expression, broadened or developed autobiographical paradigms. Most of all, and this is the main focus, we might expect articulation between the definitions of lesbians by non-lesbians and vice versa, and for the modes of discussion to reflect and define the ideas of sexuality promulgated in the respective periods.

Lesbian readers are hungry readers. If auto/biography[1] as a genre is in general popular, consumption of statements about lesbian lives in whatever form is especially voracious, yet not uncritical. For a heterosexual woman, the idea that she should seek out evidence that there are others around is nonsensical. Detecting testimony of other lesbian existence is an occupational habit of lesbians. Signs of life are sought in many places. This sounds desperate: it is often celebratory, and most of all it is habit-forming. Auto/biography is read beyond the pages of a single text about an individual life, therefore: it takes many forms of attestation to the way the life was led, with whom and with what choices of expressiveness of sexuality.

For women, particularly, auto/biography is often 'tucked away in other forms' (Heilbrun 1988, p. 75). This is the case for lesbians especially: and signs of life are seen as indicators of activity, of 'identity', beyond the moment. From a fragment, even an illusion, a philosophical construct is built. Lesbian Lives are not exemplary, they are just treated as if they are, with different motivation by lesbians and non-lesbians alike. There is a hagiography by detractors and by the empathetic, and the two interact in the formulation of lesbian iconography. I use the term 'auto/biography' in its broadest sense, therefore, to look at evidence of lesbian lives and the social construction put upon them across the century, as well as in the formal genre(s) of autobiography and biography themselves, to look at how lesbians are self- and other-presented.

The study of auto/biography needs to be broadly contextualised. In understanding why lives are depicted as they are when they are, we need to know not only about the subject of the Life herself, but also about the historical location of the author, and the political exigencies within which each, or both, operated. 'Lesbian history is not just the study of lesbian lives in the past but also the study of heterosexual patriarchy ... which determined the form that they took and the form of their resistance' (Auchmuty *et al.* 1992, p. 100). Much of this book, therefore, is contextual, analysing and describing the pressures of the period of inception (of both the subject life and the object Life, and to some extent of the reading life). This includes political, scientific and legislative backgrounds to the representation.

Naturally, it also includes consideration of the art of auto/biography, and of the lesbian as a subject within the genre(s). Here an early definition of terms is required. The 1920s and 1930s saw a wide range of trends in literature in English, many of them commonly encompassed within the term 'modernism'. Its experimentalism with new forms and styles was intended to disturb the reader and draw attention to the text itself. Fictional disruption of continuity and chronology, use of dislocated imagery, multiple points of view, affected notions (or vice versa) of the self. We might expect to see an effect in auto/biography and within it the depiction of lesbian, as other, lives.

Postmodernism is perhaps a more disputed term, related to Western culture from the 1980s, though 'if it is to be taken seriously [it] is not to be understood as a simple periodizing term ... Rather, the postmodern calls into question the very manner of thinking history' (Docherty 1996, p. 116). It is said, amongst other things, to be characterised by disconnection, fragmentariness and dissolution of originality. It may be seen as a continuation of alienations propounded within modernism, yet whereas modernism may have sought to find some coherence within its sense of chaos, the postmodern may claim an indifference to the point of this.

Such ideas of dissolution/disillusion may seem to be antithetical to the very unities and drives upon which ideas of the self are based. How can individuation be conceived of in such contexts, and how can auto/biography be written? How, in particular, is sexuality represented when ideas of gender and the definition of 'woman' as a collectively meaningful term within the feminist postmodern are so hotly contested? We might expect that the writing of a coherent Life would be well-nigh impossible, and that auto/biography as a genre would implode, or collapse like individual identity, beneath the weight of ontological angst. Yet the genre thrives. Bookshops are full of life studies which are the late twentieth-century bestseller, and studies of lesbian lives are included in that expansion.

The timebands offered by the concepts (and vice versa) are convenient to sample the lives of lesbians. The impact of these self-consciously literary-cultural and philosophical ideas on the formulation of a Life is, perhaps, more problematic.

I have already suggested that the notion of a Life should be expanded to include forms of representation surrounding it. Finally, we might ask, is there an individual and identifiable genre of lesbian auto/biography?

When ... the child becomes familiar with the cow's udder whose function is that of a nipple, but whose shape and position under the belly make it resemble a penis, the preliminary stage has been reached ...

Freud, *Standard Edition*, vol. 11, p. 87

Introduction

Bulling Heifers

Cows were a familiar sight in rural Warwickshire when I was growing up there in the 1960s. As now, in fields throughout the land, it was not unusual to see groups of young heifers cavorting with each other, one climbing on the back of the other. On being asked what they were doing, my mother would answer assertively, 'They're just bulling heifers.'

Presenters of the *Today* programme on BBC Radio 4 on 29 August 1997 did not use the phrase, but might as well have done so. Making it clear that this was the silly season for news, and that the item on homosexuality in birds otherwise would not have been included, John Humphrys exclaimed, 'Whatever next! I thought I'd seen it all. Are there other examples of this extraordinary behaviour in nature? ... Bearing in mind we are a family programme ... what do these creatures actually do?' The German scientist replied, 'Well, in herds of cows with a bull, it is rather like in a harem with one male to many females. In order to obtain the attention of the bull, the females act as if they are lovemaking. One assumes the position of the bull.' 'Whatever next!' cried John Humphrys again. 'And I thought you were a farmer!' said Sue MacGregor, moving on to the next item.

The discussion set up a series of implied oppositions which are common in anti-homosexual statements: inferred tension between natural and not, between real and pretend, between welcome and interloper. There could be no explanation made of the activity of the heifers without the presence of the bull whose attention was more desirable. The females make do with each other in his absence, or use each other cynically to attract or divert him. Lesbian heifers are presented as they are constructed, within the male heterosexual gaze, inexplicable without its presence. Theirs is not an alternative sexual expression, but a parody, an approximation. They only 'act as if' they are lovemaking: it is 'inconceivable that a woman's sexual pleasure could be significant if the male were absent' (Faderman 1981, p. 29). It follows that this 'phallogocentrism' of language has eliminated meaningful words for autonomous female sexuality (Cixous 1981; Irigaray 1977). Hence, the word 'heifer' has an inscribed heterosexual meaning or it makes no sense.

Starting Points: The Class of '94 and Lesbian Biography

This radio exchange gave me reinforcement for a framework of ideas which had begun to form some time before, with the observation that lesbianism is frequently obscured by normative smokescreens.

In 1994 I had asked a group of adult learners, studying for a degree in humanities, to read an auto/biography of their choice in preparation for a study of philosophies of the self. Of the group, five had chosen works about women who had had at some time in their lives at least one relationship which is commonly construed as lesbian (definitions of which are discussed on pp. 10–13): Elizabeth Bowen, Marlene Dietrich, Katherine Mansfield, Vita Sackville-West, Virginia Woolf.

We talked about how individual identity, including sexual, was manifested. The students had not picked up the possibility that the subjects were lesbians. We might consider that they simply had not read the texts carefully, but that turned out not to be the case. One did concede that she expected that Katherine Mansfield might have been bisexual. And another concurred that this might have been the case with Elizabeth Bowen. Maybe the students were too embarrassed to use the word 'lesbian'? But they showed no signs of being constrained. Rather it seemed that their eyes had been deceived by the quickness of the biographical pen, by the prestidigitation of matrimony. Of Virginia Woolf and Vita Sackville-West's relationships with women, one student commented, 'but they were married weren't they?' and 'they didn't name themselves lesbians'. Here, as in the biographies themselves which often do not name lesbian relationships, we can see both the 'perceptual screen of heterosexism' (Zimmerman 1986, p. 202), and the justification for invoking it.

'Lesbian' and 'Auto/biography'

This student debate pinpointed the dilemma for the whole discussion of lesbian lives. It immediately raised a question of the identification of lesbians, and the language of representation. 'Identity' itself is a problematic term (discussed on pp. 8–10) and its use always raises a question about upon whose definition that identity (if it exists) does exist. The student use of 'lesbian' was within parameters which had been defined by others in the absence of, or in counterpunction to, the women's self-definition. This is precisely the subject of this book: it explores the nature of the relationship between self and other definition. It is a study of the interconnectedness between what is expressed *of* lesbians in cultural discourse, and its effect on lesbian self-expression, and vice versa; of the interaction between social and cultural language of the other (broadly biography) and the ontology of self (broadly autobiography).

Since the strength of the debate is often in the hands of the determining, this can often appear a one-way process. Frequently, the power to define is in the pens or mouths of the non-lesbian. Hence I have included in my discussion texts produced by heterosexual females and males, since these may be seen to (try to, or actually) determine aspects of lesbian definition. Language is a site of power, and that which categorises sexuality seeks to define and control parameters of both action and description. The languages of eroticism tell us about ways that power is distributed, mediated and produced. Foucault has contended that techniques of control of sexuality were introduced in the nineteenth century, and that this resulted in the 'hysterization of women's bodies', the 'pedagogization of children's sex', the 'socialization of procreative behaviour' and the 'psychiatrization of perverse pleasure' (Foucault 1978, pp. 104–5).

To accept that there are power structures within conceptualisations of sexuality is not to say that I have adopted a Foucaultian stand. Nor do I consider without reservation that the state alone has defined homosexuality in order to control and legislate against it. Whilst there is undoubted advantage for the anti-homosexual to believe that sexuality can be categorised, Foucault has been felt to infer that the power always flows in one direction, that determination is by the dominant culture which, through its various manifestations of education, medicine, law, religion and the family, and via homosexual self-patrol, shapes and defines the practices of homosexuality.

Frequently, however, within the dominant paradigm of heterosexuality, lesbians self-define in ways which either subvert (a word which is itself suggestive of still remaining within an outsiders' discourse) or which establish alternative modes. Foucault's inference of homosexuals as passive and other-defined has been challenged, for example, by Oosterhuis in his critique of the hit-and-run: 'As far as individuals who are labelled as "perverts" are concerned, they have mainly been presented as passive victims of a medical juggernaut, having no other choice than to conform to medical stereotypes' (1997, p. 70).

While Foucault is alleged to have considered that early twentieth-century sexologists 'created' the homosexual by introducing the category, lesbian writers themselves aver

> that the so-called scientific production of the category homosexual as a congenital or pathological being in fact originated in a strategic effort by homosexual activists ... to define homosexuality in their own interests ... shaped by dominant culture ... while also attempting to shape that culture ... (White 1991, pp. 70–1)

It is possible, therefore, to see the process as two-way. Whilst those who claim the moral high-ground may seem to have the gravitational advantage of a waterfall, Escher-like and contrary to perception, the flow is in both directions.

In addition, the introduction of systematised taxonomies of sexuality may have had, whatever its intention, a liberating effect: 'once the social role – the label – is available, it enabled individuals to make meanings out of their experiences for themselves and others' (Wilton 1995, pp. 40–1).

My focus, then, is on the interchange of conceptions, how the language of the determiner (heterosexual or lesbian) and the (self-)determined (lesbian) relate, and how a protean notion of identity emerges. It has been important to include other-definition as well as self, in order to analyse the contested space. This may seem counter to lesbian-feminist aspirations: 'Never let your oppressor define you – that's what has hurt us all along' (CLIT Collective 1974). Here, the interest is how they *do* define, as a means of rolling back their language of oppression.

Locations

Several explorations of lesbians in various arenas have already been written.[1] Here, the primary focus is on narratives of the self, in autobiography and biography, genres which are themselves expandable to include modes such as obituary and life interviews. If 'The purpose of lesbian fiction is to "map out the boundaries of female worlds"' (Zimmerman 1992a, p. 21, quoting Lesbian Nation), then my purpose is to map the mapping done by the language of self- or otherhood.

Again, there is tension between directional flows: lesbians depicted in fiction may be used as authority for non-fiction statements about identity. Stephen Gordon, in *The Well of Loneliness* (1928), for example, frequently has been read as an autobiographical reflection of its author, Radclyffe Hall, from its early reception as 'an excellent description of the female invert' (Wolbarst 1931) to contemporary response (Walter 1997, p. 14). Clearly, too, there is leakage in other ways between autobiography manifested in fiction and non-fiction. A writer may use an autobiographical voice, or explore aspects of her life in a fictional text (Griffin 1991; Hanscombe 1991). On occasion, therefore, the relationship is explored here between a Life and the artistic embodiment of experience: fictional forms bear out ideas of autobiography, or vice versa. Works such as Virginia Woolf's *Orlando* (1928) and Daphne du Maurier's *Rebecca* (1938) operate on several boundaries, where autobiography and biography, personal history and fiction, intersect. Inclusion of such works reflects, too, the impact that fiction may have on the formation of the reader's self-consciousness:

> If you asked me to write a list of the first ten homosexual people with whom I had conversations, then the first eight of them would be fictional characters … Our relationship to fictional, fantastical or historical material is different to that of heterosexuals. (Bartlett 1994, quoted in Smyth 1996, p. 109)

But, for the most part, with exceptions like those mentioned, this is a study of non-fictional components, not because I deny the inter-relatedness, but because I have had to draw a line somewhere, however shaky it may appear.

Limits

Similar limitations have had to be set to the scope of discussion. I have primarily used material in English and about Britain. In any period this poses difficulties, let alone one in which the whole issue of nation and of 'Englishness' is so contested (with political devolution; issues of autonomy within the European Community; amidst transatlantic relations and postcolonial discourses). Material and events not in English,

or from outside Britain, naturally have an impact beyond the boundaries of the nation-state, just as fiction and non-fiction conflate.
Individual lesbians cross geographical boundaries, and cliques of influence and communication relate. Borders are not real, yet representation
is often culturally contingent, so generalisations cannot be made from
individual lesbian lives whose social privilege enabled stylistic osmosis
not available to others. The complexity of intercontinental and inter-
class crossings in lesbian style would be the subject of another study.
Translation occurs, too, in both linguistic and cultural senses. Where
particular events or texts affect definitions of lesbianism in English,
therefore, these will be used.

Equally problematic are time contours. Inconveniently, ideas leak
across time-frames. Unlike Virginia Woolf's hero Orlando, we do not
find at specific and exact periodic intervals, such as decade or century,
that 'A change seemed to have come over the climate of England' (1928,
p. 146). Whilst I began to work on a notional comparison of modernist
and postmodernist representation (crudely 1920s and 1930s; 1980s and
1990s), and this remains at the heart of the arrangement and study, this
became increasingly difficult and misrepresentative. Antecedents of
both 'movements' appear in earlier periods, and ideas of selfhood
change, endure and metamorphose. Some, but not many, references are
from between these periods, especially where this bears out the larger
narrative, or where an obituary appears for a lesbian whose life or statements of the 1920s or 1930s are of especial interest to self-definition.
Clearly, sexological discussion which arose from later nineteenth-
century debate had an impact on lesbian life definitions, and such
material is included as essential to the discussion of definitions.

'Race'

'Lots of black lesbians I know won't use the word lesbian, because they
see it as a white word' (quoted in Ainley 1995, p. 70); 'the white lesbian,
has become the quintessential representation of lesbian experience, of
the very concept of "lesbian"' (Omosupe 1991, p. 108).

Initially, I had planned to discuss the idea of representation as it
affects general conceptions of lesbians. I wished to incorporate material
by and about white lesbians and lesbians of colour. However, as a white
writer, whilst I do not claim that examples of white lesbian self-definition are 'exemplary', increasingly I felt that with black material I was in
danger of the Audre Lordeisation of material:

her work compactly represents that generally repressed matter towards which white feminists wish to make a gesture of inclusion, but since Lorde conveniently represents so much at once she can be included without her presence threatening the overall balance of the white majority vision. (Wilson 1992, p. 77)

Lesbian-feminists are not 'exempt from imperialist original sin' (Zimmerman 1992a, p. 175) in their assumptions, and have frequently sought to transfer, unproblematised, values from one arena to another. Oppression is not portable, however. Though some inferences may be read across and between racial contours, I have limited my discussion for the most part to white lesbians. I do not always use the denominator 'white' as a prefix, however, and propose to let the reader decide if discussion is racially apposite, or flawed by assumptions bound to punctuated nationhood.[2]

There is, however, discussion within the book about the assumed affinity within sexological debate between race and sexuality. Ideas of both, and of their intersection with class, run together in white sexological discussion, where the (inferior) 'other' is expressed in terms of 'exotic' and 'stranger'. Some oppressions may have originated from definitional sameness: as Alice Walker observed, 'the original "crime" of "niggers" and lesbians is that they prefer themselves' (1984, p. 289).

Representation

These 'exclusions' (alternatively, embracements of potential sameness sometimes unstated) suggest the limitations to 'representation', which otherwise may appear to be an all-embracing term, though Judith Butler, amongst others, has noted the instability of terminology surrounding this:

> On the one hand, *representation* serves as the operative term within a political process that seeks to extend visibility and legitimacy to women as political subjects; on the other hand, representation is the normative function of a language which is said either to reveal or to distort what is assumed to be true about the category of women. (1990, p. 1)

'Reveal' or 'distort' are relative terms, they depend on perspective. My interest here is in determining what axe a representor has to grind: identification of that, goes some way to disarming the tool-shaper.

Identity

'Identity', too, is a contested term within the buttery dictionary of the postmodern. Its definition may seem suspiciously straightforward, referring to self-perception, 'the enduring sense of oneself as a sexual being which fits a culturally created category and accounts for one's sexual fantasies, attractions and behaviours' (Savin-Williams 1995, p. 166).

The phrase 'culturally created' suggests the problem. Debates have ensued about whether a woman is born with an inherent and intact sexual nature or instinct (essentialism), or whether she is able to become (or resist becoming) a lesbian because of social conditions (constructionism); whether it is a matter of 'being' or of 'doing'. Essentialism infers that there are transhistorical and 'intrinsic culture-independent facts' about sexual orientation, whereas social constructionism denies that there are such facts in the absence of particular historical cultural conditions (Stein 1990, pp. 4–5).

Accordingly, essentialists contend that lesbians have always existed, and in all places. Constructionists, on the other hand, operate as nominalists, who consider that categories have been established for social purposes, and who identify the lesbian emerging at a culturally conducive moment from her chrysalis, when conditions in the nineteenth century allowed some social determination for women, a relative economic and sexual independence from men. Women came together in new ways at this time, it is argued, and same-sex relationships could take new form (Faderman 1981; Vicinus 1985).

The Lesbian, as a constructed category, therefore, is said to appear philosophically in the late nineteenth century. She only has a verifiable life, like any species, when she is named, when sexologists define her in an effort to control her by reference to difference: she is not, in constructionist/nominalist terms, a timeless type but has been 'actively constructed in a society which ... is predicated on male subordination of women through prevailing ideas of "femininity" including the requirement that the "feminine" woman be heterosexual' (Kitzinger 1995, p. 139). In other words, the lesbian is born to sexologist parents who despise her, who conceive her only in order to teach their 'normal' children a lesson.

The contestation surrounding 'identity' and its adjunct 'sexual' has led theorists to question the usefulness of the term: 'To what extent is "identity" a normative ideal rather than a descriptive feature of experience?' (Butler 1990, p. 16). Essentialism has become unfashionable:

theorists deny they espouse its ideas as hotly as the righteous deny that they are racists or feminists. Terms dissolve in the deliberately stoked crucible of definitions within the postmodern.

At a time when lesbians most clearly began to articulate their sense of personal and political identity, then the academic postmodern began to deny the primacy of the individual author (Barthes 1968; Foucault 1972, discussed on p. 144). This occurred when 'we [had] just begun to name our own world and to consider the full implications of women's friendships and the crucial role played by female networks of love and support' (Cook 1979, p. 720).

For muted groups who seek, via theories of the self or life narratives, to claim a social or personal place or history, the idea of the dissolution of knowableness within the postmodern is particularly challenging. Faced with a theory of dissipated self, which essentialism can no longer contain, the lesbian seeking a language of selfhood has sought to establish a politically resistant dimension, based on seeming contradiction within lesbian-feminism which

> relies *both* on the assumption that there *is* a 'lesbian identity' that we can search for and uncover both historically, and within our own lives, *and* that we all experience lesbian desire differently from our own specific social and cultural position, according to our class, our race, our economic and other circumstances. Identity politics are an ideological contradiction, and a political necessity. (Raitt 1995, p. xi; and see Zimmerman 1992a, p. 51)

Linda Hutcheon's model is partly helpful, it 'gives equal value to the self reflexive *and* the historically grounded' (1989, p. 2, my emphasis). Though she implies by the tension around 'and' that the self-reflexive may be incapable of historical grounding, her approach allows for the interplay of inner and outer pressures on ontological formations. It can 'investigate the determining role of representations, discourses and signifying practices. It can, in other words, address the matter of power' (Bertens 1995, p. 79).

The focus can then be on the embracement, or elusiveness, of power; on the fluctuations in the confidence with which lesbians assert an individual, or collective, identity, and on personal or collective epiphanies, without implying a singular or fixed 'identity'. Shifts of language, troughs and peaks of self-expression can be detected in individual attestation, within a broader context of an eroticised or supportive women's movement.

Within these spaces, individuals use language of social and sexual self, combined with 'lesbian', in various ways. To encompass these affidavits, my approach here is one not of evasion of the problematics of 'identity' but of movement into the turbulent arena of identity politics: 'We cannot escape the problem of identity, but only displace it and stage it as a problem' (Lejeune 1989, p. 44).

'Identity', then, may be (but is not inevitably) moveable and unfixed; individual testimony is not held to be representative of all (white) lesbians at all times and in all places, but rather is a snapshot, with cultural commentary, based on historicised meanings. Of course, even the subjects of photographs sometimes deny the veracity of a photo as a true likeness. Stilled for a moment, the subject will move after the shutter has flapped: identities are held, not indefinitely fixed, nor are they readable without some knowledge of the cultural or personal moment within which an individual has (re)positioned herself. Hence, there are hesitations in transferring ideas of identity between classes, and of an individual across time.

'Identity' is used, then, with the possibility of denial (the emphatic not-me-guv embedded in every cultural assertion). Like 'lesbianism' in Stimpson's terms, it 'might represent a space in which we shape and reshape our psychosexual identities, in which we are metamorphic creatures' (1990, p. 380). It is in this sense 'a matter of "becoming" as well as "being"' (Hall 1990, p. 225).

Reshaping may be individual (within one lesbian over time) or historical (within Lesbians as a category). Claims of a lesbian cultural identity are open to dangers pointed out in relation to international image markets: reduction to 'a national label stuck on what is essentially a transnational copy'; complacency in claiming our lesbian identity 'as standard-bearer for an alternative cultural imperialism'; or, most importantly, a reflex essentialism 'When the defence of cultural identity becomes confused with the defence of a fixed past [when] it runs the risk of fulfilling a strictly conservative role' (Mattelart *et al.* 1993, p. 429).

'Lesbian'

'Lesbian' is no exception to this rule of (non-) fixity. To use the term is to enter still further into the lexicographer's lions' den. I write 'term' rather than 'word' deliberately. Maybe 'phrase' would be closer still to the sense of the issues coagulating within and around 'lesbian'.

'A lesbian who does not reinvent the word is a lesbian in the process of disappearing' (Brossard 1988, p. 122). On this basis, there is no danger of imminent oblivion. Though popular discourse operates as if the word is self-explanatory, there continues to be debate about meaning.

Blanche Cook has argued that 'women who love women, who choose women to nurture and support and to create a living environment in which to work independently and creatively are lesbians' (1979, p. 739). This is broadly in line with definitions given by Lillian Faderman, for whom attachment of exclusively sexual phenomena is rejected as a component of male fantasy: for her the word 'describes a relationship in which two women's strongest emotions and affections are directed toward each other. Sexual contact may be part of the relationship to a greater or lesser degree, or it may be entirely absent' (1981, pp. 17–18).

Adrienne Rich has likewise sought to define beyond sexual preference, and attaches the word to 'a politics of *asking women's questions*, demanding a world in which the integrity of all women … shall be honored and validated in every aspect of culture' (1979, p. 17). Her description of lesbianism as a woman-to-woman cathexis has been felt to be problematic, since her notion of 'lesbian continuum' (1980) embraces all intensities between women. This dilutes awareness of the historical and social moment of an individual's formation of a sense of sexual(ised) self, and therefore fails to identify specific oppressions experienced by lesbians, according to Sheila Jeffreys for whom the question 'Does it matter if they did it?' is paramount (1989).

This question raises a plethora of further queries even if the answer is 'yes': ' … exactly what differences are at stake when acts, rather than identities are targeted for cultural attention' (Frandenburg and Freccero 1996, p. xx)? Does one act count? Does desire but no physical action suffice? And should it be desire over a lifespan (Kimmel and Sang 1995)? Does spasmodic desire qualify? And, if it is consummated desire, what is the nature of the activity to count as sexual? If lesbianism is behaviour in which 'carnality distinguishes it from gestures of political sympathy with homosexuals and from affectionate friendship' (Stimpson 1981, p. 363), what, then, if the 'lesbian' wavers? Some definitions would then cast her out: a lesbian 'does not fuck men. It does not mean compulsory sexual activity with women' (Leeds Revolutionary Feminists, quoted in Groocock 1995, p. 109). Axiomatically, nuns fall into this category along with all celibate others.

'Lesbian' is bound, too, with ideas of predestiny/free will. 'Choosing to be a lesbian' suggests choosing to act as one, to stage one's identity: internalised facets of sexuality become proven, a lesbian cannot merely be (and presumably, therefore, could not lead an isolated existence if her identity were not reinforced by others in front of whom she enacts) but has to do in order to be authentic or believed. Yet, in doing, she becomes a mystery, the truth of which is public.

The question of sex is conspicuously at the forefront when non-lesbians seek to understand lesbian sexuality. And yet there is a paradox here: to know someone as a lesbian is apparently to know everything about her (that she has sex with women), yet nothing (what do lesbians actually *do?*). This knowing of everything and nothing is therefore a source of double resentment. The same-sex-identified woman enters the room with a ventriloquist lesbian dummy: nothing she says is not lesbian, but what is she saying? 'The lesbian subject is not all I am and it is all I am. A shadow of who I am attests to my being there, I am never with/out this lesbian' (Meese 1990, p. 70).

Foucault's observation for the male homosexual is apposite:

Nothing that went into his total composition was unaffected by his sexuality. It was everywhere present in him: at the root of all his actions because it was their insidious and infinitely active principle; written immodestly on his face and body because it was a secret that always gave itself away. (Foucault 1978, p. 43)

Hence the paradox: lesbians are everywhere, lesbians are nowhere (Jagose 1994). Moreover, the same one is in both places at the same time.

Within this book, I am not concerned to make decisions about whether individuals engaged in sexual activity, but I am concerned about what it is said that they did, and what they claim for themselves as defining their identity. I am interested in perceptions, and how these are constructed within ideas of the sexual self; in the language of those who write of lesbianism (their own or others) and how they conceptualise the doing as a signifier of sexuality. Here it is evident that lesbians, because they are often talked about as if they are not present in the room, are in a particular power relation to the speaker. Lesbians are frequently objects, or conceptualise themselves as counterpoint to the dominant discourse. Hence, a lesbian is not only (or necessarily) a woman with same-sex emotional focus, but also one 'who has a sexual minority identity, that is, recognises through the use of language or symbolic expressions that her sexual orientation places her apart from a sexual mainstream, even though she may not use the term lesbian per se' (Brown 1995, pp. 9–10).

Within this book, my aim is to identify cliques of lesbian utterance (or silence). These do not necessarily relate to lived 'communities' such as groups of individuals who lived in certain geographical locations (like Smallhythe in Kent, or Paris in the 1920s and 1930s). Rather I am interested in ideas of transmission of identity, and how patterns of utterance emerge, either from antagonistic (anti-lesbian) statements or from the language of self-definition. Gombrich's model is useful, rejecting as it does the notion of collectivity which has so bedevilled notions of 'group' identity:

> The behaviour of insect colonies appeared to be so much governed by the needs of the collective that the temptation was great to postulate a super-mind. How else ... could the individuals of the hive respond to the death of the queen? The message of the event must reach them through some kind of telepathic process. We now know that this is not so. The message is chemical; the queen's substance picked up from her body circulates in the hive through mutual licking rather than through a mysterious mental fluid. Other discoveries have increased our awareness of the relation between the individual and the hive. (1967, p. 50)

This may seem to suggest my interest is indeed in physical activity as a signifier! Rather, it should indicate my curiosity about how individuals go about constructing an identity, what messages they pick up and from whom, how 'lesbian' is constructed as an adjective and a noun.

Selection and Self-selection

If I elide the definition of 'lesbian', how can I select material about which to write? I have chosen to consider women who identify as lesbian themselves; are labelled as such; whose life suggests a woman-identification; about whom discourse operates within lesbian innuendo (meant as a positive term for accretion of aspersion[3] which may be meant to be negative but which creates lesbian space by default). I have asked Judith Schwarz's questions of lesbians, 'Did they know? And did they act on that self-knowledge? And if they didn't, did they still, to all intents and purposes, live their lives as if they had?' (1986, p. 85).

I have followed the assumption that the word 'lesbian' has a certain stability that can be historically investigated when

> It is hard for me to believe that the question of 'lesbian being' should be exempt from the Derridean critique of being in general – something we presume and assume, attributing it to some essential or transcendental state, in order to speak about it ... 'lesbian being' is

something which is 'there', when 'there' shifts and exchanges itself to suit the speaker, who also exchanges herself (making more of us). (Meese 1990, p. 81)

Selection has not ended with others, of course. I have struggled, too, about which grammatical persona to use, the first or third person. This is not merely in recognition of the shakiness of the ontological 'I', or in deference to the postmodern danger that the I who begins to write may disperse en route and fluctuate over the book's course. My real issue has been one of ease of speech. I have frequently found myself knotted up around the 'I' in the lesbian 'we', and indeed the 'we' in that. My approach is not one of case studies 'which claim a representative status for their subjects' experiences' (Montefiore 1994, p. 71).[4] It is instead one of individual attestation, however transitory that might be, and the effect of that testimony on other discourse. This is not unproblematic:

> What or who is it that is 'out', made manifest and fully disclosed, when and if I reveal myself as a lesbian? What is it that is now known, anything? ... To claim that is what I *am* is to suggest a provisional totalisation of this 'I'. (Butler 1991, p. 15).

Some lesbians reject use of the first person singular. Janet Flanner, for example, asserted 'The trick is never to say "I". You're safer with one or it. "I" is like a fortissimo. It is too loud' (Wineapple 1989, p. 104). This is no use. Using 'one' is clumsy in English, and suggests an aloofness of royal disdain. Somehow, referring to a lesbian as 'it' is even less conducive.

Monique Wittig was partly helpful. She considered how the use of personal pronoun, and gender, mutually reinforce, and offers 'j/e' to underline the false unity contained in 'je' (1975). 'I' is less easily severed. In any case, my hesitation about first person was not *only* in observation of rhetorical non-unity, and was also in deference to a destabilised, solitary subject in poststructured women's narratives of self.

For several reasons, then, I have settled for using the third person. This is clearly not to claim impartiality. It does, however, serve to remind that I am writing about what is said of 'the lesbian'. And, most of all, it saves me disappearing into linguistic tail-chasing, when for example, ontology gets complicated, when at moments I, she and we conflate, or when I am writing about how 'we' (lesbians) write about what 'they' (non-lesbians) say about 'them' (lesbians as other).

I will write about 'the lesbian' and 'she' to differentiate between me and the subject. None the less, it is undoubtedly an 'I' who seeks to construct ideas of definitional communities. They did not magically self-select.

Sources

It may be redundant within the postmodern to justify use of 'popular' sources. Belief in a hierarchy of documents, we might feel, is a feature of past theory. Certainly, in exploring ideas of the Lesbian, newspapers and advertisements, TV programmes and magazine photographs are all indicative of cultural attitudes, whether held, reinforced or promoted for whatever political purposes. So language of the self is constantly reinforced or disrupted by cultural references from disparate sources.

Personal testimony, likewise, is as legitimate as theorised positions of selfhood within a feminist discourse. To underline this, writers often interweave autobiography and theory to create open and fluid critiques of gender and sexuality.[5]

Because my interest is in what is said *of* a person, as well as by them, my sources are often unashamedly secondary. I also use primary material, such as wills and obituaries. The distinction between primary and secondary is difficult here: obituaries are primary sources but by definition secondary to the subject. In the bibliography, I list all sources together for ease of the reader, though archival sources are mostly indicated within the text since their listing is problematic (sometimes the author is not named).

Evidence

Both personal and other testimony has its problems. 'Every group in power tells its story as it would like to have it believed, in the way it thinks will promote its interests' (Becker and Horowitz 1972, p. 48). This is true of those who are labelled by anti-lesbians and those who self-define, depending on their power at that time. It is also true of individuals not in power, who, when oppressed or fearful may present themselves in the best way to the listener to avoid trouble. In the language of both powerful and powerless, however, can be heard 'the voice and longings' of each (Brown 1984, p. 277).[6] The context for these longings, and the sounds that they make, and a possible explanation of why, constitutes an historicised sense of lesbian meaning.

I have chosen to write about a range of women whose lesbian existence is evidenced by their friendships, employment, living
arrangements, book dedications, by their posthumous life (wills, rituals
of death and burial spaces, and obituaries) and by aspersions cast in,
and after, their lifetimes.

Friends

Sometimes it may seem as if identification of the lesbian is 'through an
inexhaustible accumulation of connotations, never proven, but
perhaps more or less probable' (Hart 1994, p. 66). That probableness
can be realised, or reinforced, through research of networks of women
whose professional and daily lives intersect, to obtain a sense of 'a
social self lodged within a network of others' (Stanley 1992b, p. 194).
Rosemary Auchmuty (1989) in this way has delineated a 'community'
in North Lambeth from 1880–1940. Her title, 'By their friends shall we
know them', is apt.

Some groups of friendships intersect, and we can gain a sense of
lesbian intergroupings, across continents in some cases. Speedboat
champion Joe Carstairs's friends included the actors Tallulah Bankhead
and Marlene Dietrich, and the writer Radclyffe Hall, amongst others,
some of whom were her lovers (Summerscale 1997). In turn, associates
of Radclyffe Hall and her lover Una Troubridge include Gwen Farrar, an
actor, who gave a dance in June 1923 at which they met Teddie Gerard,
'a wild girl who took drugs, drank too much, and loved women hard
and fast' (Baker 1985, p. 158). She, too, was friends with Tallulah
Bankhead, and introduced her to Hall and Troubridge.

A further circle opened up with the move of Hall and Troubridge to
Rye, where there were several lesbian households nearby, among them
Edy Craig living with Christopher St John and Tony Atwood; Lady
Maud Warrender with Marcia van Dresser; and Mary Allen, pioneer
policewoman, with 'Miss Taggart'.[7] The Kent–Sussex circle included
Vita Sackville-West and through her, Virginia Woolf. Ethel Smyth was
friends with Edith Somerville and Virginia Woolf, who was acquainted
with ('that goose') May Sarton, who in turn was intimate with Elizabeth
Bowen (Sarton 1976). The lesbian 'hive' (in Gombrich's term) is thus
configured. This is not, of course, to deny the existence of those who
lived beyond such groupings, but to suggest a model by which identities were transmitted.

In visiting Paris, English lesbians came to know members of the
circle there, around Natalie Barney and Gertrude Stein (Benstock 1987).

And women such as Marlene Dietrich who travelled widely intersect with various groups: Ginette Spanier had a relationship with Dietrich and with Nancy Spain, who in turn had association with Elizabeth Bowen and Jackie Forster, amongst others (Collis 1997).

More satisfying for the lesbian detective are the more obliquely documented associations. Sarah Reddish and Sarah Dickenson, friends in the Womens' Trade Council in the early twentieth century with Eva Gore-Booth and Esther Roper, always appear together in contemporary records. Though Dickenson was married, her husband appears little in records of her life, in contrast to Reddish, and this has led to the conclusion that the two were lesbians (Hamer 1996, p. 60).

Similar particular woman-centredness is seen in references to a nurse, Ethel Dunbar, and to other women in obituaries and life records (discussed on p. 98).

Employment and Occupation

Formal employment can suggest social-sexual preference, especially when it intersects with circles of friendship. The historian Veronica Wedgwood was Stevie Smith's editor at Cape publishers and became her friend (Spalding 1989, p. 165). Wedgwood wrote leaders almost weekly for *Time and Tide*, known as the 'Sapphic Graphic', founded in 1920, owned and edited by Viscountess Rhondda and her partner Theodora Bosanquet, and informed by 'intense feminism' (Keith-Cohen 1987). *Urania*, another lesbian magazine, founded in 1915, attracted a circle of women to its publication, including Eva Gore-Booth and Esther Roper, amongst others.

Particular signals of independence, often associated with lesbianism, can be seen in the occupation of Joe Carstairs as a motorboat pilot, and Eve Balfour and Margot Gore as air pilots (*Daily Telegraph*, 16 January 1990; *The Times*, 25 September 1993, respectively). Evelina Haverfield and Vera Holme worked together in a women's hospital unit in France, then travelled to Serbia, where Evelina Holme died in 1920 (Hamer 1996, p. 56); they, like Toupie Lowther, who founded an all-woman ambulance unit in 1917 (pp. 50–3), were in some personal danger. We cannot infer lesbianism from gallantry, of course, but can recognise independence as a signifier, and that lesbians themselves may have used this to express a sense of self, in fulfilment of Richard von Krafft-Ebing's characterisations of lesbians who find 'pleasure in the pursuit of manly sports, and in manifestations of courage and bravado' (1894, p. 355).

Living Arrangements

Domestic arrangements, though not decisive, are indicative of emotional focus.

Mary Allen, policewoman, lived with Margaret Damer Dawson between 1914 and 1920, when Dawson died. Records from the early 1930s show Allen living in the house left to her by Dawson, with a Miss Taggart (Baker 1985, p. 267). Eve Balfour, organic horticulturist, in a 1989 *Country Living* article is recorded as living alone, 'since the death of her close friend of fifty years' (Collis 1994, p. 154); and Lilian Barker, prison governor, lived with Florence Francis for some 40 years (Gore 1965, pp. 61–6). Rosa Bonheur's living arrangements are of interest: she lived with Nathalie Micas for many years, and then with Anna Klumke. Though Bonheur's French nationality takes her beyond the subject of this study, the ways in which her cohabitation is desexualised by Germaine Greer (1979) is of interest in formulations of sexuality in English (discussed on p. 128). The politics of domesticity, and the way they are countenanced, are of great importance when determining lesbian identity.

Angela Burdett-Coutts lived with Hannah Brown for 52 years (Auchmuty 1989, p. 79); Ivy Compton-Burnett with Margaret Jourdain for 31 years; Edy Craig lived with Christopher St John from 1899 until Craig's death in 1947, with Tony (Clare) Atwood joining them from 1916 (Cockin 1998, p. 61); Eva Gore-Booth with Esther Roper for 30 years, in Manchester and in Hampstead (Hamer 1996, p. 58); Octavia Hill with Harriot Yorke for 35 years (Auchmuty 1989, p. 80; 1992, p. 9); Christine Murrell with Honor Bone and with Marie Lawson for over 30 years (St John 1935, p. 35) and Elizabeth Robins with Octavia Wilberforce from 1908 until she returned to the US in 1940 (Whitelaw 1990, p. 113). If this sounds like a Who's Who of relationship longevity, it should also be remembered that *not* living together, of course, does not indicate lack of lesbian identity. Several married women who lived with their husbands had lesbian lovers (Virginia Woolf and Vita Sackville-West, for example) and doubtless many *un*married women did not live in a home with their lovers. Domestic cohabitation is not a definitive sign. None the less, the life records of numerous women attest to their women-centred daily existence.

Book Dedications

Ascriptions in books leave particularly notable records of relationships.

Sheila Jeffreys dedicated *The Lesbian Heresy* to Sandy Horn, 'In warmest lesbian friendship' (1994, p. vii). Similarly transparent in its association is Virginia Woolf with *Orlando* (1928), 'To V. Sackville-West'.

Other dedications are more oblique. Maureen Colquhoun's autobiography *A Woman in the House* (1980) has a 'Dedication – for B.T.' (Barbara Todd) (see p. 153). Clemence Dane's *Regiment of Women* (1917) is dedicated to 'E.A. / Here's Our Book / As it grew. / But it's Your Book! / For, but for You, Who'd look / At My Book? / C.D.' (Elsie Arnold was her lover for many years).

Other inscriptions suggest wider networks. Micky Jacob's circle is revealed by the nexus of dedications surrounding her. She dedicated *Me – and the Stags* (1964) to Angela du Maurier, who is also recalled in Nancy Spain's *Poison for Teacher* (1949) which features a school called Radclyffe Hall. Nancy Spain dedicated her novel *Out Damned Tot* (1952) to her lover Joan Werner Laurie 'with much love and gratitude'.

Cannily, Christopher St John had a dual dedication, to Honor Bone and Marie Lawson, in her biography *Christine Murrell M.D.* (1935). Written at the request of Honor Bone, Murrell's lover, the book acknowledged the fact that Murrell, like St John herself, lived with two women, both of whom had loving significance for her.

More recently, one lesbian biographer records another in a biography of a third: Lis Whitelaw's work on Cicely Hamilton (1990) is 'In Memory of Rosemary Manning'.

Posthumous Association

The rituals of death can reinforce, or challenge, the sense of a woman in life.

Letters written after the death of their partners reflect the acceptance of enormous grief, a sign that the status of their relationship was recognised. Honor Bone received a 'vast number of letters' when Christine Murrell died (St John 1935, p. 129). Ivy Compton-Burnett, generally intensely private, wrote on the death of Margaret Jourdain, 'It is the loss itself that I cannot get over, and I find it hard to look forward' (Sprigge 1973, p. 131). Eva Gore-Booth's sister, Constance Markievicz, recorded of Esther Roper, 'I feel so glad that Eva and she were together and so thankful that her love was with Eva to the end'. She wrote to Esther

Roper herself in 1926, that Esther's grief was of a different order as she 'was so much nearer her body than I was' (Roper 1934, pp. 314, 315).

Death-bed scenes are suggestive of associations, and not only of the deceased. When the poet W.B. Yeats died in 1939, at his bedside were Edith Shackleton Heald, his lover who later lived with the lesbian painter Gluck, and Dorothy Wellesley and her lover, Hilda Matheson (Cullingford 1993, p. 269). When Hilda Matheson herself died in 1940, Wellesley placed a plaque at her home which reads 'Amica Amicorum' (Hunter 1994, p. 174). In a distraught state, she was herself comforted by Vita Sackville-West, who had been Hilda's lover in 1928 (Glendinning 1983, pp. 305–6).

Significantly, many lesbians are buried with their partners. Père Lachaise cemetery in Paris commemorates Rosa Bonheur, Nathalie Micas and Anna Klumke in the same grave. Their tombstone is inscribed 'L'amitié, c'est l'affection divine'. Gertrude Stein and Alice B. Toklas are likewise interred together. Their tombstone records Stein, who died first, on the front, and Toklas on the rear.

Edy Craig (d. 1947) is buried in Smallhythe, Kent, with Christopher St John (d. 1960) and Tony Atwood (d. 1963); and Eva Gore-Booth (d. 1926) is buried in Hampstead with Esther Roper (d. 1938), their headstone bearing a quotation, said by Esther Roper to be from Sappho, 'Life that is Love is God' (Hamer 1996, p. 74).

Radclyffe Hall purchased a catacomb in Highgate cemetery on the death of her lover, Mabel 'Ladye' Batten (1916), and she is buried there with her. Hall had tried, too, to erect a tablet in Batten's memory, on the church wall in St Wulfstan's, Malvern Wells, but her request was turned down, ostensibly because the priest disliked wall tablets, but 'We may guess the real reason, for the relationship between the curious occupants of White Cottage had been the subject of persistent rumours in the village' (Baker 1985, p. 80).

Una Troubridge, Hall's subsequent partner, wished to be buried with Hall and Batten: her will of January 1944 specified that her coffin-lid plaque should read 'Una Vincenzo Troubridge / The Friend of Radclyffe Hall / Arrive at last the blessed goal / When he that died in the Holy Land / Would reach us out the shining hand, / And take us as a single soul' (Baker 1985, p. 349). As it turned out, Troubridge's will was discovered too late for her wishes to be followed. She died in Italy, and in Rome's Verano cemetery her grave reads 'There is no death (Radclyffe Hall)'.

Octavia Hill (d. 1912) and Harriot Yorke are buried together in the churchyard at Crockham Hill, near Edenbridge in Kent; and on

Valentine Ackland's death (in 1969) Sylvia Townsend Warner erected a gravestone with both names, her own dates left blank. When she died (in 1978), an envelope marked with Valentine's name was cremated with her (Harman 1989).

Wills, likewise, leave evidence of emotional ties. Several lesbians left legacies to their lovers: Mary Allen was left a home by Margaret Damer Dawson (Baker 1985, p. 267), Margaret Jourdain bequeathed Ivy Compton-Burnett her estate and royalties (Sprigge 1973, p. 131). Clemence Dane's will of 1956 reflects her shifting romantic attachment, and names Olwen Bowen-Davies as an executor and major beneficiary, to inherit her house in St John's Wood in which her previous lover, Elsie Arnold was at that time living, with the rider that Elsie could live in the house for life if she so wished (Hamer 1996, p. 87).

Few lesbian requests associated with death are so enticingly exact as that of actor and suffragette, Vera Holme. On the death of her lover, Evelina Haverfield, in 1920, she was required by the executors to remove her belongings from their shared house, and she sent to them a list of requests for particular gifts. It mentions '1 bed with carved sides [inscribed with] EH and VH' (Hamer 1996, p. 56).

If lifetime attestations suggest a relative assertiveness on the part of lesbians, we cannot assume that posthumous accounts over which they had no control are so straightforward as evidence of their sexuality. A bereaved lesbian partner, for example, may be disenfranchised by her lover's family: 'I went to the flat – I had waited too long, everything had been stripped, no trace of our things ... everything cleared out ... as though we had never been there' (in Neild and Pearson 1992, p. 79).

Similarly, in accounts of funerals, the bereft can often seem 'not there' or a less significant other, such as Radclyffe Hall in lists of attendees at Ladye Batten's funeral (see Chapter 3, note 9). Sometimes, on the other hand, such accounts are useful at least for establishing a sense of lesbian association. The report of the mass for Micky Jacob in *The Times* (5 October 1964, FL) listed members of the congregation, including representatives of the International Alliance of Women, the Suffragettes' Fellowship and other alliances. Women appearing here may be linked to others, cross-referencing aspersion, and adding to the 'accumulation of connections'.

The report of the funeral of Cicely Hamilton in *The Times* (13 December 1952, FL) included a range of women with feminist connections, including Theodora Bosanquet, partner of Lady Rhondda. From these lists, historians can establish networks, make cross-connections.

Cicely Hamilton's will recorded her gratitude for Lady Rhondda's friendship, and the latter wrote an obituary of Hamilton (Whitelaw 1990, pp. 108, 112). When Lady Rhondda shows up again, for example, in *The Times* announcement (16 June 1958, FL) of the inaugural meeting of the Octavia Hill Society, sending sprigs of rosemary for remembrance, then we can begin to derive a real idea of lesbian affiliation.

Obituaries, by definition, are out of the hands of the deceased. The language they use to describe, or not, the personal relationships and sexuality of departed lesbians is a facet of auto/biography, and the subject of a particular and separate study (pp. 95–103).

1
Historicised Contexts:
Lesbianism in the 1920s and 1930s

> Both muted and dominant groups generate beliefs or ordering ideas
> of social reality at the unconscious level, but dominant groups
> control the forms or structures in which consciousness can be artic-
> ulated. Thus muted groups must mediate their beliefs through the
> allowable forms of dominant structures. (Elaine Showalter, quoted
> in Rose 1986, p. 249)

Gayatri Spivak (1988) has asked 'Can the subaltern speak?', a question
about the capacity of a member of a marginalised group to use
anything but her master's voice, to be an agent as well as a (potentially
resisting) subordinate. She has answered herself (1990) in recognising
the 'subject-effects', the ways in which the subaltern can organise
narrative resistance. Showalter, too, has argued that a 'double-voiced
discourse' can be heard in which a member of a muted group is both
passive and active, both shares in the language of the determining and
in her own formation of reality.

Such double voices can be heard in lesbian autobiographical narrative, where the writer both negotiates around received statements and
establishes her own language. In an economy of words, language is
borrowed, if only temporarily, and returned with interest.

By the 1920s a number of theories of sexuality were in the public
arena, through magazines and books (Brimstone 1991, p. 95). Whilst
we cannot generalise about circulation of this material on the basis of
ownership by a social elite, we know, for example, that the writer Vita
Sackville-West owned several books on the psychology of sexuality.
These included works by Havelock Ellis and Edward Carpenter, as well

as Otto Weininger's *Sex and Character* (1903), her copy of which is inscribed with 'V.N. Polperro 1918' on the flyleaf (Glendinning 1983, p. 405).[1] It was to Polperro, in Cornwall, that she went that year with Violet Keppel, at the beginning of their sexual relationship (see Chapter 2, note 13), about which Sackville-West wrote, a narrative subsequently contained in *Portrait of a Marriage* (1973). The very title suggests the context of her negotiation of realities. Just so are theory and practice dramatically related in the formation of a lesbian aesthetic.

Sexology

It has commonly been said, after Foucault's *The History of Sexuality*, that 'the homosexual' was discovered when ideas about sexuality were formulated for the first time in the late nineteenth and early twentieth centuries, in an attempt to control sexual activity. It is clearly not the case that same-sex relationships only began to *happen* at that point, but that they were *described* in certain new ways. There is increasing evidence[2] to chart pre-nineteenth-century lesbian 'emotions, desires, tastes and behavioural tendencies that make up an identity' (Donoghue 1993, p. 3).

Assertions that notions of 'the lesbian' did not exist before the period are belied by the women themselves. Ida Wylie, for example, an Austrian-born lesbian who worked in England (described as 'spirited, volatile ... promiscuous', Baker 1985, p. 221) reviewed *The Well of Loneliness* for the *Sunday Times* (5 August 1928). She stated there that the male prototype of homosexual had always existed, and now was acknowledged in women (Hamer 1996, p. 103). She inferred that the female was a copy of the male[3] and operated within both an essentialist framework, as though homosexuality had always existed, and a constructionist one, as though the phenomenon was only now identified.

The early sexologists themselves indeed wrote as essentialists, as though 'deviant' sexuality was not new, but newly explained. Yet they are critiqued as if they were the original constructionists, creating the category. They formulated their ideas within the context of a rise of the case study and of classification systems more broadly, in parallel to Darwinian taxonomies, for example.[4] Within a range of cultural imperialist philosophies, sexological methodologies and concepts of species and hierarchy attained an influential authority.

Richard von Krafft-Ebing's *Psychopathia Sexualis* (1894, expanded several times to 1924, and frequently translated) is one example of such classification. It studied non-procreative sexuality, and provided a psychiatric evaluation of deviancy, for the use of lawyers and doctors, discussing sexual crimes, and advocating a general pathology (neurological and psychological) of sexual anomalies. Around 200 case studies of deviant sexual behaviour follow this analysis, and homosexuality is placed among other manifestations, including necrophilia, bestiality and coprophilia. The writer's declared purpose was for homosexuality to be considered as an illness rather than as a crime, so to be treated with compassion in the justice system.

Along with Karl Westphal, who in 1870 coined the phrase 'contrary sexual feeling', and Karl Heinrich Ulrichs, whose 1864 pamphlet formulated the idea of the third or intermediate sex (Miller 1995, pp. 13–14), Krafft-Ebing's work was highly influential in systematising white European ideas about sexuality. Notions of lesbianism thus became medicalised. This is an approach taken up, too, in English by Havelock Ellis in his *Studies in the Psychology of Sex*, first published in 1897.[5] Ellis's theories were also based on case studies from which were extrapolated general features of deviancy. Lesbians he characterised as suffering from character inversion, and he identified common characteristics, based ostensibly on observation of morphological differences:

> The brusque, energetic movements, the attitude of the arms, the direct speech, the inflections of the voice, the masculine straightforwardness and sense of honor ... will often suggest the underlying psychic abnormality to a keen observer. In habits not only is there frequently a pronounced taste for smoking cigarettes, often found in quite feminine women, but also a decided taste and tolerance for cigars. There is also a dislike and sometimes incapacity for needlework and other domestic occupations, while there is often some capacity for athletics. (quoted in Miller 1995, p. 19)

He also observed that green is a favourite colour of inverts, but not the general population; that a large percentage of male inverts are unable to whistle, a manly trait, but female inverts can whistle admirably; and that inverts of both sexes are youthful and have a childlike appearance.

Each of these writers conflated ideas of sexuality with those of gender, its related attributes and activity, and they established a normative framework in heterosexuality. Homosexuality, moreover, was construed as cross-gender confusion, combined by some writers with a spiritual component: lesbians embodied male souls (Krafft-Ebing 1894, p. 355) and Oscar Wilde was 'a feminine artist in the body of a man' according to Edith Ellis (1924, p. 53). Without actually describing the 'touchstone' sexuality, therefore, lesbianism was conceptualised as a subset of both heterosexuality and of masculinity, against an inferred, but rarely described, normality. Heterosexuality was equated with nature via ideas of procreation: the further association of women with nature (Showalter 1990) meant that homosexual women were somehow a double aberration which reinforced the normal by default. The idea of norm is thus safe from analysis because it is only defined by homosexuality's failure to meet its typological standards: it only exists in contrast to the case-studied deviancy. Furthermore, this established heteroness as healthy by contrasting homosexuality as illness. Sexologists thus moved ideas of lesbianism from crime to medicine, and embodied them in a language bound up with moral ideas of selection:

> They could not foresee that translating contempt for pity, punishment into treatment would not increase social acceptance for homosexuals but side-track scientific investigation for generations. To try to cure what is not an illness in the first place is like trying to weed a field without knowing the nature of the crop. (Rule 1975, p. 15)

'Not-weed' is defined by default. Psychological discussion likewise embeds notions of the norm through avoiding its catalogue. Sigmund Freud classified homosexuality as 'a variation of the sexual function, produced by a certain arrest of sexual development' (Letter, 9 April 1935, Abelove 1993). Many texts (such as Jones 1927; Wolfe 1935) classified female homosexuality as a retreat from adulthood, and considered that unsatisfied sexual impulse, typical within lesbians, led to frigidity and neurosis (Meagher 1929). Women were constructed as less sexed than men (Rosanoff 1929). Generalisations were made from the male heterosexual prototype to the female homosexual (Roof 1991, p. 204; and see O'Connor and Ryan 1993).

Even some books of the period which discuss lesbianism in relatively positive terms do so from a defensive impulse. Hence, the title of Laura Hutton's *The Single Woman and Her Emotional Problems* (1935) suggested its approach. She wrote of 'intense emotional relationships ... [where] emotional conflicts and tensions will inevitably arise' (p. 28). Though she was trying to justify female friendships, her tone was pejorative: 'some sexual experience may indeed play quite a useful part in society at the present day' (p. 121), 'It is fairer to describe such women as sexually abnormal (or anomalous) rather than perverted, bearing in mind always that the abnormal is not necessarily diseased' (p. 131).

Medicalisation of sexuality was not new to the twentieth century. Examples of biological assessment of lesbians can be seen, for example, in the eighteenth century, when masturbation, and physical symptoms such as an enlarged clitoris, were equated with same-sex desire (Brown 1986, p. 18; Dekker and van de Pol 1989, p. 52). Likewise, binary dialogues can be detected at least as early as 1742.[6]

If the configurations themselves were not entirely new, the production of texts in the early twentieth century established a space for lesbian discussion. Several journals published material. Among them, *The Freewoman*, a feminist journal, printed the correspondence in 1912 between Kathlyn Oliver and Stella Browne, on sexual desire. *Urania* (founded in 1915) and *Time and Tide* (founded in 1920) both contained articles on the subject (see Hamer 1996, pp. 23–7, 67–74): 'the discourse of medicalisation gave other women a language to define and celebrate lesbian eroticism and to form identities and communities on the basis of their shared sexuality' (Carlston 1997, p. 192).

The Law

Normalisation is embedded in the law which postures as neutral. It is often asserted that, since lesbianism as such was not illegal, lesbians have not suffered from the legalised persecution of male homosexuals. This is not strictly true. The term 'sodomite' was applied to both sexes, and working-class women, particularly, were routinely arrested for prostitution, an 'umbrella term for women's sexual transgressions' (Robson 1992, pp. 31–2).

In 1921 there was British parliamentary debate about whether to introduce legal sanctions against lesbianism as such (extracts from which are discussed on p. 104). The would-be legislators considered that introducing a law would itself draw attention to the existence of an otherwise unheard-of offence, rather as if establishing the category of forbidden fruit itself led to the fall. In other words, they 'presumed that the act would not flourish in the absence of a signifier. Naming the activity threatened to produce the category ... [Yet] If the act could not precede the signifier, then what was the content that necessitated concealment?' (Hart 1994, p. 3).

The Church

Articles of religion of the period likewise have a performative[7] effect, but by their silence. Like the law, state religion seeks to protect the sanctity of marriage yet, within articles of faith, lesbianism is presented as oddly innocent. Sexual acts, by definition of contemporary religion, required a penis, so the church 'effectively erased lesbianism through the agency of language' (Glasgow 1992, p. 242). Here, too, the inherent racism of Christian imperialism operated to free the British lesbian. Whilst guides for missionaries to South America warned that lesbianism existed there, white women were somehow exempt. The church, like sexology, therefore underscored a theorised link between race and sex.

Because sexual activity was seemingly not thinkable in a church designed for procreation, many lesbians in the early part of the century converted to Catholicism with alacrity, and did not see it as contradictory to their sexuality. Asked how she reconciled faith and lesbianism, for example, Una Troubridge replied 'There was nothing to confess' (Baker 1985, p. 357).

Lesbian configurations thus silence in conscience-salving ways; yet also serve to make the unthinkable unutterable.

Class

As with the law and the church, lesbians are conceptualised as beyond the determinators' ken. They are of a different milieu, literally another class(ification).

Ideas of the working class and their association with lesbianism were not new to the twentieth century. Mary Wollstonecraft referred to ideas of cross-class perversion in *Vindication of the Rights of Women* (1792). A double transgression is represented by these same-sex defilers when female servants introduce their mistresses to the sin of mutual masturbation. This is an excuse for social apartheid 'as many girls have learnt very nasty tricks from ignorant servants, the mixing them thus indiscriminately together, is very improper' (1792, vol. V, p. 197).

In the late nineteenth and early twentieth centuries, both class and homosexuality were associated with degeneracy: 'The wild beast is ... slumbering in us all', wrote Edward C. Spitzka (1888, p. 778). Frequently, ideas of animal behaviour are reflected in the representation of deviant or excessive female sexuality,[8] and in connection with prostitutes and working-class women (e.g. Ellis 1895, p. 156). In this discourse of strangers constructed from a middle-class white mentality, references to deviant others focused frequently on race as a determinant of difference. In a landmark nineteenth-century legal case, a judge associated lesbianism with corruption by Indian servants (Faderman 1985, p. xvi).

Race and Imperialism

Medical frameworks of the early modern period had already connected racial and sexual anomaly. In 1671, Jane Sharp in *The Midwife's Book* wrote of 'lewd women': 'In the Indies and Egypt they are frequent, but I never heard of one in this country' (Aughterson 1995, p. 129).

Early twentieth-century writers claimed, similarly, that 'primitive' women and lesbians both had physical symptoms of aberration (Lichtenstein 1921; Gibson 1997). If ideas of racial-sexual deviancy were evident much earlier, with Darwinian and bourgeois theory they found their model, in association with ideas of selection and purification in eugenics. Darwin himself had written: 'We do not even in the least know the final cause of sexuality. The whole subject is hidden in darkness' (Rosario 1997, p. 9). Sigmund Freud had equated race, mystery and women's sexuality: 'We know less about the sexual life of little girls than of boys. But we need not feel ashamed of this distinction; after all, the sexual life of adult women is a "dark continent" for psychology' (the words 'dark continent' were written in English: 1926, *Standard Edition,* vol. 20, p. 191).

Both Edith Ellis and Havelock Ellis, too, had an interest in eugenic promotion of racial health. Havelock Ellis wrote a praising introduction to Dickinson and Beam's *A Thousand Marriages: A Medical Study of Sex Adjustment* (1931), a study in which 'Sexual normality, whiteness and authorship were more than coincidentally juxtaposed' (Carter 1997, p. 155). In his own work, Ellis claimed that lesbian activity was especially prevalent among 'negroes and mulattos of the French Creole countries', as well as in New Zealand, South America and Egypt. He asserted that black women raped black girls (1895, p. 143), thus linking lesbianism to race, criminality and paedophilia. Other writers (such as Chideckel 1935) likewise connected inferiority, racial and sexual *ab origine.* Tribades, like 'coloured girls' and children, were said to use vulgar language:

> racialised others invariably have been compared and equated with children, a representation that conveniently provided a moral justification for imperial policies of tutelage, discipline and specific paternalistic and maternalistic strategies of custodial control ... [Children, in nineteenth-century childcare manuals] are animal-like, lack civility, discipline and sexual restraint ... they are, like racialized others, not fully human beings. (Stoler 1995, p. 151)

Lesbians, and deviant, subhuman others, were to be understood (rather than to understand) via the intellect. The normalised thus established themselves as guardians of nature which 'has as its other and opposite a fear of the powers of the unknown, the animal, the unlawful, the insane, the masses, women, blacks. These "others" become objects to be known and thus civilised and regulated' (Walkerdine 1990, p. 201).

Isolated individuals, or a nation, could constitute a psychological crowd. Within modernist configurations of the intellectual versus these masses[9] spinsters were grouped with low-life crowds, themselves characteristically female, immature and illiterate savages (Carey 1992, pp. 27, 52). Clive Bell, in *Civilisation* (1928) accordingly considered that single women could not be civilised, because a woman must have sex with a man, preferably several men, before the 'exquisite' is available to them, and before the 'subtlest and most impalpable things of the spirit' can penetrate their mind (Carey 1992, pp. 80–1). A spinster or a lesbian would thus be unable to know herself, and even if she could, her language would be crude and invalid in the civilised scheme of things. Lesbian narratives of self in this paradigm, would be, indeed, a contradiction in terms.

Such epistemes of other are frequently founded on a paradox of grudging respect/contempt. Lesbians, like male homosexuals, are posited as a threat which may invade the civilised world, yet they are simultaneously primitive, and easily colonised. Havelock Ellis (1895, p. 147) described 'hypertrophied friendship' in lesbians as threatening to overwhelm the social and physical order. Feminists were suspect lesbians axiomatically, and both 'sets' are described in the language of thrall.

Arabella Kenealy, a member of the Eugenic Society, in 1920 claimed that:

Feminism disrupts [the] complementarity of the sexes. The result of women's competition with men is the development of 'mixed type', more or less degenerate, structurally, functionally and mentally, which imperils the race ... Masculine mothers produce emasculate sons by misappropriating the life potential of male offspring. (p. 74)

Such ideas were formulated by members of an imperialistic continent. Britain itself governed around 26 per cent of the total world population (Bygrave 1996, p. 235), in Asia, Africa and 'other' European countries (Ireland, Greece, Spain). Sexological schema, and their apparent ready acceptance, are an extension of such 'a Western style for dominating, restructuring, and having authority' (Said 1978, p. 3). The exotic and the erotic intersect, and homosexuality is associated with racial impoverishment and rampant non-procreation. All non-white races (South America, New Zealand and Egypt, in Ellis's writing) become one melded orgiastic continent whose promiscuity threatens barrenly to counter-colonise the civilised world.

The setting, and breaching, of borders is an essential tenet of colonialism. Social images of outsiders 'signal imperfection or a low ranking in the hierarchy of being. Exclusionary discourse draws particularly on colour, disease, animals, sexuality and nature, but they all come back to the idea of dirt as a signifier of imperfection and inferiority' (Sibley 1995, p. 14). Such claims often appear confident, but reveal anxiety. Gertrude Stein suggests that there was a feeling of impermanence within modernist imperialism, a precariousness to the claim of superiority which arose from being an incomer. White races assert at once an ownership, yet signal a lack of belonging: 'Native always means people who belong somewhere else, because they had once belonged somewhere. That shows that the white race does not really think they belong anywhere because they think of everybody else as native' (1937, p. 27).

Two texts of 1928 repeat this idea of jejune invasion. They stand counterpassant with Radclyffe Hall's *The Well of Loneliness*, published in that same year, and they operate as reasons for the suppression of the book, invoked in discourse if not in actuality. *Sexual Inversion* by John Addington Symonds is written from the paranoia of the imperialist:

> [Homosexuality] throbs in our huge cities. The pulse of it can be felt … Endowed with inextinguishable life, in spite of all that has been done to suppress it, this passion … penetrates society, makes itself felt in every quarter of the globe where men are brought into communication with men. (1928, p. 6)

Marie Stopes, in her *Enduring Passions*, wrote to provide 'solution to sex difficulties, with especial reference to the problems of middle life' (as advertised in *The Times*, 27 November 1928, FL). She condemned lesbianism, particularly manifest amongst independent women: 'This corruption spreads like an underground fire in the peaty soil of a dry moorland' (1928, p. 29).[10] Again, there is the paradox. Lesbianism is in danger of being un-put-outable but it is set obliquely in contrast to the title of *Enduring*-ness within heterosexuality, wherein lies the true happiness of procreation. This sets up an implied tension between lesbians and family life which recurs throughout twentieth-century representation.

Lesbian Representation: The Family as Fictive Space

The end of the nineteenth century had seen increasing public debate, and formation of moral-reform organisations, concerned with marriage, following the 1878 Matrimonial Causes Act.[11] Numerous articles were published, by women, on the institution and its effect on them. These included, for example, Marie Corelli's 'Does marriage hinder a woman's development?' (March 1899, in Calder 1976, p. 168), and Mona Caird's 'The morality of marriage' which refer to 'self-immolation' of married women and 'mental coagulation' of mothers. In the latter, marriage is remade in 'the modern spirit ... husband and wife regard one another as absolutely free beings; they no more think of demanding subordination to one side or the other than a couple of friends who have elected to live together' (March 1890, in Calder 1976, p. 167).

In this public debate, it has been noted that men had little to say about marriage as such, though the press 'scoffed at the New Woman and ridiculed the blue-stocking' (Calder 1976, p. 168). This is an established strategy, and one repeated in the late twentieth century, to not define oneself but to attack or mock detractors.

Corelli and Caird both indirectly posit a theory of auto/biographical individuation for women, suggesting an independence, a maintenance of self-identity. They defend marriage, none the less, seeking reform, separating then remelding female identity to the larger good. Marriage is recognised to be a choice, and this suggests an historical situation in which other social alternatives were possible.

In general, however, 'heterosexual' behaves as if it is a cultural given. Used to describe the relationship between members of the opposite sex, its proponents tend to use the word as though it is an historically enduring touchstone, in an essentialist framework. But conceptualisations of heterosexuality, as of any other term describing social institutions, are formed at non-neutral moments in history. Feminist critics since Adrienne Rich (1980) have recognised 'compulsory heterosexuality' as a key mechanism which perpetuates patriarchy. Writers identify its construction of an 'artificial' femininity with subordination of women's sexuality to procreative ends (Chodorow 1978; Irigaray 1977) as one aspect of a system of empiricist dominance. This subordination carries over into representations of lesbians: it is too simplistic to see a hetero–homo binary opposition in sexual construction, since heterosexual discourse treats lesbians differently from male homosexuals, just as it treats male and female heterosexuals with difference. A lesbian is typologically a subset of both the male homosexual and of the female heterosexual: both subgroups which are defined by their differentiation from the male heterosexual as the primal and essential 'given' from which all other life forms deviate. Eve's genesis, from Adam's rib, ingrains itself in a Western cultural hierarchy within which the lesbian is doubly fallen, as woman and as deviant woman.

This had spatial-cultural implications, associated with expulsion from sacred spaces. From the seventeenth century at least, the family was a metaphor for the nation (Hobby 1988, p. 29), so invasion of one suggests danger to the other. The early twentieth century saw a hetero-sexual encampment in the high ground of morality. And yet heterosexuality can equally be seen as itself moving into lesbian space in its effort to describe and classify. The resistance to this effort, and its counterdiscourse, characterises aspects of the language of self-descrip-tion in lesbians of the 1920s and 1930s:

> To achieve recognition is to rechart and then occupy the place in imperial cultural forms reserved for subordination, to occupy it self-consciously, fighting for it on the very same territory once ruled by a consciousness that assumed the subordination of the designated inferior Other. Hence, *reinscription*. (Said 1993, p. 253)

'Reinscription' takes various forms depending upon who is resisting what or whom. In the 1920s and 1930s lesbians developed a language of self-description which cleared space within, and without, operative heterosexual paradigms.

Robert Dickinson and Lura Beam's *The Single Woman* (1934) operates on both borders. It includes 28 lesbian 'cases' of whom questions are asked to refute prevailing stereotypes. Posed with a query, 'Do you take the male part?', a lesbian replies 'We don't think of it like that' (Carlston 1997, p. 192). The counter both contradicts and reinforces, via denial, the normative. This suggests that, primarily, the deter-mining metaphor was one of hetero-space, which was formed along gendered lines and with a full establishment of 'the bourgeois home ... [which] drew a clear line between the inside and the outside ... the inside provided protection against outside spaces filled with potentially hostile forces' (Weissberg 1996, p. 105).

Capitalism is said to have changed the structure of the white family, to have created divisions between public and private and, conversely, to have created potential intimate space beyond the familial, as indi-viduals moved outside for work:

the relationship between capitalism and family is fundamentally contradictory. On the one hand, capitalism continually weakens the material foundation of family life, making it possible for individuals to live outside the family, and for lesbian and gay male identity to develop. On the other, it needs to push men and women into families, at least long enough to reproduce the next generation of workers. The elevation of the family to ideological pre-eminence guarantees that a capitalist society will reproduce not just children but heterosexism and homophobia. (D'Emilio 1992, p. 13)

Home, in this nineteenth-century American capitalism, and in Britain, became, therefore, an idealised space, described, like marriage, in terms of paradise: 'Home – that blessed word, which opens to the human heart the most perfect glimpse of Heaven, and helps to carry it thither, as on an angel's wings' (Child 1843).[12]

Marriage, of course, was not a new institution, had altered fundamentally during the course of its history, and had been reinvented in different periods to fulfil political purposes. From its early definitions in Middle English *familie*, from the Latin *familia*, for household and extended 'family' of servants and dependants, the term had undergone a heterosexual codification to signify consanguinity and kinship, a means of property control based on ancestry and lineage. Changes in ideas of marriage in Western society had occurred as a result of social shifts brought about by the English Reformation and the industrial revolution, amidst individualistic ideologies within both (see Tilly and Scott 1978; Weeks 1981, pp. 30–80). In the later nineteenth century, the increasing numbers of women outside marriage, pursuing independent careers, put pressure on those who benefited from the institution to define it as secure and inviolable.

In consequence, this period saw attempts further to embed marriage and family in ideas of idealised nationhood, of procreation and of evolution:

The Family is the Country of the heart. There is an angel in the Family who, by the mysterious influence of grace, of sweetness, and of love, renders the fulfilment of duties less wearisome, sorrows less bitter. The only pure joys unmixed with sadness which it is given to man to taste upon the earth are, thanks to this angel, the joys of the Family. (Mazzini 1844, ch. 6)

And is it not a high vocation to make homes, like gardens, bloom in the wilderness of life; to be the centre around which hearts gather, and the fondest affections cling; to strengthen, brighten, and beautify existence; to be the light of others' souls, and the good angels of others' path? ... And what to be a mother? To give birth to young immortals! To guide and train the opening minds of those who shall influence the coming generation ... Sacred, blessed motherhood! Is not yours a high and holy mission? (Joseph Shillito, *Womanhood: Its Duties, Temptations and Privileges*, 1877, quoted in Calder 1976, p. 169)

Marriage had become a kind of literary trope, a fictive backdrop against which life was lived out. It was mythologised in Judeao-Christian concepts of paradise, as Mazzini's and Shillito's narratives describe, and this was culturally embraced with alacrity. Marriage is, in this sense, a utopic space and the family is a parade ground for cadet heterosexuals:

The family is the basic cell of government: it is where we are trained to believe that we are human beings or that we are chattel, it is where we are trained to see the race and sex divisions and become callous to injustice even if it is done to ourselves, to accept as biological a full system of authoritarian government. (Steinem 1981)

Marriage is 'triumph of evolution' (Carter 1997, p. 155) within which hierarchies are correspondingly natural:

a woman *is* positively and distinctly created in order that she may become a wife and mother. If she misses this destiny, there is something wrong somewhere ... You may take an old maid, or a nun, or a nurse all her life of her; but if you do, she is qua woman, a failure, whatever great and noble things she may do, or whatever she may accomplish to raise the standard of human effort and kindle the flame of human hope. (*The Girl of the Period Miscellany*, No. 9, 1869, p. 277, quoted in Auchmuty 1992, p. 141)

The iconography of Florence Nightingale as a lamp-bearing signifier and embodiment of acceptable femininity bursts from this passage. As a single woman, even in an acceptable occupation such as nursing, she is a failed woman, a controlling metaphor for female accomplishment within (non-) marital zones.[13]

The family was accordingly seen by intellectuals to be under threat from the masses, including independent and single women. Wyndham Lewis, expressing views on the 'family and feminism', considered it had been consigned to a kind of theme park for mass recreation:

> With a new *familiarity* and a flesh-creeping 'homeliness' entirely of this unreal, materialistic world, where all 'sentiment' is coarsely manufactured and advertised in colossal sickly captions, disguised for the sweet tooth of a monstrous baby called 'the Public', the family as it is, broken up on all hands by the agency of feminist and economic propaganda, reconstitutes itself in the image of the state. (1926, ch. 4)[14]

The threat to territory came from dubious elements within, a perverse discourse of homeliness, within which Freud developed his conception of the Uncanny (1919), *Unheimlich* ('unhomely'), a threat to the family home. Lesbianism is frequently associated with the Uncanny in literature, and is characterised in this way by its opposition to the home. Literary lesbians disturb the happy infrastructure of homes (as in Marie Stopes's manual). They stalk the corridors[15] of nuptial bliss, like Mrs Danvers in Daphne du Maurier's *Rebecca* (1938).

In the light of this, we can understand Olive Schreiner's *Women and Labour* (1911).[16] A South African political activist who lived also in Britain, Schreiner was on close terms with both Havelock Ellis and Edward Carpenter, and drew on ideas within social Darwinism in claiming that 'It is the woman who is the final standard of the race ... as her brain weakens, weakens the man's she bears; as the muscle softens, softens his; as she decays, decays the people' (p. 109). Heterosexuality can be seen on the defensive, paradoxically as a result of the insults attaching innuendoes of lesbianism and its attendant dangers with education and independence.[17]

Other writers, likewise, discussed the institution of marriage in less or more positive ways. Christabel Pankhurst's *The Great Scourge and How to End It* (1913) can be understood in the light of the political promotion of marriage as a site for psychological and physical health.[18] Prostitution, like lesbianism (with which it was often associated in law and language), was treated as antonymic to family, and had been seen as a threat to the health of the nation. In her text, Pankhurst provocatively associated marriage itself with sexually transmitted disease. According to her statistics, a high percentage of ruling-class men passed venereal disease from prostitutes into their families: for women, avoiding marital intercourse was therefore healthy. Pankhurst's text entered into linguistic dialogue with ideas of health surrounding normalised heterosexuality.

Cicely Hamilton, in *Marriage as a Trade* (1909) similarly suggested that motherhood and sex threatened women, advocating celibacy as the answer. She argued that marriage was in effect itself a form of prostitution. This is an inversion, like Christabel Pankhurst's, of the dominant thesis which had set the family (idyllic, saved) in opposition to the fallen.[19] Similarly configured in a framework of morality, but inverting the fall/redemptive language, is a statement which reveals another lesbian counterdiscourse. Kathlyn Oliver,[20] a lesbian who wrote to Edward Carpenter to express enthusiasm about his book *The Intermediate Sex* (1908), had been under pressure to marry for financial reasons after the death of her father:

> But tho' I had other 'chances' to marry & tho' I was at times rather tempted to sell myself in marriage as a way out of work which I hated, I am indeed glad today that I did not yield to the temptation. (25 October 1915, CC).

This is a nice sacramental reversal: the lesbian envisages those who marry as yielding to sin.

In general, unmarried women in the early twentieth century living apart from their biological family, were perceived to be a threat to the social structure. The suffrage campaign was always associated with ideas of female independence. The full-time organisers of the Women's Social and Political Union (WSPU) were almost all unmarried, and membership donations shifted from 45 per cent unmarried in 1906/7 to 63 per cent in 1913/14 (Vicinus 1985, p. 261). The women's movement was blamed for the ruin of families (e.g. Carey 1928; Faderman 1986, p. 31). Signs of female independence, grounded on education, as ever, aroused suspicion of sexual separatism.

One text will serve as a jumping-off point about this continuing polarity between family and single, educated woman set up by heterosexual discourse in the period. I found it unexpectedly, in a centenary celebration volume produced by my old school, set up in 1879 as an endowed single-sex institution to improve the education of women. It is an extract from the 1920 school magazine, 'The Ilex', written by one N. Pearce, who would have been around 15 years old at that time. Entitled 'Should boys and girls be educated alike?', she weighs up arguments:

[Parents] still often believe a girl has not carried out the purpose for which she was born if she does not marry ... after the Great War, there are some five million surplus women who have no chance of getting married, unless British men take to keeping harems. These surplus women will have to earn their own living in some way or other, and in doing so they will probably have to compete with men. If they have the same education they will be more likely to hold their own and keep their positions ... Even if a girl's parents are well enough off to keep her at home ... she should have practically the same education so that she can take an intelligent interest in things, and perhaps, if she's not one of the five million, make an interesting and intelligent mate for some man. (Browett 1979, p. 70)

Like Schreiner (1911), the writer envisions a male-centred home which will be enhanced by the educational improvement of women. We have here a sense of the heterosexual paradigms within which even a highly academic girls' school operated. We have, too, insight into the contemporary educational debate about girls' schooling in case it excludes them from suitability for feminine pursuits of matrimony. Education and separatism are thus linked, and gendered identity is associated with evidence of academic capacity. Contemporary psychological discussion underlines ideas about this. Many women analysts engaged with views about the acquisition of femininity. Some of these pre-empt, and some are in subsequent dialogue with, Freud's statements about women's psychology. Helene Deutsch (1884–1982), for example, considered 'All observations point to the fact that the intellectual woman is masculinized; in her, warm, intuitive knowledge has yielded to cold unproductive thinking' (1944; and see Deutsch 1933).

In Freudian analysis, intellectual qualities are aligned with the masculine: the crucial event that precipitated homosexuality was Oedipal disappointment, failure to be as strong in the mother's affections as the father. Lesbians are characterised by their determination not to be inferior to boys: 'the active inverts exhibit masculine characteristics, both physical and mental' (1905, *Standard Edition*, vol. 7, p. 145).

The school magazine extract provides two useful points of excursion: into association of ideas of the masculinisation of women with education, and of this with lesbianism; and into the notion of family and its contrast to lesbian life. Both notions are contained within the phrase 'surplus women'. If 'heifer' carried the imprint of heterosexual, then 'spinster' is almost indecipherable without lesbian connotations.

The early twentieth century saw particular manifestation of distaste for the phenomena of the 'surplus'.

After the 1914–18 war, there were indeed many more unmarried women. The 1921 census revealed a higher number of spinsters than previously in Britain (Auchmuty 1992, p. 141). Heterosexist explanation of this phenomenon is that, because so many men had died during the war, women who otherwise would have married were alone. In the Warwickshire village where I grew up, there were numerous unmarried, elderly women who had 'lost their fiancés at the Front', whether truly or in explanation to avoid a stigma associated with their spinsterhood, I am now unsure. It is no coincidence that lesbians at this time are castigated as medically deviant in an effort to depoliticise the challenge of independent women (Kitzinger 1987, p. 33). As with the bulling heifers of the Introduction, 'spinster' conveys rejected rather than rejecter, and female autonomy is to be pitied because it inadequately compensates, and only arises, in the absence of the male. Hence, Marie Stopes writes of 'deprived women' using lesbianism as a 'practical solution' for their frustration (1928, p. 29); and in corresponding with Jacques Raverat about 'loving one's own sex', Virginia Woolf received a reply in precisely these terms: 'Sapphism seems to me much more attractive [than male sodomy which he equated with arrested development], & with all those surplus, unattached women about, they must find, shall we say some outlet for their passions, poor things' (February 1925, in Lee 1996, p. 493).

Pitiable they may be, but these women are nevertheless dangerous and sap the strength of the nation-body, here personified as male (in contrast to Schreiner's maternally nurturing ideal):

> I write of the High Priestess of society. Not of the mother of sons, but of her barren sister, the withered tree, the acidulous vessel under whose pale shadow we chill and whiten, of the Spinster I write. Because of her power and dominion, she, unobtrusive, meek, soft-footed, silent, shamefaced, bloodless and boneless, thinned to spirit, enters the secret recesses of the mind,[21] sits at the secret springs of action, and moulds and fashions our emasculate society. She is our social nemesis. (*The Freewoman*, 23 November 1911, in Jeffreys 1985, p. 95)

Sheila Jeffreys (1985) has claimed that the 'spinster class' emerged in mid-nineteenth-century England. However, the independent female as a societal emasculator was a castigated type much earlier in British culture. Commenting, in 1801, on the encroachment on the male preserve by women and the decline of the culture of the nation, for example, Henry Fuseli, President of the Royal Academy in London, referred to his 'effeminate age': 'in an age of luxury woman aspires to the functions of man, and man slides into the offices of woman. The epoch of eunuchs was ever the epoch of viragoes' (1801, p. 144).

In the early twentieth century, the barren-rabbit oxymoron remained: 'Today', wrote Vera Brittain in 1935, in language which also reflects the association of displaced spirituality and nunhood in 'spinster', 'there is a far worse crime than promiscuity: it is chastity. On all sides the unmarried woman today is surrounded by doubt cast not only upon her attractiveness or her common sense, but upon her decency, her normality, even her sanity' (1935, p. 91).

Aspersions of spinsters usurping their place in the natural order, even to 'sainthood',[22] were strongly expressed: 'The claim of the teacher feminist was no longer for equal rights, but for the canonisation of the spinster' (*Times Educational Supplement*, 26 April 1924, p. 180, quoted in Oram 1989, p. 107). In their infertility, they try to corrupt the offspring of the fruitful: 'The women who have the responsibility of teaching these girls are many of themselves embittered, sexless or homosexual hoydens who try to mould the girls into their own pattern ... these thin-lipped, flat-chested, sadistic creatures' (*Daily Herald*, 5 September 1935, in Oram 1989, pp. 105–6).

The spinster-lesbian, sexless 'frigides' (Gallichan 1927, p. 13), invade the marital home, emasculating:

> If a married woman does this unnatural thing she may find a growing disappointment in her husband and he may lose all natural power to play his proper part ... No woman who values the peace of her home and the love of her husband should yield to the wiles of the lesbian whatever her temptation to do so ... The bedrock objection to it is surely that women can only *play* with each other and *cannot* supply each other with the seminal or prostatic secretions they ought to have. (Stopes 1928, pp. 29, 30).[23]

From marriage manuals, paradoxically, the prototype lesbian emerges: she has a home-wrecking Eve typology, seduces the content wife away from the Edenic sanctuary of her home, and causes impotence and marital mayhem whilst herself is only capable of a mere parody of the real act of procreation.

2
Lesbian Lives in the 1920s and 1930s

Lesbians and Familial Spaces

Marie Stopes's *Enduring Passion* was published, then, in 1928, the same year as *The Well of Loneliness*. It was advertised ('by the author of *Married Love'; The Times,* 27 November 1928, FL) in newspapers which also had carried articles condemning Radclyffe Hall's novel, and in which lesbianism was configured as virulent in its attack on the nation's healthy offspring:

> I have seen the plague walking shamelessly through great social assemblies. I have heard it whispered about by young men and young women who do not and cannot grasp its unutterable putre-faction. Both aspects of it are thrust upon healthy and innocent minds. The contagion cannot be escaped. It pervades our social life ... I would rather give a healthy boy or a healthy girl a phial of prussic acid than this novel. Poison kills the body, the moral poison kills the soul (*Sunday Express*, 19 August 1928, in Cline 1997, p. 243)

The language of antipathy nicely reinforced Marie Stopes's idyllic vista of the familial home, a private space from which the lesbian is (to be) cast out, occupying as she does crowds and 'assemblies'.

Some 'desirable' lesbians are (re)claimed by proponents of the family as one of their own. Octavia Hill, for example, was associated with many reputable establishment groups, including housing organisations and the National Trust. At the centenary of her birth, several national news-papers paid tribute to Hill. They depicted her ostentatiously within a family setting. Under the subheading 'Family life', the *Manchester Guardian* (29 November 1938, FL) reported that Hill's mother and sisters 'were her chief confidantes', not mentioning Harriot Yorke with whom she had cohabited for some 35 years. Elsewhere, Reginald Rowe, President of the National Federation of Housing Societies[1] wrote, under the subheading 'A happy family', that Hill was '"the man of the five [sisters]"; but there was nothing masculine about her unless it was her remarkable business aptitude' (*The Times*, 3 December 1938, FL).

Another writer that year referred to Hill's thwarted engagement, broken off

> for reasons that remained the secret of those two; both remained unmarried to the end. The memory was regarded as so sacred that the engagement has not been hitherto disclosed. The passage of time permits its mention now, since it helps to explain more than one misconception. (*The Times*, 27 December 1938, FL)

The writer does not enlighten us about what these misconceptions are, though his motive of scotching rumours of her lesbianism seems highly likely. He uses the language of 'sacred': the sanctity of Hill's heterosexual credentials are at stake here, and through family references her reputation is reinvested. In the face of anxiety, heterosexual claims can be equated to riding a bicycle, matrimony, which is always in danger of toppling over and in a constant state of being righted.

In the (re)constitution of marriage as upright, lesbians played their part. Individual lesbians reinforced the sense of roles within marriage, whilst distancing themselves from 'women'. Mary Allen (1878–1964) who campaigned for women's entry into the police force, for example, received extensive publicity after her visit to the US, to give traffic-control training to women police there. Interviewed on her return in 1924. 'Miss Allen added that in America the prettiest women were used as decoys ... she thought that a mean trick which would never be done in this country' (*Daily Chronicle*, 7 November 1924, FL). Ten years later, she described how she had gone fact-finding in Germany to learn 'the truth of the position of German womanhood ... It would be a mistake to ban women completely from public life, but I realise that many of them would be more suitably employed in the home' (*Evening Standard*, 29 January 1934, FL).

'To be a good wife and mother is the finest work a woman can do', said Radclyffe Hall to Evelyn Irons, one lesbian to another, in her interview for the *Daily Mail* (26 July 1927, in Baker 1985, p. 248). A lesbian talks aloud to another, using a vocabulary based on assumptions of role and separating herself from notions of womanhood.

Lesbians refer to themselves here as inhabiting a different spatial zone from women, and yet also from other lesbians. Vita Sackville-West had herself spoken to Evelyn Irons about Edy Craig (a lesbian to another of a third), recalling her as 'the most tearing old lesbian – not unlike your friend Radclyffe Hall ... seeing me trying to sharpen a pencil, she came up, and took it away, "Here give me that", she said, "no woman knows how to sharpen a pencil" ... ' (1932, in Glendinning 1983, pp. 250–1). Acts change as these women construct themselves, dressing as it were, in front of each other.

Married Lesbians

This sense of 'public speak', and, in Showalter's terms, 'double-voiced discourse' (see p. 23), was repeated literally when Vita Sackville-West contributed to a BBC discussion on marriage in June 1929, with her husband Harold Nicolson. She had been invited by Hilda Matheson, Director of Talks, with whom Vita was having a sexual relationship at the time. In the broadcast, Harold described marriage as a living organism, 'a plant, not a piece of furniture. It grows; it changes; it develops'; Vita countered that men 'regard *themselves* as the plant and the woman as the soil', that this 'taught men to be domineering and inconsiderate, and it taught women to be sly. What *you* call feminine' (*Listener*, 26 June 1929, in Glendinning 1983, p. 215). Gender is thus a role adopted under the pressure of expectation and in order to conceal.

The interview has often been regarded as an emphatic, and hypocritical, endorsement by Harold and Vita of marriage as an institution, whilst both conducted extra-marital homosexual relationships. This claim is made without a sense of the careful construction of the listener, which both radio as a medium and the personal context of the broadcast demand. Vita Sackville-West can be seen to steer a clever path through expectation and assertion of personal fidelity. Neither Nicolson nor Matheson needed to be unduly alarmed by her statements which hover over and between public/private knowledges. Her previous sexual relationship, with Violet Trefusis, was well known publicly. And husband and wife each knew that the other conducted homosexual relationships. Harold Nicolson accordingly indicates that marriage could change and adapt, it is not an unyielding tree which snaps in the winds of change. It could, he reassures, encompass their emotional tensions. Their statements, therefore, are made in the tacit public and personal acknowledgement of their own challenge to the institution. In addition, the immediate dimension of Hilda Matheson as listener cannot be forgotten. For her benefit Vita shows the tension in heterosexuality of expectations and fulfilment, and marriage is shown to operate in a different space to lesbian relationships which are immune from the pressure caused by expectations of gender differences.

Suzanne Raitt sees the broadcast as 'reiterating one of the least tenable myths of heterosexual marriage: that within it radical differences are transcended or resolved ... Conceived as an intermittent sexual or emotional orientation, [lesbianism] could flourish happily in the interstices of heterosexual existence, hardly threatening it at all' (1993, pp. 8, 7). This does not appear to acknowledge the careful construction of listeners that Sackville-West had arranged, her alternative negotiation of a space within lesbianism for a heterosexual existence. Marriage does not threaten her lesbian identity, nor is it, in turn, threatened.

An alternative view to a marital paradigm is possible, one similar to that observed of Elizabeth Bowen's relationships with women where 'lesbian experience [is] bracketing the heterosexual experience of marriage and children' ... 'marriage is both the unlikely and inevitable center at either end of which is the more likely and less destined involvement of women with their own kind' (Rule 1975, p. 15). The broadcast brackets need to be moved from (lesbian) to (married).

For Sackville-West, marriage was construed as a safe haven, an idealised space, to which she could intermittently return. In 1913, newly married, and in love with Rosamund Grosvenor, she described Harold Nicolson as 'like a sunny harbour to me' (quoted in Glendinning 1983, p. 68). Later, whilst in the throes of her passionate relationship with Violet Keppel, Vita wrote to her husband 'You are my anchor ... I feel like a person drowning who knows there is an absolutely safe boat somewhere on the sea' and 'You are my only anchor' (25 May and 1 June 1918, in Sackville-West 1973, pp. 137, 151). These have consistently been taken as statements in support of marriage, with no sense again of the constructed moment, of the listener – her husband whose value, at a time of crisis, she reinforces.

Lesbians who are married tread a careful path in reassuring their lovers and their spouses. They aspire to the fictivity of marital security while telling each other that marriage is no threat to their relationship, it operates in a separate sphere: 'in all London, you and I alone like being married', wrote Virginia to Vita (16 November 1925, in Woolf 1975/80, vol. III, p. 221) just days before they became lovers. At her most flirtatious, in 1926, Virginia reminds her lover of their marital state, within and outside which their own relationship exists: her long letter is deliberately circumlocutory, deviating to other subjects, sometimes mid-sentence, about the possibility of the two women meeting soon:

> if it were feasible to you, and you had no lovers friends mothers, poisoned dogs, or young men proposing to you (though you are a married woman as you so often and so surprisingly assert) in the house, then I should be divinely happy, and sit on a seat and chatter ... Oh Vita I must stop writing.
>
> Yr VW.
>
> Leonard says he can't come because of the Press etc – but would like to.
>
> (19? July 1926, in Woolf 1975/80, vol. III, pp. 280–2)

Reference to marriage is used here as a ploy to reassure and yet to provoke uneasiness, and therefore desire, for erotic encounter. It draws upon an idea of lesbianism as a place of potential bliss ('divinely happy') and yet of marriage as a space of safety: 'I snuggled in to the core of my life, which is this complete comfort with Leonard & there found everything so satisfactory & calm that I revived myself, & got a fresh start; feeling entirely immune' (14 June 1925, in Woolf 1977/84, vol. III, p. 30). The language is striking, given that lesbians are accused of infection of marriage as a healthy state. Virginia Woolf invokes here the topos of marriage as protector. This is not to say that neither she nor Vita did not experience its safety as reality. Rather it is to see that they reinforce the fictivity of its safety in order to enjoy lesbian excursions outside its walls.

With Sackville-West, Woolf's marital/lesbian language underwent transformation as her relationship shifted. As the passion assuaged, she wrote (in a letter to Ethel Smyth), 'Vita was here for a night. I always fall into a warm slipper relation with her instantly. Its [sic] a satisfactory relationship' (12 October 1940, in Woolf 1975/80, vol. VI, p. 439). Domestic familiarity, interestingly, has become a metaphor for the now cosified lesbian relationship, in contradiction to the commonplace that 'the fiction and the marriage shelter and conceal the volatile depths of Woolf's lesbian feelings' (Stimpson 1984, p. 199).

Lesbian love and heterosexual marriage operate in separate zones, but, as Woolf's statement shows, the lesbian can traverse and carry values across their seeming boundaries. Likewise, 'the liaisons which you and I contract are something perfectly apart from the more natural and normal attitude we have towards each other, and therefore don't interfere', wrote Vita to Harold after their marriage (31 May 1926, in Sackville-West 1973, p. 145). This distinction was there from the outset. Vita described her feelings for Harold in 1920: 'It never struck me as wrong that I should be more or less engaged to Harold, and at the same time much in love with Rosamund. The fact is that I regarded Harold far more as a playfellow than in any other light' (1973, p. 35). This was an aspect of Vita's marriage which Virginia Woolf recognised when she described the relationship between Orlando and her husband as playful: 'She was married, true; but if one's husband was always sailing round Cape Horn, was it marriage?' (1928, p. 173).

Violet Keppel, similarly, saw marriage as a showground, and her love of Vita as real. When Vita's engagement was announced in the newspapers, she wrote Vita a facetious letter:

> *Accepté mes félicitations* les plus sincère *à la nouvelle de tes fiançailles!* I never could write letters on this subject in any language but somehow it sounds less sickening in French. I wish you *every possible happiness* (et cetera) from the bottom of my heart (et cetera). Will you and Mr Nicholson [sic] come and have tea with me? (5 August 1913, in Souhami 1996, p. 110)

When Sackville-West and Nicolson went to the wedding of a friend, Keppel was likewise mocking, and described a comic scenario of mayhem at the ceremony, of flies tickling the bridegroom, an organ playing on its own, noses being tweaked and hassocks snatched away. Despite the playfulness, the language is none the less of damnation in the context of this sacrament of faith: 'Tomorrow you will go to a charming wedding. You will blend facetiousness and sentimentality most suitably. You will be reminded of your own – damn you – and mine – damn me' (Souhami 1996, p.169).

Expressions of personal pain by Violet and Vita, as their relationship struggled under the pressure of marriage, showed how unhappy could be the tension between heterosexual and homosexual mores. The way in which Sackville-West's autobiography described events can be interpreted in terms of ideas about lesbianism disturbing male homosociality. In Eve Kosofsky Sedgwick's thesis (1985), English literature (and assumedly auto/biography as a genre) since the late seventeenth century has been structured around the erotic triangle of male homosocial desire. Female bonding destabilises this. The idea has not been applied to Vita Sackville-West's auto/biography, but could be, to read *Portrait of a Marriage* as, indeed, a destabilising text. The events of Sackville-West's relationship with Violet Keppel (later Trefusis) are dramatically retold there (pp. 109–24): the two women left England together, and were pursued by their husbands who acted together to 'recapture' their wives.

Usually, as in Nigel Nicolson's commentary on the text, interwoven when he published it, the work has been discussed as if 'female bonding' is something which 'dismantles the real ... in a search for the not-yet-real, something unpredicted and unpredictable ... As a consequence, it often looks odd, fantastical, implausible, "not there" – utopian in aspiration if not design ... ' (Castle 1993, p. 548). The lesbian relationship consistently has not been taken seriously because it is 'not-yet-real', whereas for the women themselves, it represented the intensely real space within which they lived.

Marriage and Lesbians

Marriage operated for *non*-married lesbians likewise as a fictive space. Some aspired to occupy it in their erotic bonding with other women, an aspiration which is sometimes delivered with stereotypical notions about gender. Radclyffe Hall, for example, stated that 'In the heart of every woman is the desire for protection. In the heart of every man is the desire to give protection to the woman he loves. The invert knows she will never enjoy this and because of her affliction will face social ostracism' (*New York Telegram Magazine*, 15 December 1928, in Baker 1985, p. 248). In 1929, she wrote that 'what I ultimately long for is some sort of marriage for the invert' (Letter to Audrey Heath, 19 March 1929, in Baker 1985, p. 254).

Other lesbians autobiographically describe themselves as if they are married. The artist Gluck addressed Nesta Obermer as 'my own darling wife', and 'Darling Heart, we are not an "affair" are we – we are husband and wife':

> I think we are like a perfect apple cut in half – the most lovely and significant of fruits and I am sure for that reason chosen as of the Tree of Knowledge ... It's shocking how he misses his rib when Eve is not by his side, his heart nearly pops out through the gap that's been left. (1936/7, in Souhami 1988, p. 128)

The language of Eden, again, has here been inverted to apply to a lesbian marital mode.

Amy Tasker, a lesbian who corresponded with sexologist Edward Carpenter, wrote to him of her lover, 'I loved her as the mother of my children'. When the woman became engaged to a man, 'I am widowed as no man was ever widowed' (2 July 1913, CC, see Chapter 1, note 20). Such use of marriage as a metaphor to describe lesbian partnership has often been treated as if it is literal. Rather, it may be that marriage offered a linguistic allegory for a stable and loving relationship. Heterosexuality will permit no other. Yet statements of it are frequently read as 'true', constative rather than performative:[2] 'A parable does not so much passively name something as make something happen ... A true performative brings something into existence that has no basis except in the words ... ' (Miller 1991, p. 139). By using 'marriage' of their relationship, lesbians confer a stability that is understood by outsiders.

The history of lesbian representation is based upon a systematic, or orchestrated, misreading of performative statements as if they are constative. To do otherwise would be to afford lesbian language a power to transform, which the heterosexual hegemony could ill-afford in its linguistic hold on the creative faculty. Furthermore, lesbians who describe themselves as being married are automatically credited with male/female affection because the married are heterosexually tattooed to have any meaning at all. To some extent, lesbians appear to collaborate with this part-play: they 'acquire and assemble meanings, skills and values from the people around them' (Gagnon 1977, p. 15). Sexuality, in this view, is a social construct, regulated by 'sexual scripts' which are variable and fluid, subject to editorial control of a range of possibles at any one time open.

Lesbian lives, like black women's narratives, mediate between personal experience and the prescribed language of expressiveness:

> The coherence of black women's autobiographical discourse does incontrovertibly derive from black women's experience, although less from experience in the narrow empirical sense than from condition – the condition of interlocking structures of gender, class and race. But it derives even more from the tension between condition and discourse, from the changing ways in which black women writers have attempted to represent a personal experience through available discourses and in interaction with imagined readers. (Fox-Genovese 1988, p. 65)

Lesbians can break away from the scripts given to them, into improvised ad-libbery. Like other writers of 'minority group autobiographies', individuals can 'move beyond alienation within the dominant culture to construct meaningful lives in writing and otherwise' (McKay 1988, p. 175).

In statements of lesbian lives around, and within sight of, marriage as an institution, we can see a lesbian 'reinscription'. Some lesbians use language already available within a dominant mode in order to construct life statements; some mimic heterosexual possibilities; others use performative potential in language of matrimony. Similar features can be seen within lesbian adoption of the language of masculinity and of femininity in the 1920s and 1930s.

Masculinity and Performance

Masculine identification by lesbians was not, of course, new to the late nineteenth and early twentieth century. Anne Lister, in July 1823, described her own desire, aroused while she was working in the hayfield: 'All this ordering & work & exercise seemed to excite my manly feelings. I saw a pretty girl go up the lane & desire rather came over me' (1988, p. 267). In 1820 she had written, 'Yet my manners are certainly peculiar, not all masculine but rather softly gentleman-like. I know how to please girls' (1988, p. 136). The binary code delimits the possibilities of her self-definition: she construes herself as somehow mid-way, gentlemanly soft, in an effort, in her diary, to explain herself to herself.

Such masculinised self-definition was treated, by early twentieth-century sexologists, as if it were constative, that is real. The hypodermal lesbian is thus a man occupying a woman's body. She is in someone else's proper and intimate space, by definition an interloper. Instead, within a limited framework of opposites, masculinity was perhaps one form of role which lesbians may have adopted in order to be understood and to understand themselves, paradoxically, *as hetero*sexual, or as attracted to women: in psychoanalytical terms this had been explained as 'the daughter's masculine identification with the father [which] mimes a male heterosexual attraction' (Roof 1991, p. 204). Gender, and tensions around it, are part of the mimicry: 'Women always experiment at certain moments in their life with the view that "femininity" is a pretence. The garment that they must don often transforms itself into an unbearable shell' (Plaza 1978, p. 27).

Beyond this, the lesbian configures herself in additional acting terms. The idea of a homosexual social role has been attributed to Mary McIntosh (1968, p. 187).[3] Since then, other writers have explored notions of performance as it relates to a social self-construction. Judith

Butler, for example, considers gender to be an act of fabrication or impersonation. Her observations can be extrapolated for a construction of sexuality: 'As in other ritual social dramas, the action of gender requires a performance that is *repeated* ... [It] is an identity tenuously constituted in time, instituted in an exterior space through a *stylized repetition of acts* ...' (1990, pp. 136, 140–1). Teresa de Lauretis has argued for a particular type of enactment in sexual identity which is

> neither innate nor *simply* acquired, but dynamically (re)structured by forms of fantasy private and public, conscious and unconscious, which are culturally available and historically specific ... I consider sexuality as a particular instance of semiosis, the more general process joining subjectivity to social signification and material reality. (1994, p. xix)

Autobiography as a genre can be seen as an act within an act, a theatrical commentary in which the author self-describes her own performance, projecting a *dramatis persona* within a *curriculum vitae*. In Philippe Lejeune's terms, it is an act of staging: 'l'écriture y est mise en scene' (1971, p. 73). From this, Nancy K. Miller asks, 'What conventions govern the production of the female self as *theater*? How does a woman writer perform on the stage of her texts?' (1988, p. 49). And the lesbian writer may add to this: How does the *lesbian* both perform and describe herself in the act? What historically specific possibilities are open to her, or are created by her, in order to self-describe? Sexuality is both a site of performance, and a means to it. Lesbianism in this context is both noun and verb: 'to lesbian' describes the act as well as the script.

Manifestation of 'identity', accordingly, can be read as if it is unfixed. Literary theory can be applied to lesbian performance to see the codes as textual, and having, in Barthes' (1970) terms, *scriptible* potential. In this, the text of sexual expressiveness (masculinity or dress) has an open meaning, or at least a more open meaning than is suggested by proponents of the philosophy that language only contains true and false statements. A *scriptible* text involves its reader, expects her to produce meanings from a series of hints which engage her as a co-writer. So, the observer of lesbian dress is involved in interpreting the identity of the person inside the clothes, and may experience *jouissance* (Barthes 1973), an unsettling but stimulating kind of response, as opposed to *plaisir*, a comfortable reassurance of our existing values.[4] Observers of lesbians show themselves frequently as ideal modernist readers, unsettled in the face of a performance. This happens because they continue to see dress, and the sexual identity it tries to convey, as if it is real rather than descriptive.

Radclyffe Hall, for example, often wore a jacket, collar and tie with a skirt. Her observers found it difficult to place her, and they projected this onto her: 'It was always said at a dinner party, when women left the table, Johnny Hall ... found it hard to make up her mind whether to go with the women or remain with the men' (Rupert Hart-Davis 1925, quoted in Cline 1997, p. 67). Beverly Nicholls, in the *Sunday Herald*, described her 'British policeman act':

> hands clasped behind the back, chin thrust up, knees bent and jerked outward in a springy aggressive motion ... It was her boast that she knew nothing about housekeeping. She must have regarded this as a sign of virility, because she often referred to it. 'Couldn't boil an egg', she would proclaim gruffly, jerking out her knees with extra gusto. (21 March 1926, FL)

Role play, real or perceived, within gendered and marital paradigms thus leads to an attribution of male and female parts to lesbian partnerships. Harriot Yorke was given the wifely role when she was described in 1935 as Octavia Hill's 'ever-present but self-effacing fellow-worker' (*The Times*, 28 February 1935, FL). Similarly, in 1920, Leo Stein observed of the relationship of his sister Gertrude and Alice B. Toklas that the latter is 'a sort of all-important second fiddle' (Wineapple 1996, p. 297). Here we can see a constatively construed correlation between what Gertrude Stein said of herself and what was said of her at the time: 'consistently the language of self was male and masculine. Stein was "husband" to Toklas' "wife"' (Stimpson 1977, p. 496).

Beyond this, well-adjusted lesbians are described as combining male and female characteristics, a corporeal marriage of parts: Eve Balfour had 'masculine manners in spite of a feminine heart' (Lutyens 1920, in Lutyens 1972, p. 8), while Angela Burdett-Coutts was 'a woman of great strength of mind as well as tenderness' (*Times Literary Supplement*, 2 March 1951, FL). Angela du Maurier, herself a lesbian, described Micky Jacob in the 1920s as 'an extraordinary woman ... wearing a velvet dinner jacket, and with a head like Beethoven ... In spite of her masculine appearance, Micky was extremely feminine in many things; she was a very good cook ... ' (1966, pp. 52–3).

Christopher St John, in her biography of Christine Murrell, likewise seems to feel the need to stress an identity equilibrium (1935, p. 100; see p. 87). To Vita Sackville-West, St John had written:

I can never think of your sex, only your humanity. I could love you in breeches, or in skirts, or in any other garments, or in none. I know you must be a woman – evidence your husband and sons. But I don't think of you as a woman, or as a man either. Perhaps someone who is both, the complete human being who transcends both. (10 November 1932, in Glendinning 1983, p. 253)

Hence, lesbians are constructed, and construct themselves, through the eyes of another: 'The subject never really sees herself ... accept through the gaze of the other' (Diamond 1995, p. 152), and the other heterosexualises in describing the lesbian performative act.

Not only do lesbians of the period describe themselves, or act as, male, they also refer to themselves as boys. This is presumably in reflection of Freud's designation of homosexuals as immature, of Havelock Ellis's treatment of inverts as having 'young faces'. Daphne du Maurier, in love with a woman, felt she was 'a boy of eighteen all over again'. In a letter to her beloved, Ellen Doubleday, she asked her to imagine her 'never being a little girl. Always being a little boy. And growing up with a boy's mind and a boy's heart' (10 December 1947, in Forster 1993, p. 221). Gertrude Lawrence, whom she also loved, would 'never be an adult, which is why I find her so fascinating' (p. 240). One of her inner selves du Maurier called Niall, 'identifying myself with my boyish love for my father' (p. 421).

Edith Ellis was described by other sexologists in terms of her boyish immaturity (Havelock Ellis 1940, p. 263; and see Edward Carpenter and Daphne Bax, in their prefaces to Edith Ellis's work, 1921, pp. x–xi). Katherine Mansfield, recalling her love for Edie Bendall, in her journal of 1907, wrote 'I am a child, a woman, and more than half man' (Alpers 1980, p. 49). Of Maata Mahupuku, a Maori, older than herself, she noted: 'I feel savagely crude – and almost powerfully enamoured of the child' (p. 49). Here the language of gender, immaturity and race conflate. Katherine Mansfield embraced, or reflected, the idea of same-sex identity ascribed by sexologists.

Other lesbians self-ascribe a masculine identity through their names. Mary Allen was known to her friends as Robert (Baker 1985, p. 267), and Radclyffe Hall as John (Cline 1997). After her conversion to Catholicism, Christabel Marshall preferred her baptismal name of Christopher St John (Hamer 1996, p. 31), and Clemence Dane took her new name from a church in the Strand (*Daily Telegraph*, 29 March 1965, FL). By 1918, Gluck was calling herself Peter (Souhami 1988, p. 36); and Naomi Jacob adopted the name Micky, 'as Naomi was too feminine a name for so robust and dominating a personality' (Obituary, *Daily Telegraph*, 28 August 1964, FL). Other lesbians were given male designations by other people: Edith Ellis was named Johannes by Daphne Bax, to indicate her role in the wilderness (Ellis 1921, p. x).

Naming is a strong statement, and the power of designation over another suggests an assertion of right over identity. Gender is thus conferred through renaming of self, or by being named, and the lesbian recreated in this way can enact her male persona.

Dress Codes

Dress is a primary badge of sexuality. Like heterosexuality, it is not neutral. It operates as an outward sign of an inner statement of self. The contours of the possible are monitored by an heterosexual hegemony to culturally coerce conformity to posited norms.

Cultural cliques (of which heterosexuality, like homosexuality is a large set), identify themselves by what they wear in an effort to conform or to signify non-conformity. Within an alien hegemony, dress plays a particularly strong part in signification. Commendation or criticism of this, like any code, depends on whether you approve or not of the assumed motives of the dresser:

> If the term 'style' is thus used descriptively for an alternative way of doing things, the term 'fashion' can be reserved for the fluctuating preferences which carry prestige ... Moreover, since considerations of prestige sometimes carry with them the suspicion of insincerity and snobbery, the same movement may be described as a fashion by its critics and as style by its well-wishers. (Gombrich 1968, p. 354)

Lesbians and their mode of dress in the 1920s and 1930s have been treated with suspicion, not of *insincerity* but, indeed, of *sincerity* in their use of 'male' clothing. In the modernist history of signification, there are dual standards operated by the heterosexual determiner: in an effort to control, and to stimulate a sense of threat, the thing and the sign of the thing were presented as one:

> Cultural modernism is characterised by the tendency to translate things into signs, ontology into epistemology, *prematurely*. It collapses the materiality of history into the immediacy of a consciousness which is validated by consensus and thus by a philos-

ophy of Identity in which the 'I' finds itself mirrored and legitimized in the 'you' of 'society' or 'culture'. (Docherty 1996, p. 27)

Or, alternatively, the 'I' finds itself delegitimised by its non-conformity to dominant cultural typology. Here, the reader of the lesbian script is deliberately disingenuous in the penetration of lesbian 'disguise': a wolf in sheep's clothing is generally recognised as just that, suspected at once of having an ulterior motive, not of wanting to *be* but of wanting to take advantage of the dissemblance. Mannish lesbians, on the other hand, were treated as if they aspired to *be men*, which ignored the historical moment, 'the evaluation of expressiveness [which] will largely depend on a knowledge of choice situations' (Gombrich 1968, p. 358). The 'choice situation' of the period is one of women in general expressing independence via dress, a primary tool of dominance. 'The lesbian' and her aspirations, evidenced by appearance, was constructed as a threat to fictive norms.

The epideictic function of all sartorial codification has especial importance around sexuality. As soon as imperialism had embedded a notion of difference, then what lesbians wore became crucial. It was then, in the early twentieth century, that different cliques within and without lesbianism self-asserted via dress. Independent women showed their independence by wearing mannish gear. Such a preference for cross-dressing was not new (Newton 1984, p. 558). Lesbians may assert identity in and beyond this, to signify sexual as well as social independence, possibly via exaggerated style.

They align with, or rebut, the logic of a game played by all social cliques. Here, again, differentiation was made between *real* game-play and *pretend*. Lesbian cross-dressing was treated differently, for example, from male stage or professional impersonation. This was a genre of representation which was well known from life and from art. There was an enduring interest in 'James Barrie', for example, a woman who had passed as male until her death in 1865 in order to work as an army doctor. In the 1930s there were a number of newspaper articles about Barrie: 'One of the strangest facts in her story is that ... she was by no means masculine in appearance' (article by Agnes Allen, c. 1938, source unknown, FL). Stage male impersonators such as Vesta Tilley (1864–1952), the professional name of Matilda Powles who dressed in uniform and in 'Burlington Bertie' style, were likewise of unhostile interest (Maitland 1986; and see *Observer*, 8 November 1970, FL).[5]

More threatening masculine dress was mocked, on the other hand. Micky Jacob commented, 'I remember the [First World War] when women who wore uniform – unless they were nurses – were regarded as something strange, eccentric, and a fine target for jokes' (1940, p. 208). Other lesbians were attacked more blatantly. 'Colonel' Barker (Lilian Smith) was treated with hostility in the press in 1929 because she had used her disguise to perpetrate sexual fraud, and had been married to a woman for three years (Baker 1985, p. 254). General Sir Nevil Macready, Commissioner of the Metropolitan Police Force, in 1918 obtained a photograph of members of the Women's Police Service, amongst whom he claimed there was a man in woman's clothes. On the basis of this evidence he argued against the formal incorporation of the service into the official police, 'to eliminate any women of extreme views – the vinegary spinster or blighted middle-aged fanatic' (Lock 1979, p. 110).

Such derision wilfully ignored the logic of 'the game of "watch me"':

Satirists have inveighed against what they call the Follies of Fashion: but the folly of the game does not preclude rationality on the part of the players. For fashion can be described in terms of a rarity game. At one time it may be the display of rare lace that arouses attention and competition, at another a daring decollete, the height of the coiffure or the width of the crinoline ... occasionally the game catches on and reaches a critical size where all join in. Whether we have our hair cut or put on a tie, whether we drink tea or go skiing, we all join in the game of 'follow my leader' (Gombrich 1974, p. 63).

A lesbian in this Logic of Vanity Fair, like any other person, acts *de tempori*, gives in to, or rejects, the fashion of the times. Not to do something fashionable is as much a statement as to do it. And lesbian style, like any other, can be seen as a 'history of preferences, of various acts of choice between given alternatives'. (Gombrich 1960, p. 18)

Lesbians self-police at crucial historical moments, showing anxiety about appearance. Toupie Lowther, for example, after the trial of *The Well of Loneliness*, cooled her relationship with Radclyffe Hall and was noted by Una Troubridge to be shunning the company of 'her own ilk' and wearing 'scarlet silk "confections" in the evenings with accordion pleated skirts and low necks' (21 November 1932, in Baker 1985).

For other lesbians, there was a freedom gained from the loosening of the constraints of femininity. Agnes Hunt, with affection, recalled her lover Emily Goodford: 'Had she been well-dressed and her hair done in a later fashion, she would have been an exceedingly handsome woman. As it was she was unique' (1935, p. 77). Cicely Hamilton was recalled, too, by Lady Rhondda, off to meet a duchess in the 1930s, 'in a very old coat newly cleaned with a large cleaners' label hanging down her back' (*Time and Tide*, 13 December 1952, FL). Adoption of mannish gear was liberating. Gluck wrote to her brother in 1918:

> I am flourishing in a new garb. Intensely exciting. Everybody likes it. It is all black though I can wear a coloured tie if I like and consists of a long black coat, like a bluecoat boy's with a narrow dark leather belt. It was designed by yours truly ... It is most old masterish in effect and very dignified and distinguished looking. Rather like a Catholic priest. (Souhami 1988, pp. 35–6)[6]

Similarly, Eve Balfour, in an interview late in life, recalled that she had worn trousers since the First World War when 'she discovered the freedom of breeches' (*Country Living* 1989, in Collis 1994, p. 154).

In 1920 Vita Sackville-West gave an exuberant description of her earlier self, on the day on which she and Violet Keppel became lovers:

> An absurd circumstance gave rise to the whole thing; I had just got clothes like the women-on-the-land were wearing, and in the unaccustomed freedom of breeches and gaiters I went into wild spirits; I ran, I shouted, I jumped, I climbed, I vaulted over gates, I felt like a school*boy* let out on holiday ... I remember that wild irresponsible day. It was one of the most vibrant days of my life. (27 September 1920, in Sackville-West 1973, p. 99, my emphasis)

Other lesbians adopted what has been termed a 'Byronic posturing' in the style of the male libertine (Castle 1993, p. 103; and see Gilbert and Gubar 1989, pp. 350–3). Sackville-West recalled in 1927 her friend Valerie Taylor, who stayed late 'after dressing up earlier in the day as Lord Byron' (Glendinning 1983, p. 180).

Lesbians positioned themselves, and were positioned, within a prevalent discourse around dress. In a similar manner, they used, and are described within, the language of race.

Race and the Language of Lesbian Identity

The interplay between race and sexuality is partly reflected in such dress. Byronic posturing is associated with ideas of the foreign (for example via an 1813 portrait of him by Thomas Phillips, in the costume of a corsair, in the National Portrait Gallery, London) and Orlando is given androgyny by assuming similar clothing from overseas (Woolf

1928, p. 115). Otherwise, references to lesbians frequently contain an association of sexuality and racial difference. This seems to have derived from sexological language. Eve Balfour 'had an Egyptian face' recalled Elizabeth Lutyens (1972, p. 8); Gertrude Stein had 'a beautifully modelled and unique head. It was often compared to a Roman emperor' (Alice B. Toklas, of her first meeting in 1907, 1963, p. 26).

Foreigners are represented as seductive. French women are especially alluring. This connection is not new to the early twentieth century: Charlotte Brontë, for example, in reference to her relationship with Ellen Nussey, in 1836 called herself a 'Frenchified fool' (Miller 1989, p. 49). The connection, though, had especial resonance after sexologists categorised race and sexuality so closely.

Virginia Woolf gave her lesbianly Sally Seton in *Mrs Dalloway* (1925) French characteristics perhaps in reference to Vita Sackville-West's Norman ancestry: 'Sally always said she had French blood in her veins, an ancestor had been with Marie Antoinette … she had it still, a ruby ring which Marie Antoinette had given her great-grandfather' (1925, pp. 166–7). This is particularly powerful reference because there had been persistent rumours from the nineteenth century that the queen was a lesbian. Charlotte Moberly and Eleanor Jourdain had written in 1913 about 'visions' of her, at Versailles, in a *cause célèbre* of the period, from which evidence Terry Castle describes Marie Antoinette as 'a code-figure for female homoeroticism' (1993, p. 140).

Daphne du Maurier in that same year, 1925, wrote: 'I have quite fallen for the woman I told you about, Mlle Yvon. She has a fatal attraction … she's absolutely kind of lured me on and now I am coiled in the net … Venetian [her code word for lesbian] I should think … I only hope I haven't got Venetian tendencies.' Of herself, she wrote: 'at eighteen this half-breed fell in love' (Forster 1993, pp. 28, 222). When Gertrude Lawrence died, du Maurier wrote to Ellen Doubleday, with whom she was also in love, saying that she had experienced with Lawrence the 'strangest bond' beyond language: 'I think, if one was Gauguin in the South Seas, or loved a native girl, and never spoke their language, in a way that would be like that. Yet there was a mutual language. Something all mixed up with theatre and writing' (18 September 1952 in Forster 1993, p. 265).

Spanish and other European elements appear in descriptions. 'Miss Alice Toklas … looked like a Spanish gipsy and talked like a Bostonian' (c. 1927, in Stendhal 1995, p. 104). Vita Sackville-West wrote a biography in 1937 of her Spanish grandmother, *Pepita*, which is partly an autobiography also. In it she tries to explain aspects of her own 'foreign' personality (discussed on pp. 81–2). Orlando, Sackville-West's biographical embodiment, allied herself to a 'gipsy tribe' (Woolf 1928, p. 135), as Violet Keppel had written in her letter to Vita Sackville-West, 'You know we're different – gipsies in a world of landed gentry' (15 September 1918, in Sackville-West 1973, p. 138).

Keppel contained her sense of otherness in a language of spatial and cultural colonising:

> I tell you, there is a barbaric splendour about you that conquered not only me, but everyone who saw you. You are made to *conquer*, Mitya [Vita], not to be conquered ... You could have the world at your feet ... They said this evening after you had gone, that you were like a dazzling Gypsy ... A Gypsy potentate, a sovereign ... but still a Gypsy ... Everyone is vulgar, petty ... beyond all words, in comparison to you ... I have shown myself naked to you, mentally and physically and morally.
>
> Good God alive! No one in this earth has as much claim to you as I have. *No one in this world.* (Undated 1918, in Jullian and Phillips 1976, p. 158)

Like Ladye Batten and Radclyffe Hall, who used 'dear abroad' as a catch-phrase for the glamour and freedom of their relationship (Baker 1985, p. 37), Vita Sackville-West and Violet Keppel found that their relation-ship could be played out away from England. Social and spatial freedoms confer an existential liberation.

Foreignness and sexual freedom mutually reinforced, and the language of guilt was accordingly associated with both, yet inverted as lesbian and marital paradigms clashed. Violet Trefusis, discussing marriage, described herself as 'dumped down in a jungle of entirely foreign and soul-shattering emotions' (1919, in Souhami 1996, p. 170). After an excursion with Violet, after which she returned to her family, Sackville-West described her feelings of alienation, she 'felt blackened' (1920, in Sackville-West 1973, p. 112).

This displacement of ideas of sexuality on to the area of race can also be detected in disperals within class and body.

Class and Body: The Language of Identity

Some lesbians described self-alienation in terms of their body, espe-cially hands, a literal sexual site. Daphne du Maurier's characterisation of Rebecca, in her novel of that name (1938), was based on Ellen

Doubleday, in the face of love for whom she described herself as a little boy 'always biting her nails' (10 December 1947, in Forster 1993, p. 221). Aspects of du Maurier's autobiographical self can be seen cast in the second Mrs de Winter who, faced with the more overtly lesbian characters in the novel, Rebecca (the first wife), and Mrs Danvers, the housekeeper, describes herself: 'I went on polishing my nails. They were scrubby, like a schoolboy's nails' (1938, p. 156).

Du Maurier's views on class and sexuality intertwine in her fictioned self. When the second wife meets Mrs Danvers for the first time, 'I guessed at once she considered me ill-bred' (p. 72). After she has broken a china cupid, she is confronted by her husband, in ghastly conspiracy with Mrs Danvers to humiliate his wife:

> It was like being a child again ... it was like being a prisoner, giving evidence ... 'Is not that the sort of thing the between-maid is supposed to do, Mrs Danvers?' 'The between-maid at Manderley would never be allowed to touch the valuable things in the morning-room, sir', said Mrs Danvers. (p. 149)

> 'I am like a between-maid,' I said slowly ... That's why I have so much in common with Clarice [another under-servant]. We are on the same sort of footing. And that's why she likes me ... I knew now why Clarice did not disdain my underclothes as Alice [her maid] had done. (p. 151)

Here, du Maurier seems to echo Radclyffe Hall's description of Stephen Gordon's first same-sex encounter in *The Well of Loneliness*, significantly with Collins the housemaid. Power relations, again, are inverted:

> Stephen wanted to touch her, and extending a rather uncertain hand she started to stroke her sleeve. Collins picked up the hand and stared at it. 'Oh my!' she exclaimed, 'what very dirty nails!' Whereupon their owner flushed painfully crimson and dashed upstairs to repair them. (1928, pp. 13–14).[7]

'Their owner' is objectified, and watches herself as if from beyond her own body. When du Maurier wrote to Ellen Doubleday, her contradictions were bound up with similar issues, bound up, too, with ideas of language: 'Kissing your hands is like writing a poem'. If Ellen saw her as 'just one more Venetian [lesbian] wanting to make a pass' she must say so, when Daphne would throw herself in the river because she refused 'to be classed with that gang' (15 July 1948, in Forster 1993, p. 231). She encodes her lesbian feelings to Ellen in the third person, and writes about 'the boy in a box' who is sometimes let out:

> she opened up the box sometimes and let the phantom, who was neither girl nor boy but disembodied spirit, dance in the evening when there was no one to see ... I pushed the boy back into his box again and avoided you ... like the plague. (December 1947, in Forster 1993, p. 222).

> Women ought to be soft and gentle and dependent. Disembodied spirits like myself are all *wrong*. (September 1948, in Forster 1993, p. 235).[8]

Du Maurier refuses to name herself as lesbian, or, indeed, to use the word itself in full: 'nobody could be more bored with the "L" people than I am ... I like to think my Jack-in-the-box was, and is, unique' (21 February 1948, in Forster 1993, p. 229). She cannot bring herself even to use available language, and morphologically relocates, in both senses of form (organisms/body and words). In these respects, her autobiographical struggle reflects women's narratives of self more generally:

> To appropriate by means of the word has been a divine privilege rarely accorded to women. Although every speaking and writing subject is in a sense a stranger in a strange land, the feeling of power derived from even provisional occupation of certain linguistic or textual space ... has been a characteristically male delusion ... Whether male or female, the autobiographer is always a displaced person: to speak and write from the space marked self-referential is to inhabit, in ontological, epistemological, and discursive terms, no place. (Brodzki 1988, pp. 243, 244)

For a lesbian, doubly marginal in alien space, the act of claiming is particularly difficult. Sexual identity may rest on especially bodily definitions, and, in rejecting a corporeally defined selfhood, it is not surprising that du Maurier faced bodily-spiritual dispersal. Her negatively construed self-image she expressed by reference to working-class or racial groups, and she displayed in her writing a 'fear of the proletariat' (Kelsall 1993, p. 310). This is evident in an interview she gave in later life, in which, she emphasised her family credentials and links with royalty (she was at Buckingham Palace on the night that Prince

Charles was born), and claimed to be 'deadly against Enoch Powell', who had recently made his speeches on black immigration:[9] 'But I dare say if the little village of Polkerris was swamped by coloureds I might feel the same as I do in the summer when tourists swamp the beach and there's no rock left to undress behind' (*Evening Standard*, 14 June 1969, FL).

Du Maurier's racial and class antipathy are exposed here, in association with bodily anxiety. Her concern is about invasion, and about the other taking over: she feared that her identity includes what it claims, or desires, to exclude, and she struggles (like other lesbians, see p. 83) with what Derrida describes as the 'logic of identity'. He identifies in much of Western philosophy an effort to establish unity which excludes difference. This unity contains truth, towards which there is a struggle in auto/biographical writing that strives to describe the wholesomeness of self. Good, healthy features are attributed to an identity which excludes the false and pathological (Derrida 1976; and see Spivak 1990; O'Connor and Ryan 1993, pp. 17–18). For du Maurier to feel herself incorporating or threatened by that which she disdains socially, it is no wonder that she collapsed in her own self-meaning: 'The foreigner is within us', notes Kristeva (1991, p. 191), du Maurier's fear made flesh.[10]

Lesbians of the 1920s and 1930s frequently expressed alienation from their own bodies, in terms which express dis- and relocation. For some, translation offered liberation: Joe Carstairs, rich heir to a fortune, established a garage of female drivers in London after the First World War. They were frequently believed by their employers to be working class. 'This confusion of status appealed to Joe. She was a woman in the guise of a man, an heiress in the guise of a servant: such ambiguities not only played to her sense of theatre, they were also tools to disconcert and outwit' (Summerscale 1997, pp. 59–60). Other lesbians were less comfortable, and show dysmorphia not euphoria.

Radclyffe Hall's alienation from herself has frequently been said to be manifested in *The Well of Loneliness*, where fiction and non-fiction blur. Stephen Gordon looks at her own body in the mirror with hatred, and touches it with her own hands. It is 'like a monstrous fetter imposed on her spirit'. In the scene she struggles to find a new language, 'finding few words that seemed worthy of prayer, few words that seemed to encompass her meaning – for she did not know the meaning of herself' (1928, pp. 186–7). Teresa de Lauretis considers that this shows an ideological division between body and mind, a

groping blind and wordless toward an Other who should provide the
meaning, but does not, only leads her back to the real of her body
... [Her] 'healing' can be cast only in terms of renunciation and
salvation, in an order of language that occludes the body in favor of
the spirit. (1994, p. 211).

Non-body Language

Kathlyn Oliver had used similar language to describe her wish to meet
others of the 'same temperament', 'kindred spirits', in her letter to
Edward Carpenter after she had read *The Intermediate Sex*. But she
expressed reincorporation to a classification that had been established
within an exclusionary discourse: it had 'lately dawned on me that I
myself belong to that class' (25 October 1915).

Oliver is active, therefore, in (re)appropriating for herself a term
which arose from negative ascription. Unlike Virginia Woolf who
wrote, 'These sapphists *love* women' (21 December 1925, in Woolf
1977/84, vol. III, p. 51), or du Maurier who called them 'that gang',
Oliver reinscribes, and hence shows herself to be in a complex relationship to ideas of logos within a Platonic-Christian framework of
Western philosophy. In general, 'Woman does not take an active part
in the development of history, for she is never anything but the still
undifferentiated opaqueness of sensible matter' (Irigaray 1985, p. 224).
Consequently, woman is 'lacking in all power of logos' but 'offers
unawares an all-powerful soil in which the logos can grow' (pp. 162,
224). Such a statement, of the heterosexualised earth, was used by
Sackville-West in her statement about marriage in her 1929 broadcast
(see p. 43).[11] Oliver, who had rejected marriage, recognised the non-
closure of classification, the intertextual fluidity afforded by others'
definition where 'the text is not a line of words releasing a single "theo-
logical" meaning (the "message" of the Author-God) but a
multi-dimensional space in which a variety of writings, none of them
original, blend and clash' (Barthes, cited in Culler 1983, pp. 32–3).

Other discussion sought to consign lesbians to a non-carnality by
reference to spiritual worlds.[12] Radclyffe Hall was recalled at a 1932
Foyle's literary luncheon, with other 'kindred spirits with close-cropped
feminine heads, some stiff collars and monocles' (Roberts 1952, p. 96).
Such statements seek to deradicalise the possibilities of transgressive
physicality. Other lesbians use ethereal language as part of their mutual
fantasy. Virginia Woolf wrote to Vita Sackville-West:

let us dine together in the new place where they have a great variety of food and drinks; and they give you roses, and there are looking glasses which reflect the most astonishing scenes – a fat woman gobbling – in such a way that one feels one is dangling among octo-puses at the bottom of the sea, peering into caves, and plucking pearls in bunches off the rocks. (19 July 1926, in Woolf 1975/80, vol. III, p. 282).

Mercedes de Acosta described an evening with Greta Garbo in May 1935 in similar terms:

The evening was a sentimental one. We did the traditional things, ordering caviar, champagne and our favourite tunes from the orchestra ... in that rococo room with its pink-shaded lights, its soft string orchestra and its old-world atmosphere, I felt that I was moving in a dream within a dream. (Souhami 1994, p. 130)

Lesbians inhabit each other's extra-physical worlds. Violet Trefusis, in 1919, wrote to Sackville-West of being 'haunted by you day and night',[13] 'the house is haunted by your presence, and the sound of your voice calling me' (Trefusis 1989, pp. 151, 164), whilst Virginia Woolf wrote to her: 'We'll dine; we'll haunt the terrace' (1927, in 1975/80, vol. III, p. 396; and see Castle 1993). Such statements may displace to the unearthly a sense of discomfort which was suggested by contemporary notions of a lesbian bodily affliction, related to degeneracy. The *Sunday Chronicle* (19 August 1928, in Cline 1997, p. 245) referred to lesbianism as 'one of the hidden cankers of modern life'. Elsewhere, it was said that 'The Lesbian cult exists, but it is like those anaerobic bacilli which cannot endure fresh air' *(New Statesman*, 25 August 1928, in Cline 1997, p. 249). Some lesbians felt the force of this disapproval: 'This is unclean I know, but true', wrote Katherine Mansfield of her desire for Maata Mahupuku (journal, 29 June 1907, in Alpers 1980, p. 49). Others resisted its implications, again in a language of spirituality: Valentine Ackland recalled her feelings in 1922, on being questioned by her father about her relationship with a woman in Paris:

I remember vividly the expression of disgust on his face ... He asked if I knew what a filthy thing I had been doing? No, it had not been at all filthy. It was something very strange, but not at all wrong ... I thought one or other of us must have been wrongly made ... I said that Lana ought to have been a man; I thought she must have been one in a previous incarnation ... (1949, p. 67)

This suggests that Ackland had espoused, or instinctively herself interpreted her lesbianism, in the manner of the mystical male-soul-in-woman's-body description of Krafft-Ebing.

Hilda Matheson, like Ackland, acknowledged at once the antagonism and her own feelings which transcend it. She was not only resistant, but expressed an internalised sense of the life-giving properties of same-sex affection, when she wrote to Vita Sackville-West:

Love – all you've given me – all the physical side of it too – seems to me to be life in its very highest expression – it's mixed up for me with any decent thinking or feeling I've got or ever had – with everything in fact that is true and beautiful and of good report. And yet I suppose some people would regard it as shameful and vicious. (1929, in Glendinning 1983, p. 210)

There are other techniques of counterdiscourse, observable within the metaphorical language used by lesbians of themselves and each other.

Elemental Imagery of Identity: 'You grant me space, you grant me my space'

Lesbians of the early twentieth century had not, of course, heard of Luce Irigaray, but they seem to have written ahead of her ideas of *Elemental Passions* (1982). Though her poetic monologue is a chant of pleasure to a male lover, its basis is in the natural elements within which lesbian images of self and other were formulated in writing of the early twentieth century. It is a further act of reinscription to use her phallocentric text as an organising principle, to show that a lesbian's self-language parallels anti-lesbian theory.[14] In addition, lesbian usage of elemental imagery suggests at once an individuation (adoption of particular, peculiarly personalised inferences) and a remerger to more widespread signification. Self-conscious use of such language places an individual lesbian apart from, yet within, a sexual mainstream: this configuration is less clear-cut than the either/or of orientation. Lesbians take and restyle an existing language of love, and negotiate within the pressures of man-made and self-styled formulations. The tensions were not always resolved, none the less the lesbian writer sought to establish a means to writing of self which had emerged from her encounter with literary traditions that sought to exclude her.

> **a woman's voyage as she goes in search of her identity in love ... Between nature and culture, between night and day, between sun and stars ... she seeks her humanity and her transcendency.** (Irigaray 1982, p. 4)

In lesbian elemental imagery, 'she' and self articulate in mutual (re)creation: 'if you make me up, I'll make you' and 'What I am; I want you to tell me', wrote Virginia Woolf to Vita Sackville-West (23 September 1925, 26 January 1926, in 1975/80, vol. III, pp. 214, 233). In her diary in 1926, having just received a letter from Sackville-West, Woolf queried: 'Who am I, what am I, and so on: these questions are always floating about in me: and then I bump into some exact fact – a letter, a person, and come to them again with a great sense of freshness' (1977/84, vol. III, p. 86).

In the process of writing her biography, *Orlando*, though not in the narrative itself, Woolf 'killed off' her friend and lover. As she finished writing the book she wrote:

> Did you feel a sort of tug, as if your neck was being broken on Saturday last [17 March] at 5 minutes to one? That was when he died – or rather stopped talking, with three little dots ... Now every word will have to be rewritten ... I've lived in you all these months – coming out, what are you really like? Do you exist? Have I made you up? (20 March 1928, in 1975/80, vol. III, p. 474)[15]

In finishing the work, the author must start again. Endings are not real but presage new beginnings. Woolf is interested here in the prerupted, and this is integral to her literary preoccuption with narrative endings, especially for the female subject whom the patriarchal literary tradition had consistently punished for transgression. This was a subject about which Woolf wrote to Sackville-West as their relationship developed, in relation to Tolstoy's *Anna Karenina*, the emblem of female infidelity. On 13 April 1926, Woolf wrote:

> There is a book called Father and Son, by Gosse ... A parable this, of what we have done to the deposits of family happiness. But I'll flood you with all this when you come. When? ... I will tell you about Anna Karenina, and the predominance of sexual love in 19th

Century fiction, and its growing unreality to us who have no real condemnation in our hearts any longer for adultery as such ... (1975/80, vol. III, pp. 254–5)

In another letter, of 8 September 1928, Woolf complimented Sackville-West for her essay on Tolstoy, significantly in the same letter referring to Radclyffe Hall and the difficulty of supporting her appeal against the prosecution of *The Well of Loneliness*. Later, Woolf wrote:

> Practically every scene in Anna Karenina is branded on me ... *That* is the origin of all our discontent. After that of course we had to break away. ... How could we go on with sex and realism after that? ... It is one brain, after all, literature; and it wants change and relief ... (8 January 1929, in 1975/80, vol. IV, p. 4)

Anna Karenina is the epitome of female waywardness and its punishment: she commits suicide, the only possible solution to the unresolved pressures of patriarchy. Woolf (ironically enough) is interested to explore alternative endings, and offers rebirth to *Orlando*'s subject-object, for whom the biography was associated with the personal loss of Knole, her childhood home, on the death of her father, since she could not inherit as a woman. The themes of self-loss, gain and continuity are explored in *Orlando* across hundreds of years, not only in relation to a specific biography, but also in relation to wider, and literary, notions of female disjunction. Feminist, lesbian and writerly interests are thus behind the embodied polygamy of the biographical subject.

Orlando him/herself undergoes a transformation, and is reborn, as it were from death, awaking as a woman (1928, pp. 132–3). For Sackville-West, losing her home had been expressed as amputation: 'I felt as though a knife had been plunged into my heart the day Dada died, and as though a great chunk of flesh had been cut out, and had now fallen bleeding to the ground' (Letter to Harold Nicolson, 10 October 1928, in Raitt 1993, p. 102). In writing *Orlando*, Woolf was able to offer re-embodiment. She had created the ideal modernist reader in Sackville-West, and restored a sense of self by disrupting it, having dislocated the subject-reader who wrote to Harold Nicolson that she was 'in the middle of reading *Orlando*, in such a turmoil of excitement and confusion that I scarcely know where (or who!) I am' (11 October 1928, in Sackville-West 1992, p. 205).

The women frequently describe their writerly lesbian struggle, and the discourses intermesh: 'the language of sexuality not only intersects with but transforms the other languages and relations by which we know' (Sedgwick 1990, p. 3). Sackville-West herself had written of her early relationship with Violet Keppel, 'I felt like a person *translated*, or re-born; it was like beginning one's life again in a different capacity' (29 September 1920, in 1973, p. 103, my emphasis). The theme is explored in *Orlando*, which reconstitutes moments of personal and narrative struggle. Language fails the hero at key emotional moments: 'words went dashing and circling like wild hawks ... til they crashed and fell in a shower of fragments to the ground' (pp. 250–1).

Neither permanently fixed, nor shifting and fickle. Nothing solid survives ... (Irigaray 1982, p. 13)

Lesbian articulation of lovingness of self and other women moves between heterosexualised conceptions of home and desire for new habitation. Dimensions of home (shelter, hearth, heart, privacy, root, abode, paradise – Sommerville 1992; and see Valentine 1998, p. 320) are inverted, fluctuating between notions of real/rooted/fictive/heterosexual and real/liberated/paradisical/lesbian.

On 30 August 1928, Woolf wrote to Sackville-West about her feelings of self-uncertainty: as in the 'floating about' image of 1926, the letter contains language of water and of earth. She describes being 'dissipated', her soul is

floating, like duckweed, down a dirty river. I am very hot. I have been mowing the lawn. It looks now like a calm sea through which several large ships have passed leaving wakes behind them ... For many days I have been so disjected by society that writing has been only a dream – something another woman did once. What has caused this irruption I scarcely know – largely your friend Radclyffe Hall ... I am observing with interest the fluctuations of my own feelings about France [where she planned to travel with Sackville-West]. Leonard says he can't come. Like an angel he says but of course go with Vita ... And then [I] visualise myself saying goodbye to him and cant [sic] face it; and then visualise a rock in a valley with Vita in an Inn; and *must* go. So it goes on ...

I accept no responsibility for anything I write or do. I like your fecundity. And; surely, for the last ten years almost, you have cut back and pruned and root dug ... Please write your novel, and then you will enter into the unreal world, where Virginia lives – and poor woman, can't now live anywhere else ... (1975/80, vol. III, pp. 520–1)

The letter is quoted at some length since it epitomises both a sense of flux and of rootedness. The writer stands back from herself ('something another woman did once', 'I am observing', 'the unreal world'). Writing has *been* a dream. Other moments are anticipated, through visualisation and temporal shifts.

The context is important. The year 1928 saw the coincidence of personal and national event: the passionate relationship between the two women continued (they took their trip to France in September), Knole was lost to Vita, *Orlando* was completed, and *The Well of Loneliness* was seized on the charge of obscenity. Hence, Radclyffe Hall, and Woolf's feelings for Vita, caused 'this irruption'. Their relationship, through writing and sexuality, is embedded in a language of change, of space, of creativity and the lack of it, of marriage to 'an angel' (though male) in the manner of Marie Stopes. Woolf describes her bodylessness, like Daphne du Maurier, when she struggles to describe feelings bound up with sexuality, the issues around it, and her own sense of self through writing.

> **You have transformed my gaze into a sky of truths ... Your infinity? An uninterrupted sequence of projected points. With nothing linking them. Emptiness ... What terrifies you? That lack of closure.** (Irigaray 1982, pp. 37, 71)

Lesbian physical dislocation appears to run counter to the association of men with the mind and women with the body in the history of philosophy: 'the female sex becomes restricted to its body, and the male body, fully disavowed, becomes, paradoxically, the incorporeal instrument of an ostensibly radical freedom' (Butler 1990, pp. 12, 11, discussing de Beauvoir). The (self-) representation of lesbians afforded an opportunity for liberation. Subversive possibilities are opened up for the 'deviant' because she is categorised as transgressive other.

Vita Sackville-West's bodily escape was configured in a language of dress and vibrancy when she became 'a schoolboy let out on holiday' (p. 56). Reclothed in new possibilities, she, like other lesbians, was able to enter what previously had been male spaces. They are able to inhabit the elements as a new sphere, though they recognise that constraints still exist: 'she is afraid and custom hedges her in, I feel', wrote Katherine Mansfield in her journal (June 1907, in Tomalin 1987, p. 36) about her feelings for Edith Bendall. Violet Keppel used similar language of constriction, within heterosexual mores, to Vita Sackville-West, frustrated by their failure to be together: 'They've forced you to sleep beneath a self-respecting roof with no chinks to let the stars through … ' (15 September 1918, in Sackville-West 1973, p. 138). 'All the time I see how different it might be – the wild hawk and the windswept sky. I can see you splendid and dauntless, a wanderer in strange lands … ' (22 October 1918, p. 139). By 14 April 1919 she was urging, 'Mitya, fly, fly, fly – fly with me now; before it is too late … Away we'd go, away from the pretty countryside with its neat hedges and decent revelry. Away! Away!' (p. 150); and 'Cast aside the drab garments of respectability and convention, my beautiful Bird of Paradise, they become you not. Lead the life Nature intended … ' (1919, in Jullian and Phillips 1976, p. 166).

Convention came to contain Violet, too: married to Denys Trefusis on 16 June 1919, she wrote to Vita on 23 June 1919: 'Oh give me back my freedom! I was so happy once, so irresponsible and free. What am I now? A heartbroken nonentity, a lark with clipped wings' (Sackville-West 1973, p. 152).

> I am overwhelmed by the all-pervading sense of dissolution, finality – the sense of flight – migration of birds, winds, leaves … I feel out of place, like a green leaf on a withered stem. I feel that I too must be going … The hunter tingles at its bridles, the hound strains at its leash … I, too, must be away … there is a Gypsy caravan not far from here. (10 October 1919, in Jullian and Phillips 1976, p. 188)

The women interweave images which they used of and to each other in their letters and their fictionalised autobiography. For Woolf, to write is itself to engage with a male tradition, from which she derives motifs in order to reinvest them. The predatory bird image, for example, used by Woolf in *A Room of One's Own* (1929, p. 58) to describe male acquisitiveness, was contained in Chaucer's *Troilus and Crisyede* (II, ll. 924–931), where Troilus the eagle tears Criseyde's heart in her dream. Woolf had herself written to Sackville-West:

> I have finished Troilus and Cressida [sic] (by Chaucer) … Next Spenser; then Daniel; then Drayton, and so on, down one long road after another … Well Vita, you must be ready to lead me by the hand into daylight … (29 December 1928, in 1975/80, vol. III, pp. 569–70)

Woman-to-woman cathexis can lead the writer from the determining tradition into new spheres.

In *Orlando*, itself occasioned by issues of patriarchal theft, the frightening bird images of the earlier sections become less oppressive as the novel proceeds. The hero becomes more comfortable in herself, though they do trouble yet towards the end: 'Haunted! Ever since I was a child. There flies the wild goose. It flies past the window out to sea ... I fling after it words like nets' (p. 299). The language of language comes again: 'refluent like the tide' (p. 282), 'words like nets', the struggle to define and hold meaning.

The imagery infuses Sackville-West's own sense of self. In 1932 she was involved in a complex love-triangle with Evelyn Irons and Olive Rinder, and her poem 'No Obligation' opens with the line 'Come on the wings of great desire' (in Donoghue 1997, p. 128).

In her later life, 'birds' still haunted her: after Violet Trefusis had been to visit her in 1940 at Sissinghurst, some twenty years after their passionate relationship had ended, Vita wrote to her:

> It is as though great wings are beating round me – the wings of the past. Am I at Carcassonnée? At Avignon? In Venice? ... I don't want to fall in love with you all over again ... My quiet life is dear to me ... (1973, p. 167)

Note again the temporal shifts as Vita's mind moves back and forth, relocates in other countries and struggles to express and control.

Deep, deeper than the greatest depths your daylight could imagine, once again I caress you. Luminous night, touched with a quickening whose denseness never appears in the light ... Your light shone out so high beyond the night, so distant in the darkest depths. (Irigaray 1982, pp. 13, 37)

The women mutually enlighten and seek to explore new areas. The literary and the sexual come together. Women, denied access to inspiration, claim it, and from each other, their previous role as muse being combined with artistic agency. The female nude is, as it were, configured in a female (lesbian) gaze, and is no longer passive; the single-chambered receptacle, woman, is shown to have greater complexity:

> she will light a torch in that vast chamber where nobody has yet been. It is all half lights and profound shadows like those serpentine

caves where one goes with a candle peering up and down, not knowing where one is stepping.

So wrote Woolf about the act of writing of relationships between women (1929, p. 80). In *Orlando*, 'Slowly there had opened within her something intricate and many-chambered ... which one must take a torch to explore, in prose not verse' (p. 168).

For Woolf, Sackville-West had the quality of a beam, a 'candle lit radiance' (21 December 1925, in 1977/84, vol. III, p. 52; and see DeSalvo 1982, p. 200). The two women write to each other, and feel for substance in a darkness where object becomes subject. Approaching an impending visit by Woolf, Sackville-West wrote to her:

> I am not as solid as usual ... because there is at the back of my mind all the time ... a glow, a sort of nebula, which only when I examine it hardens into shape; as soon as I think of something else it dissolves again, remaining there like the sun through fog, and I have to reach out again, take it in my hands & feel its contours: then it hardens, 'Virginia is coming on Saturday'. (in DeSalvo 1982, p. 202)

Writing and sexuality come together. *To the Lighthouse* was published in 1927; and in that year Woolf referred to her 'as being very distant and beautiful and calm. A lighthouse in clean waters' (cited in Glendinning 1982, p. 172). In jealousy, when Sackville-West is taking other lovers, she is out in the 'bitter black night with woman unknown' (14 December 1928, in Woolf 1975/80, vol. III, p. 563).

At moments of inspiration in *Orlando*, light (or lack of it), and words (or lack of them) concur:

> Ransack the language as [Orlando] might, words failed him. He wanted another landscape, and another tongue ... The clearness [of Sasha/Keppel] was only outward; within was a wandering flame. It came; it went; she never shone with the steady beam of an Englishwoman. (pp. 45–6, and see pp. 49–50, 52, 55, 59)

Woolf thus explores the link between self-expressiveness and identity. The potential for destruction and well as creativity was located in the same elements. Light can be fire, as Sackville-West herself wrote. This elemental imagery for her operated on hetero-homosexual boundaries: she reassured Harold Nicolson that 'a thing like that [with Trefusis] happens only once and burns out the capacity for such a feeling' (17

August 1926, in Sackville-West 1992, p. 158). In that same letter she mentions her husband's fears that she will embark on a relationship with Woolf, whose mental instability makes her 'a fire with which I have no wish to play' (p. 159). Nicolson had warned, 'It is like smoking over a petrol tank' (1 July 1926, p. 150) and the wife replied 'it's not merely playing with fire; its playing with gelignite' (2 September 1926).

Some thirty years after her sexual relationship with Trefusis ended, 'we must not play with fire again' (31 August 1940, in Glendinning 1983, p. 306), and 'You and I can't be together. I go down country lanes and meet a notice saying "beware – unexploded bomb". So I have to go round another way. You are an unexploded bomb to me' (5 December 1940, in Glendinning 1983, p. 307). For Sackville-West, there can be too much of this light. Darkness is expressive of peacefulness and reunification in her own self-imaging, for example, see her poem 'Solitude' (1938).

Orlando, too, regains herself: 'Night had come – night that she loved of all times, night in which the reflections in the dark pool of the mind shine more clearly than by day' (1928, p. 312).

so distant in the darkest depths. (Irigaray 1982, p. 37)

Again, Sackville-West mediates in the 'double-discourse' established by the conflicts between heterosexual and lesbian love. 'Unless one is willing to embark on abysmal depths, and I feel at present they are too abysmal to be sounded by a plumb-line', she wrote in 1913, torn between Nicolson and Rosamund Grosvenor (Glendinning 1983, p. 68). In miserable love with Violet Keppel, in Venice, she wrote, 'Everything is black again … She is in the depths. So am I. I feel the Grand Canal, in spite of slime and floating onions, would be preferable' (1973, p. 163).

Sackville-West's novel *Challenge* was written at this time, between May 1918 and November 1919, published in 1924. It features the relationship, and ends with Eve/Violet drowning, having been abandoned by Julian/Vita in the darkness:

> she felt tiny and helpless in that great surge of water; even as she tried to scream she was carried forward and under, in spite of her terrified battle against the sea, beneath the profound serenity of the night that witnessed and received her expiation. (p. 287)

For Sackville-West, then, the water element suggests an other-world that is at times destructive. She engages, like Woolf, with the notion of narrative endings, and her lesbianly hero succumbs to the depths. Though she elsewhere referred to her heterosexual relationship as her anchor (p. 44), Sackville-West reveals a certain ambivalence at key times. Having received *Orlando*, she wrote to Woolf, 'Darling, you're my anchor. An anchor entangled in gold nuggets at the bottom of the sea' (29 November 1928, in Sackville-West 1985, p. 297), in similar terms to Woolf's fantasy sub-marine meal (p. 63). This is a fantastical anchoring, in tacit reference to the lesbian not-yet-real (p. 47).

Other lesbians more successfully subvert the patriarchal tradition via this imagery. Radclyffe Hall used Mosaic/Christian language of inspiration when wrote to her lover in 1934, 'It is as though I had struck the rock with the staff of love and at last the spring had gushed out, out of your heart into mine, beloved ... ' (cited in Cline 1997, p. 327). That lover herself wrote of Hall in 1935, 'She needed me like water, like air ... ' (p. 347). The elements are not always friendly, however. Hall wrote: 'Sometimes we are rather like two ships that get blown about for a while by winds, or washed apart for a while by tides ... ' (12 August 1938, pp. 357–8).

Virginia Woolf used the image to describe the process of both separation and coming together within autobiographical writing: 'we are sealed vessels afloat on what is convenient to call reality; and at some moments the sealing matter cracks; in floods reality ... ' (25 October 1920, 1977/84, vol. II, p. 122). Shari Benstock has located here Woolf's manifesto of self-writing, 'a process of sealing and splitting that can only trace fissures of discontinuity' (1988, p. 29). Woolf had consciously sought to save herself from drowning (again ironically) in a patriarchal sea where the female self is lost. She turned from the final (heterosexual) dryness identified by Irigaray who says to her lover, 'We are separated by so many similar things that the flow which attracts us to each other is exhausted as it beats against these obstacles. It no longer flows, held back by boundaries that are too water-tight' (1982, p. 104).

The mother is seen as the earth substance which must be cultivated and inseminated so it may bear fruit. (Irigaray 1982, p. 1)

The sexualised soil is an enduring literary motif within heterosexuality. The passive (written) receives the active (writing). Like Harold Nicolson, though she contradicted him in public (p. 43), Sackville-West used the imagery of her married self. Similar useage appears in her long, prize-winning poem, *The Land* (1926), and in a poem written for her husband (see 1973, p. 178). Virginia Woolf, on the other hand, communicated a different tradition, encompassing imagery of the earth in a same-sex context, placing lesbian desire within Edenic/Platonic spaces where the green world symbolises the place for desire. Vernal imagery is a cliché in heterosexual romance (Zimmerman 1992a, pp. 79–80), taken up by Woolf. At a time when she considered that illness and separation had diminished the passion between herself and Sackville-West, she wrote that it had 'loosened the earth about the roots' of this affection (November 1925, in Lee 1996, p. 498). To her sister, she wrote: 'You will never succumb to the charms of your own sex – What an arid garden the world must be for you' (1975/80, vol. III, p. 381).

Lesbian language within auto/biography accordingly makes use of the language of the elements, the very centre of heterosexual encampment and spatial occupation, to establish a discourse of same-sex creativity. Writers engage with commonplace metaphors, available before heterosexuality purloined them and encased them in a normalising episteme, to create a means of self-expression which extends beyond and before their own sense of selfhood. The writer-lesbian delves behind received tradition so that her language is both subaltern and postliminiary, asserting her right as a returned exile to assume former status.

3
Lesbian Auto/biography in the Early Twentieth Century

The State of the Art

Elemental imagery, used in various genres, shows one way to express a sense of self. Within the more formal genres of autobiography and biography, modes of lesbian self- and other-expression took particular and distinctive style, under pressure on both the genres themselves and of notions of sexuality.

At the beginning of the twentieth century, the tradition of biography, the written account of an individual life, was summarised by the editor of *The Dictionary of National Biography* (*DNB*) which accommodated 'full, accurate and concise biographies of all note-worthy inhabitants of the British Isles and the Colonies' (Lee 1900; 1975 edn). Earlier, he had written that the *DNB* 'commemorates ... the men and women who have excited the nation's commemorative instinct' (1896, p. 265). Nationalistic aims were the organising principle to the publication, as often with individual biographies of the period (see Chapter 2, note 1), together with an inherent sense that the enterprise of life summation was a possibility at all.

For writers such as Havelock Ellis, biography was associated with ethnography (in his 1904 text, *A Study in British Genius*, for example). Reviewers of biographies reveal what was valued in the genre, though that was not necessarily the same as the aims of the biographers themselves. Hence, a commentary on Lytton Strachey's *Eminent Victorians* praised the work for its penetration of the essence (as if timeless) of various characters. Greatness stands independently from social circumstance. The reviewer praised Strachey's 'specimens' of Victorianism which 'he treats neither as waxwork models nor criminals nor fools'. It is said that Strachey, in his portrait of Florence Nightingale, 'refuses to see the great personality obscured by the "lady with the lamp" legend ... he persists in thrusting to our notice the fiery fighter, the woman of irresistible, relentless will who made all her helpers tools, minions for the cause' (4 June 1918, in *Guardian*, 4 June 1996, p. 3) (see Chapter 1, note 13). This is a triumph of imperialism personified.

Elements of this tradition clearly did continue, and have continued, in the art of English biography in the twentieth century. Some writers have maintained an interest in individual genius and its origins. The whole urge to commemorate a life suggests at least of vestige of this belief. None the less, with philosophical changes in the early part of the century, the art underwent some shifts in the face of particular rethinking of concepts of self- and otherhood. Some such ideas might appear to be completely impossible to incorporate into the genre's main thrust. The application of modernist ideas of multiple points of view in narrative, for example, may seem incompatible with notions of biography and autobiography which seem to rest securely on the concept of unity of vision and of consensus between author and reader.

A European philosophy of self, and the writing surrounding it, had centred on the idea of a knowable, if hidden, individuality: the sixteenth-century writer Montaigne had claimed that each person possessed an 'arrière-boutique toute nostre', a room behind the shop all our own (Porter 1997, p. 3). We live behind a visage, and autobiography involves excursions and multiple forays into our own unique memory stock formed by experience and by conscious reflection on its significance, by which process subjectivity is formed. While this suggests two selves, they did not necessarily need to be co-present. The modern self might be said to have arisen when both realised that the other was there. She/they is/are both inside and outside simultaneously. In authorial terms, there was a concomitant movement away from the study of exemplary lives, described in 'objective' terms, towards an art which explored the paradoxes of uniqueness and commonality; of the transference between other- and self-consciousness; of authenticated truth of being, through, for example, fictionalised life-writing.

In autobiography, the self and the writer were not necessarily one: 'Je est un autre', wrote Arthur Rimbaud in 1871 (p. 251). His sense of inner self as other and apart from writing/written self is reflected in notions of writing both transcending and being unable to transcend the personal. The whole notion of auto/biography is predicated both on the (potential) knowableness and the mystery, hence fascination, of an individual; and on a self-consciousness, so that an author both does (write) and watches herself, is within and without her own narrative. Discourses of the modern thus divide between writer (active, moving elusive) and written (passive, set down, understood), not to mention the writing self in its continuous here and now. *Orlando* exemplifies many of these features. It ends in the time-present, which continues after the narrative has ceased; the subject has been objectified and written, yet is not understood by normative continuums in the plot. Her gender, among other seemingly fixed facets of selfhood, has changed, and who knows if even now it is fixed? The unsettledness (for subject-reader and other reader) continues after the narrative fades.

Such an interest in self-mobility, and a multifaceted construction of self, is inherent in a modern aesthetic which is concerned to demonstrate both the coming-to-knowledge and the falling-apartness of the knowable. This is also a feature of women's autobiography, in contrast to male authorial drives to the known. Within the period, it is possible to document gender-specific constructions of the self, to recognise that, while modernism destructures, decentres gender and other 'absolutes', as part of its urge to unsettle form, women often write from a special consciousness of marginality. And this viewpoint is even more manifest for those who are additionally marginal, such as lesbians.

Women autobiographers frequently apologise for assuming authority to write, and this stance may be reinforced by other elements of abjection, such as homosexuality: 'Of course I have no right whatsoever to write down the truth about my life', Sackville-West opens her autobiography (1973, p. 9). Such an approach frequently, as here, arises out of an anxiety, where self-unity is doubted, and author-ity only tentatively claimed. For women writers of the period, perhaps because of this, there is a sense of writing through others, in a literal and literary way: biography and autobiography are often confluent. In other subjects, writers see themselves, and for the quadrupally marginal Gertrude Stein (Jew, lesbian, woman, exile), auto/biography is diasporic and refrangible.[1]

Such an idea was also expressed by Virginia Woolf when she wrote of biography, 'Each of the supposed subjects holds up in his or her bright diminishing mirror a different reflection of [the author] ... It is thus, [the biographer] would seem to say, in the mirrors of our friends, that we chiefly live' (1966/67, p. 233). Accordingly, within the new art of biography, readers should not expect the subject and the reproduction the Life contains to be identical. Woolf, in her biography of Roger Fry, expressed frustration at the expectation in the English public: 'Why are they all engrossed in childish problems of photographic representation?' (1940, p. 164). She was enthusiastic about the potential of André Maurois's fictionalised life-account of Shelley (1923) which she could not 'swallow quick enough' (Letter, 24 April 1924, in Woolf 1975/80, vol. III, p. 101).[2]

Authorial stances within modernist auto/biography acknowledge the elusivity of the subject, show a move towards democratisation of relationships between writers and subjects. The author is neither omnipotent nor abject devotee:

> If we open up one of the new school of biographies, its bareness, its emptiness make us at once aware that the author's relation to his subject is different. He is no longer the serious and sympathetic companion, toiling even slavishly in the footsteps of the hero ... he is an equal. (Woolf 1966/67, p. 231)

Here, the writer of biography is not 'a neutral, objective reporter, but [has] an active, and, in psychoanalytic terms, even a "transferential" relationship to the biographical subject' (Marcus 1994, p. 90). The reader of modern biography (frequently neglected in philosophical discussion of the genre) likewise is not in a neutral position. When biography is 'fictive', the activity of reading involves a recognition, and an experience, of the fluidity of truth. This is an open truth, recognition of which is based on the collaboration of reader and writer in its pursuit. It operates on the basis of shared rules, a suspension of belief on the part of the reader in order to attain abstractions, even momentary, of truthfulness:

> The complexity of life ... is greater than our documentary, chronological, critical schemes allow for ... The Ariadne's thread is missing. It is found in no letter, no archive, no encyclopaedia ... It must be spun from one's inner consciousness ... Hence the need for *a priori* sympathy, in the exact meaning of that term: '*feeling with*'. (Barzun 1939, p. 80)

Interpreting such work about heterosexual subjects is rather different, however, from the art of reading lesbian auto/biographies where readers engage in a double process of guess-work, mediating often between open truth (that this is a fictive enterprise) and disguised truth (signs of sexuality which have been mis- or un-named). They read both the surface, where fact-fiction subtly meet, and between the lines, where inferences often suffice for both. As such, the relationship between the author and the subject of biography, and between them and lesbian readers, is not as equal as Woolf suggests. Authors often use their power to disguise issues of sexuality. Readers operate in two dimensions, using literary antennae for one activity (deciphering open truths about the biography's fictions), and using sexuality-astute skills for the other (extrapolating closed truths, showing sensitivity to signs).

The reader of a (potentially) lesbian text (and this is, by definition every biography of a woman), is often required to read the unwritten, to participate in the interchange between self as reader and subject as subtextual. She is often required, in Barzun's terms, to perform invisible mending on the text before she can catch there her sympathetic thread. For lesbian readers, therefore, there is a diaspora of the reading self as well as of the written and textual self. In modernist texts, this gave a particular dimension to those writing about their own sexual life in the form of autobiography.

There were particular (self-) constraints arising from the historical moment (itself not neutral but caused by political shifts) which affected lesbian auto/biographers, and readers, in the period. Editions of the lesbian papers of Anne Lister, produced in the 1930s, after *The Well of Loneliness* trial, for example, are felt to show prudent negotiation, 'to present only the respectable face' of their author (Liddington 1994, p. 18). In the early 1940s, further exigencies may have forestalled lesbian publication, within a Cold War association of homosexuality 'with moral unreliability, and like communism, with treason' (Wilson 1980, p. 101). The political parameters operated alongside, or within, philosophical configurations of the Lesbian as uncivilised and, by association, rude of tongue, inarticulate. Such pressures try to mute the lesbian writer, who is thus engaged in a further struggle towards eloquence.

Auto/biographies of Lesbians

Lesbian writers of autobiography in the early twentieth century accordingly faced many issues. Whilst modernist ideas of democratised author(ity), of dispersal of self through time, may have offered positive potential in life-writing, strong traditions of organisation around heterosexual rites of passage formed a narrative pattern to which few lesbians might aspire. In addition, there were theories of the sexual self to further complicate the matter. This gave rise to possible tensions between theory and practice, object and subject. What lesbians read of themselves as topics for sexual case studies may not have accorded with their own experience. Or, they may have written about themselves in certain ways because of the theories themselves, their personal experience may have been delimited, or enabled, by theorists.

For some, it was a problem to use of herself the very word 'lesbian', or to write at all in an ideology in which woman was silent and chaste (so non-lesbian, since Lesbian was categorised as whore). On the other hand, lesbians may have felt themselves to be in a relatively privileged position in relation to writing, in contrast to feminised heterosexual women: 'For a symbolic order that equates the idea(l) of the author with a phallic pen transmitted from father to son places the female writer in contradiction to the dominant definition of woman and casts her as usurper of male prerogatives' (Stanton 1984, p. 15).

From the seventeenth century, at least, women describe writing as 'manly' (Aughterson 1995, p. 231) and lesbian masculine identification, afforded in new ways in the early twentieth century, was one means to authorship. Other images of eloquence, however, may have operated as counterlever. Metaphors of childbirth, themselves ancient, were reappropriated by women to describe their process of writing (O'Brien 1981; Friedman 1987). Transfer of this image may have seemed problematic for the (potentially) non-procreative with their 'mental masculinisation' (Lichtenstein 1921). Hence, features which may have been liberating for women in auto/biography may have been less so for lesbians.

In addition, established theories of auto/biography and of sexuality suggested, with their white patriarchal confidence, that a sexual self could be known as a unified whole. Lesbians, like other minorities, may feel excluded from such claims, and experience a dual consciousness, of self as defined from outside and 'self experienced as straddling silence':

> From this division, our material dislocation, came the experience of one part of ourselves as strange, foreign and cut off from the other which we encountered in tongue-tied paralysis about our own identity. We were never all together in one place, were always in transit, immigrants in an alien land. (Rowbotham 1973a, p. 31)

Lesbians writing about themselves frequently show a quest to attain grounding and re-embodied unity in the face of an experience of dispersal.

Duality

Partly, unity might be afforded by performative marital metaphor, via a coming together with another in symbolic symmetry: Kathlyn Oliver wrote about 'my other half' (25 October 1915, CC). Agnes Hunt

(1867–1948), similarly, affirmed in her autobiography a sense of internalised unity, found through her relationship. She wrote in terms which suggest that she had in mind a Platonic ideal of matching halves as a model:

> Even now, after eighteen years, it is difficult to write of her [Emily Goodford, who died in 1920] and what she was to me. It is given to few to live and work, to laugh and play with one beloved friend for 30 years in perfect love and unity. Mother once said that I was very lucky in having such a friend, because every virtue I lacked ... Miss Goodford provided, and so we made one fairly satisfactory whole. (1938, p. 178)

The process of writing could effect a personal reconstitution. In her edition of the diary of her ancestor, Anne Clifford (1590–1676), Vita Sackville-West wrote of the process of 'reconstruction of a forgotten character from the desultory evidence at [the biographer's] disposal':

> We should ourselves be sorry to think that posterity should judge us by the patchwork of our letters, preserved by chance, independent of their context, written perhaps in a fit of despondency or irritation, divorced above all, from the myriad little strands which colour and compose our peculiar existence ... (1923, xxiv–xxv)[3]

There is interplay here between individual and history: biographers needed to revisit the moment of eloquence, to see what conditions had made it possible, or, indeed, stifled it, to look at silences as well as utterances, to read between lines of written evidence of self. In *The Diary of Lady Anne Clifford*, as elsewhere in Sackville-West's fictional and biographical work, there is a complex weaving of self and other. In *Pepita* (1937), too, Sackville-West's biography of her grandmother, generational links between the women of her family are explored, yet the work 'has no investment in creating a cohesive self over time' (West-Burnham 1994, p. 44).

It has been suggested that Sackville-West found reassurance for her inner conflicts by writing this biography which explored tensions that she attributed to her own Spanish-English ancestry. *Pepita*, it is contended, explores her 'twinned pairs of eternal opposites', gypsy-aristocrat, Latin-English, working class-aristocrat, amorality-legally coded relationships: 'It was her "Spanishness" which enabled her to accept her lesbianism comparatively easily, her "Englishness" which forbade anything so "vulgar" as a public acknowledgement of it' (Hennegan, 1986, p. vi).

Hennegan's argument is borne out by Violet Trefusis who herself observed the polarities. When she first met Sackville-West she had the impression of someone 'stolidly, uncompromisingly British. In her deep stagnant gaze there was no dawning wanderlust' (Sackville-West 1973, p. 60). Later, Trefusis had seen her as an embodiment of Spain. She wrote to her lover from there, inhabiting her linguistic and bodily space:

> Here I am in your country ... and in the country of your language ... Spain is you, you, you ... I love Spain *passionately*! ... never have you seemed so vivid. I feel like a person who has gone into a house whilst the owner is absent (July 1919, in Jullian and Phillips 1976, pp. 179–80).

In *Pepita*, Vita could herself do the visiting, of her grandmother's (and her own) foreign geography. Her personal disengagment is reflected in the *dramatis personae* she lists at the outset, divided into Spanish and English, which does not include herself. She is, in effect, an outsider and her subjectivity is disguised. She opens the text tellingly, 'Spain ... had scarcely been "discovered" by the foreigner' (p. 13). The work ends with reference to Pepita's daughter, the writer's mother. Again, she hides behind another authority, and quotes Rudyard Kipling's view of her (and, by inference, Sackville-West's own views of a biographical subject as finally elusive): 'It's outside all my experiences and of a type to which I know no duplicate' (p. 282). Self and other, having been momentarily allowed to touch within the pages of the text, are thrust apart once more. The chance to see herself in others is hastily refuted: we are all unique. She shows timorousness and temerity, in displacing herself into another's biography, an act that may have its origins in pressures within and from modernism and sexology. Ideas of fragmentation were integral to both.

Notions of sexual duality were at the heart of sexual theory. There were contradictory messages about this. Havelock Ellis, for example, based his theories on ideas of polarities, defined by gender characteristics, whereas every issue of *Urania* (FL) had at its head the following statement:

> Urania denotes the company of those who are firmly determined to ignore the dual organisation of humanity in all its manifestations.

They are convinced that this duality has resulted in the formation of two warped and imperfect types ...

If the world is to see sweetness and independence combined in the same individual, *all* recognition of that duality must be given up. For it inevitably brings in its train the suggestion of the conventional distortions of character which are based on it.

There are no 'men' or 'women' in Urania.

When Vita Sackville-West wrote her autobiography in 1920, contained in *Portrait of a Marriage* (1973), there is interplay of theory and experience: did she feel dispersal or duality because she was told that she should, or is her theory based on life? Her eloquence is formed under the pressures of antipathetic discussion in which she expresses a sense of fragmentation. Her current writing self is different, she says, from the one her husband knows, and she is differentiated from her own self. The past, with its turbulence, 'might have been the life of another person' (p. 42). Stepping outside enables her to try 'to tell the *entire* truth' because of her conviction, like *Urania* states, that the sexes increasingly resemble each other. Her 'confession' was precipitated by a crisis of identity, yet she expresses a surety. There is in her struggle an embodiment of the 'gendered opposition' (Montefiore 1996, p. 41) which characterises male/female narrative: she is her own authoritative case study and yet she writes from a position of female, and lesbian, marginality. Hence she is both in, and not in, her own narrative:

I advance, therefore, the perfectly accepted theory that cases of dual personality do exist, in which the feminine and the masculine elements alternately preponderate. I advance this in an impersonal and scientific spirit, and claim that I am qualified to speak ... because I have the object of study always to hand, in my own heart, and can gauge the exact truthfulness of what my own experience tells me (27 September 1920, in 1973, p. 102).

This echoes both Rousseau and Anne Lister in 'I know my own heart' acclamation. She strives after 'truth', yet left her manuscript unpublished. Her lesbianism was an open secret, yet, 'Having written it down I shall be able to trust no one to read it; there is only one person in whom I have such utter confidence [presumably Harold Nicolson] that I would give every line of this confession into his hands ... he would emerge holding his estimate of me steadfast' (1973, p. 9). So her autobiography is both silent and said, a confession made in a non-soundproof box to a priest who already knew, and whose absolution was expected but not tested.

This is a retrospective account, though it has the apparatus of immediacy, written as if it were a diary. The dates, though, are those on which the statement was written, about recent past events, past lives. There is a creative tension between the pretend-present and an unfolded tale. The act of retelling itself allows for a self-reconstitution, a recollection, but not from a position of tranquillity in terms of literary Romanticism. As she ends her narrative, on 28 March 1921, she is still 'writing in the midst of great unhappiness' (1973, p. 124). The seeming safety is itself only provisional, and the lie of the narrative is that it has solved anything by setting down the events. The only solution to the open-endedness is to rebegin the writing, a process which belies the process of closure in confession, an activity that suggests reconciliation, at-one-ment. Sackville-West's confession reveals, instead, the irreconcilabilty of such notions within a modernist, and sexualised, paradigm: though the confessional mode might seem to afford a liberated subjectivity, it also suggests a dependence on the very constraints of the confessional itself, that of giving authority to forgive to (a patriarchal) another, predicated on the very existence of such a listener rather than in free individuation. Again, objectivity/authority and subjectivity/submission intersect:

> On the one hand, the depiction of one's life and experiences as a woman … a homosexual, can be a potentially liberating process insofar as it expresses a public self-acceptance and a celebration of difference [in Sackville-West's case conversely via a claim that differences were diminishing] … On the other hand, the internalised cultural values which define specific identities as marginal, inferior, or deviant can come to the surface in feelings of anxiety and guilt. (Felski 1989, p. 88)

Sackville-West's assertion of confidence is contained in a narrative of self-doubt which gives it/herself away, literally and metaphorically.

These ideas and their tensions are embodied, too, in *Orlando*, Virginia Woolf's biography of her lover. For the hero, love 'has two faces; one white, the other black; two bodies; one smooth, the other hairy' (1928, p. 113). At a point of confusion, Orlando observes herself, as if outside time and space,

> censuring both sexes equally, as if she belonged to neither; and indeed for the time being, she seemed to vacillate; she was man; she was

woman ... It was a most bewildering and whirligig state of mind to be in. The comforts of ignorance seemed utterly denied her. (p. 152)

Sackville-West's autobiography begins with a figurative expression of her dilemma, her exhilaration and her quandary:

> ... it is a morass, my life, a bog, a swamp, a deceitful country ... here am I already in the middle of my infirmities ... Yesterday I was on the sea in a sailing-boat; it was very rough, and at moments I was extremely frightened, but wished I wasn't frightened, because theoretically I enjoyed seeing the ship put her nose down into the waves, seeing the spray break over the deck, and then feeling my face all wet and tasting the salt water on my lips. The world of the sea is quite a different world ... one has a whole different set of wishes and preoccupations – the wish that the boat would keep still, if only for five minutes, as a rest from the perpetual balancing ... (1973, pp. 9–10)

She is both elated and afraid, and her imagery suggests an experience of indecisive flux which is distinct from her husband's wishful thinking to his wife: 'I *know* that for each of us the magnetic north is the other – and that though the needle may flicker and even get stuck at other points – it will come back to the pole sooner or later' (Letter, 3 December 1926, in Sackville-West 1992, p. 176). In *Orlando*, Shelmerdine/Harold lectures Orlando on navigational tricks (pp. 245–6) and she gains directional understanding. In life, Harold continued to feel threatened by Vita's 'emotional storms, which are beautifully controlled, but which may be symptoms of an approaching climacteric which frightens me' (1934, in Glendinning 1983, p. 269).

If 'It is a moot question whether or not Vita allowed Virginia Woolf to read her explosive memoir [subsequently *Portrait of a Marriage*] as a sourcebook for *Orlando*' (Kellerman 1978, p. 142), the imaginative concurrence between the two books is significant. It matters less to know whether they *did* exchange written accounts, more to see in their writing an interchange of lesbian lives, a writing of selves and other in their autobiographical encounter.

Biographies of Lesbians

Biography, for the most part, despite Woolf's intention that *Orlando* should revolutionise the genre 'in a night' (Letter to Sackville-West, 9 October 1927, in Woolf 1975/80, vol. III, p. 429) continued to some extent to operate as though a Life was explicable as a unified whole. It operated, too, with heterosexuality as the unstated norm. In consequence, claims cannot be made for lesbian biography as a separate genre in this period, rather, for the most part, it was a subset of patriarchal biography, within which sexuality was confirmed or denied within the parameters of heterosexual expectation. Modernism may have provided an expressive route for biographers who were perplexed by their subject's sexuality: it may have allowed a range of choices to coexist, just as *Orlando* allowed multiple genders and times and spaces to merge. For the most part, biographers did not take the opportunity, and wrote Lives based on binary principles, as if heterosexuality gave reconciliation.

Biographies of Charlotte Brontë during this period write of her relationship with Ellen Nussey in such terms. Clement Shorter describes it as 'hero-worshipping to an almost morbid degree' (1905, p. 35; see Miller 1989, p. 52). E.F. Benson writes of the relationship as 'an emotional thread that for years was the vividest colour in Charlotte's life', assessing it directly as 'one of those violent lesbian attachments ... for a considerable period of her life, her emotional reactions were towards women rather than men' (1932, pp. 37, 48). The word 'those' suggests that the relationship is being categorised rather than described individually; and this sense of normalised philosophy is endorsed by the statement that Brontë's relationship was 'eclipsed' by her subsequent marriage to Arthur Bell Nicholls. The biographies suggest, probably incorrectly, that the passion was transitory and that it could be corrected by heterosexuality.

Biographies do not, for the most part, identify women-centredness as important. Family then marriage are assumed to be the normal route. Failure to follow this is a cause for explanation, or, more rarely, of celebration for political purposes. Gertrude Colmore's 1913 biography of Emily Davison, for example, described Davison's youthful rebelliousness, where 'defying authority' was an indicator of her latent suffragism: 'She cared nothing for dolls; it was the martial rather than the maternal spirit which was dominant in her childhood ... ' (1913, pp. 5, 7). Colmore's work described an exemplary independent female life as though it had no emotional roots to its inspiration apart from rebellion. The work has been designated as 'basically hagiography', since Colmore explains Davison's militancy through the idea of 'genius' (Morley with Stanley 1988, pp. 76–7).

Other writers do acknowledge the status of same-sex relationships to their subject, but with parenthetical commentary on their significance.

Christopher St John's biography of Christine Murrell has the importance of being a rare lesbian study of another lesbian: both women lived in a *ménage à trois* with their lovers. St John began the work at the request of Honor Bone who, with Marie Lawson, lived with Murrell; and she dedicated the finished work to both women ('For M.L. and E.H.B.'). As with her letter to Vita Sackville-West (quoted p. 52), St John expressed her own preoccupation in writing a biography based on lesbian humanism. Murrell had not married, and 'never even had a love affair': 'It was possible she was sexually underdeveloped or, as I prefer to put it, too highly developed as a human being with a nice balance of male and female attributes and qualities, to be strongly sexed' (1935, pp. 99–100).

St John gave an economic reason for women's cohabitation:

A stable friendship between two women which often leads to their setting up house together is now quite common, and accepted as an alternative to marriage. The theory that the greater economic independence of women is largely responsible for the increase in such partnerships seems to me quite sound ... Christine Murrell's and Honor Bone's ... friendship which lasted for over thirty years was cemented by their professional partnership as doctors. (p. 35)

Though St John asserts a 'happy coalescence', she poses, and sidesteps, the familiar question: 'Which personality dominated in the practice and the home is a question I lack the authority to answer' (pp. 100–1). She explained the advent of Marie Lawson to the household in similarly gendered terms. Murrell was a 'woman of massive frame, a virile woman, whose irreproachably feminine clothes seemed incongruous' (p. xvii). Honor Bone was 'hindered from supplying all that Christine Murrell needed' because of her health: 'Fully conscious that this created a problem ... she was glad when she was no longer called upon to solve it. The solution, the formation of a new friendship with someone younger, stronger and more energetic than herself ...' (p. 101). St John attested to the centrality of these relationships in her subject's life, yet tiptoed around issues of sexuality by binding up her discussion within ideas of human and economic need.

Vera Brittain's *Testament of Friendship* (1940) was written, too, to explain her 'unusual domestic arrangements', and to deny 'suspicions habitual among the over-sophisticated' (p. 291).[4] Strikingly, her justification of the uses of female friendship echoed Marie Stopes's (1928) views. Only appropriate affection between women could enhance the love of a wife for her husband, a mother and her children (p. 2). Same-sex affection does not displace, but augments.

Such works bear witness, at least, to the centrality of women to each other's lives, and St John's biography owes its genesis to their commissioning. Other biographies seem to assert a familial claim. In his edition of Octavia Hill's letters (1913), Edmund Maurice, married to Hill's sister, Emily, appears initially to aver such an ownership of Hill's reputation. He described the way that the work came about, when Hill 'expressed a strong wish that the family should keep the details of such a memoir in their own hands ... what should be published, and what suppressed, should rest with me' (p. v). Though he refers to Hill's mother and sisters as authorities, no mention is made in the preparation of the biography to any involvement of Harriot Yorke. It is as if family has taken posthumous ownership. None the less, the biography itself gives some place to the same-sex relationships which were so central to Hill's life. An early relationship with Emma Cons (in the 1851–56 period) is described as 'one of those enthusiastic friendships which exercised so marked an influence on her life': 'Octavia's fellow workers (including her sisters) were rather startled at the attraction which her new friend had for her ... Octavia saw the real power concealed for the time under the hoydenish ways ...' (p. 15). This allows for observations on Hill's fine judgement in seeing the quality in Emma Cons beneath the tomboy-gypsy (hoyden; language used of and by lesbians, see p. 40).

Hill's relationship with Sophia Jex-Blake is glossed over in this Life. The editor who elsewhere gives status to key events by his commentary, gives none here. Though she is mentioned, it is not clear that the women lived together from 1860, that they separated in 1862, at which point Octavia Hill had a breakdown. It is only from the letters that are quoted that Jex-Blake emerges. Hill tells her sisters that she 'is a bright, spirited, brave, generous young lady living alone in true bachelor style', 'Miss J.B. and I are great companions. I'm always doing things with her. You know she's teaching me Euclid ... ' (5 February 1860, 29 April 1860, pp. 177, 180).

Harriot Yorke is given special mention in the biography, though how they met is not explained:

Octavia's difficulties had, on more than one occasion, called out the help and sympathy of friends. This good fortune was remarkably exemplified when she broke down in 1877. Miss Yorke [previously unmentioned] who now came forward to give her sympathy and help, became one of the most important figures in the remaining years of Octavia's life; and, by her persistent devotion to her comfort and active help in her work, did much to encourage her new efforts. (p. 354)

At her death in 1912, Hill was supported by her women friends and sisters, among them, and predominant, Harriot Yorke:

> Her sisters were constantly with her, and Miss Yorke was devoted to her day and night ... It was a great comfort to her to know that Miss Yorke, who had lived and worked with her for 30 years, would stay on in the dear home in Marylebone Road and form a centre for fellow-workers and old friends; and, above all, that she would take the responsibility of such a large amount of the work ... she knew that each group of ladies would gather others around them. She felt she was handing on the torch to those who were animated by the right spirit. (p. 581)

Whilst he allows for the importance of these relationships, the biographer gives subtle emphasis, and subsumes Yorke into a wider community of women and to Hill's socially acclaimed work. Hill and Yorke appear self-sacrificing, ideal single women who give their lives to a cause.

There are similar features to the other biography of Octavia Hill in this period.

Moberly Bell's 1942 study has a foreword by Reginald Rowe (who appealed in *The Times* for material to assist in a biography; 29 April 1939, FL). Rowe's description admires the sense of male–female balance, and of the lesbian gaze found elsewhere in the representation of lesbians:

> I was struck especially by that notable feature of hers, her brown, and somehow bird-like, eyes, which looked straight at you and quietly into you, and was impressed as much by her quiet unassuming though decisive manner as by her compelling knowledge and good sense ... profound humility ... accompanied such powers of leadership and command ... She was completely unselfseeking, and had indomitable courage, both physical and moral. (pp. xi–xiii)

At first sight, it appears that this biography, too, will assert family ascendancy. None the less, against a constant background of Hill's family life, Moberly Bell is forthright in descriptions of Hill's same-sex relationships. He describes her feelings for Sophia Jex-Blake:

> A sudden flowering of affection was no rare experience to Octavia, and it was no wonder that she was *captivated* by Sophia Jex-Blake … Already at the age of 20, both bore unmistakable marks of *greatness*; they were built in heroic mould, of indomitable courage and capable of any *sacrifice* where their chivalry was aroused … Any relationship between them must have been a tempestuous affair … (pp. 52–3, my emphasis)

Whereas Hill's long-term friendship with Emma Cons is rather glossed over, the relationship between Hill and Jex-Blake may have been focused upon because both women were later well-known:

> Day by day [Hill and Jex-Blake] became more dependent on each other, and when Sophia went abroad for a short time, Octavia missed her acutely. 'London feels strangely desolate, the lamps looked as they used to look, pitiless and unending as I walked home last night, and knew I could not go to you'. (p. 54)

In September 1860, Hill and Jex-Blake began to discuss living together, which they did until 1862, when the relationship broke down. Bell describes this, and quotes Hill again, writing to her close friend Mary Harris: 'I am like a broken thing … feeling like a shadow, a queer feeling as if a slight touch would push me over the brink …' (p. 59). The biographer does not skirt the issue. The split is difficult:

> The decision was a hard one, and doubly so on Sophia Jex-Blake … [For Hill] her family or Sophia must be sacrificed. The sanctity of family life was one of her deepest convictions … It was a sad ending to an intimacy which promised so much happiness to both … [Octavia] wrote her tender letters, showing her affection to be unaltered but she would not attempt any reopening of the relationship, though for years Sophia could not believe this decision to be unalterable … (p. 60)

The other important same-sex relationship is likewise treated with seriousness by Bell. With Harriot Yorke, there 'arose a satisfying friendship which became the most precious possession of them both. It was such a relationship as is supposed to be peculiarly characteristic of English spinsters. For the rest of their lives they shared a home …' (p. 166).

Margaret Todd's biography of Sophia Jex-Blake is similarly forthright about the weight of the women's mutual significance. Her biography indicates a particularly emotional edge to the attachments. Jex-Blake's relationship with Hill 'was destined to make ... the deepest impression ... of any in the whole of her life' (1918, p. 84). Todd quotes from Jex-Blake's diary:

> Told Octa about Wales, – sitting in her room at the table, my heart beating like a hammer. That Carry wanted to go to Wales and I too, and most convenient about beginning of July, so ... 'Put off my visit?' said Octa. 'No, I was going to say (slowly) if you wish to see anything of me, you must come too, I think, and not put off the mountains till heaven.' She sunk her head on my lap silently, raised it in tears, and then such a kiss! (17 May 1860, pp. 85–6).

She quotes, too, excerpts of letters which show the strength of feeling:

> I look forward to bright days in which I shall learn always more about you, and watch with unending and unfathomable love and sympathy your upward growth, and we may look back together on our lives, as I do often on my own, and wonder how I could know and see so little, and wonder how, knowing so little, I should be led continually to deeper truth. (Hill to Jex-Blake, August 1860, p. 87)

When the women separate, 'dawning friendship' and 'sunshine' (p. 84) were replaced by unnatural dark. For Jex-Blake, 'It was a nightmare, an inexplicable darkness at noonday, something so contrary to all known laws of nature that it could not last' (p. 93).

Signs of Life: Reviews and Life Interviews

Book reviews and interviews are another element of biography. Their writers shape ideas of identity in relation to notions of sexuality, overt or implicit, in their subject.

Hilda Matheson's interview of Vita Sackville-West, one lesbian of another, on the BBC in June 1929, has already been discussed (pp. 43–4), with a suggestion that the listener was 'created' by Sackville-West's textual arrangement. There is a similar construction evident in another lesbian interview, Evelyn Irons's of Radclyffe Hall, for the *Daily Mail* in July 1927. This formed one of a series on 'How Other Women Run Their Homes'. There is some sense of irony, perhaps, in Irons's title and inclusion of Hall, and in the dialogue. Hall tells of her domesticity, and of household roles, in a manner which echoes her 1926 'Couldn't boil an egg' remark (*Sunday Herald*, 21 March 1926, FL, quoted above, p. 51):

> Lady Troubridge sees to the food. I am not really interested in that side of housekeeping ... My province is the house itself ... I have the housewife's 'seeing eye'. After [writing] my housework comes as a relaxation. But I cannot let the house run itself – I must supervise it personally and do my accustomed 'chores'. (July 1927, in Cline 1997, p. 220)

The openness about domestic arrangements is accompanied by lip-service to ideas of relative roles. These may or may not be truly played out in the women's lives. The sense is of Hall responding, maybe with irony but certainly with engagement, to the tacit question of 'who is the husband?' about their relationship. She almost 'normalises' it, though she infers that she, too, is a wife in part.

Other writers arrange their audience, likewise, by assuming a stance in relation to Hall's lesbianism. They adopt a tone of patronising enlightenment, to their readers and to Hall their subject; and appeal to the better nature of readers whom they construct as warily suspicious. This is even the case for woman-centred journalists. Ida Wylie's review of *The Well of Loneliness* stated of the author that 'first and last she has courage and honesty' (*Sunday Times*, 5 August 1928, Cline 1997, p. 241). Vera Brittain, commissioned to write various pieces by Winifred Holtby as book review editor of *Time and Tide*, wrote about *The Well*. She too assumed a wary readership, and called for tolerance of the 'biologically abnormal woman'. The book 'can only strengthen the belief of all honest and courageous persons that there is no problem which is not better frankly stated than concealed. Persecution and disgusted ostracism have never solved any difficulty in the world' (*Time and Tide*, 10 August 1928, FL). The Sunday-School-teacher tone not only anticipates but adumbrates a hostility to *The Well*, and invites a more considered response based on 'the devil you know' rationale. The lesbian author is thus created as much as reflected by her reviewers' tone.

The magazine *Urania* constructed a different reader for *The Well* and a different writer in Hall, based upon its own manifesto to dispel notions of gender dichotomy:

This absurd world in which two perversely imperfect types must exist, in order that by their mutual craze for each other, the perverse imperfection may be renewed, is beginning to be found out for the sham that it is ... We venture the hope that Radclyffe Hall will give us another book in which no imitation men need figure. (May–August 1929; FL)

Depending on which review we read, we are presented with a different biographical sense of Hall, as either a slightly sorry figure whom we should see as courageous in hostile world, or as one who defiantly writes a realistic book which reflects a true state of lesbian affairs, except for its unnecessary masculinising of the hero.

The idea of Hall constructed by the reviewers masqueraded as if it was Hall. The *People* (2 March 1924), reviewing Hall's book *The Forge* (published 25 January 1924) accordingly concentrated on the fact that the author owned a wardrobe which did not contain dresses (Cline 1990, p. 189). And the *Westminster Gazette*, on two successive days (12 and 13 April 1927) described the author, not her work: 'Award to Monocled Writer' and her 'only concession to feminine costume seems to be silk stockings'. The *Lancashire Daily Post* (13 April 1927) fuelled the debate in another way, and 'helpfully' pointed out that Hall rarely wore a monocle but that 'Possibly she has been confused with her very close friend', Una Troubridge (quoted in Cline 1997, p. 219). Such papers not only seek to titillate with their mention of silk stockings, but they also infer that lesbians wear male and female clothing simultaneously in a confusion of gender. They invoke Hall as evidence for their preordained notions. With the 'confusion' between Hall and Troubridge, the writer creates a lesbian community of interchangeable clones, with the normalised viewer unable to tell them apart. Biography of Hall is thus written by those whose editorial stance defines and creates their readership.

In this 1920s and 1930s biography-through-media can be seen the emergence of both the 'bad' and the 'good' lesbian. This is a figure (I use the singular with purpose, for they are frequently one and the same person, presented from different perspectives) who is evident, too, in later twentieth-century discussion. The 'bad' lesbian flaunts her sexuality, the 'good' is discrete, and turns her women-centredness to good effect. On one side of a coin was Radclyffe Hall, on the other a lesbian like Lilian Barker.

Life interviews of Lilian Barker (1874–1955) show censorship by approval. Her role, as prison governor, was lauded. Her career gave her public recognition, and she eventually became a DBE. She was a safe lesbian whose image could therefore be propounded and given dignity.

The Times (7 April 1923, FL) announced her appointment as governor at the borstal for girls at Aylesbury, and reported that Lilian Barker intended to reorganise the place as if it were a public school, conducting 'an experiment in trust'. The *Daily Telegraph* (same date and source) tells the biography of Barker, who had worked as a teacher in working-class schools, then in the 'auxiliary feminine services' when there was a 'call for women to take up men's tasks'. She is feminised: 'Very quietly, and tactfully, too, she has borne a womanly part ... At Aylesbury she will carry further that principle of women's help to women ... '

In 1925, Lilian Barker was interviewed about her lecture on women past and present at Aylesbury. For girls to read, she said, was a 'perfectly splendid thing', they should be open about their reading:

> Much of the harm that has been done in life has been because their mothers and fathers had been brought up by their mothers and fathers to be furtive, and to think of the things in life which were the most beautiful as the most disgusting. (*Daily Telegraph*, 19 March 1925, FL)

The antecedents of Daphne du Maurier's sexualised language of education (in *Rebecca* 1938; see p. 107) can be seen here. Woman is somehow construed as fallen, in a Gothic sense; and education can raise her. Barker is allowed the role of reformer, though other contemporary discourses might have delineated her as herself one of the fallen.

Her role as advocate of law and order was further emphasised when she commented on the dole later in 1925. It saved women and girls from trouble, she said in an interview, they 'would rather be law abiding citizens than otherwise, but if they are not given enough to live on, they will get food and lodging somehow' (*Daily Herald*, 30 June 1925, FL). The following year, the *Daily Chronicle* reported that she advocated thrashing (6 March 1926, FL).

A lengthy interview with her as the first woman member of the Prison Commission at the Home Office, in the *Christian Science Monitor* (5 June 1935, FL), is accompanied by a photograph of Lilian Barker with short cropped hair, side-parted, and spectacles. The interviewer describes Barker's physicality:

> She sat opposite me behind her desk on that morning, leaning back in her chair, her capable hands plunged deeply into what, had she

been a man, would have been trouser pockets ... It would be difficult to think of Miss Barker as one-sided. She has had too many experiences ... She can talk about endless adventures among women and girls, and boys too, for that matter ... Miss Barker removed her hands from her pockets and leaned her elbows on the desk ... her eyes twinkled behind her spectacles ... [They walked around the institution] Miss Barker, striding beside me in her blue homespun coat and skirt and characteristic felt hat pressed down over the short, steel gray hair, regarded the flowers with pride. 'Made that bed myself ... I got a pickax'.[5]

The magazine *Time and Tide* profiled Barker under a 'Personalities and Powers' headline:

> These are her dominant characteristics – humanity, directness and a kind of rugged strength. She is of the 'gentle-strong' type beloved of the generation of romantic novel-writers. Her voice can ring out in stern displeasure, but she will never forget the humanity in another ... She is abundantly possessed of that potent antidote to self-importance – a sense of humour ... She brings the rare qualities of the pioneer – vision, courage and selflessness. (9 October 1925, FL)

Thus her biography was created in all areas of the media in a desirable image. She passed into the establishment mythology in ways that Radclyffe Hall could not. Here was lodged the prototype of the 'bad' versus 'good' lesbian, with the attendant tropism of space (see Chapter 1, note 15). While Hall's lesbianism threatened children and was 'the plague walking shamelessly through great social assemblies' (*Sunday Express*, 19 August 1928, see p. 41), Lilian Barker, in the girls' borstal she governed, was allowed to go proudly 'striding' along the corridor (*Christian Science Monitor*, 5 June 1935, FL).

Obituaries

The art of obituary should be given a special place in biography, yet it rarely is. Published accounts of a life commonly end at the death of their subject. Yet an obituary is a revealing gauge of publicly articulated (or articulable) ideas of individuality, albeit expressed in a somewhat formulaic idiom. By definition, the obituary is public, and by its nature it is condensed. It operates on an expectation of not speaking ill of the dead, yet with a readerly frisson of pleasure that truth must out. It affords, therefore, a neat insight into contemporary ideas on the inter-clusions of sexuality.

In the early twentieth century, such writing is frequently charac-terised by its language of friendship and of professional dedication and appearance. Here is a paradoxical language of concealment and of reve-lation which at once desexualises woman-to-woman relationships, and sexualises them by its silences for the intrigued reader. Obituaries construct an every(wo)man audience in their fine-line negotiation. They can be read safely, as apparently constatively expressive of 'truth' in a neutral (neutered) language of isolation or of companionship; or they can be read as disturbing the heterosexual fixity of family, even when their soft-soap tones describe professional dedication without any hint of sexual behaviour.

Lesbian obituaries frequently mention personal appearance, in general contrast to both male and female heterosexual records where it is relatively unusual to find such description. Conspicuously, for women-centred or male-independent women, physique, and especially certain key indicators of personal appearance (hair, eyes or gaze, stance), is often emphasised.

Though obituaries suggest an immediacy since they are written usually soon after the death of their subject, in fact they are far from spontaneous or objective. The obituary often reveals as much, or possibly more, about the period in which it was written, the attitude of its writer and of the publication's editorial stance, than it does about its subject. The effect can be one of multiple interpretation, as though the deceased is beneath layers of attitudinal wallpaper. This is particularly so if she dies in older age, sometime after the period in which she had fame or reputation, when views are reassessed in view of later political imperatives. This is the case for Mary Allen (1878–1964), who co-launched the women's police force in the early part of the century. She had dubious celebrity status in her lifetime, being presented as quirkily forceful after her visits to the US in 1924, and to Germany in 1934 (see p. 42). In 1940, she joined the British Union of Fascists, and when 'Commandant Mary Allen, Head of the Women's Auxiliary Service spoke on the same platform as Oswald Moseley', questions were asked in the House of Commons (*Daily Herald, Daily Telegraph*, 26 April 1940, FL).

Obituaries of Mary Allen layer attitudes derived from her earlier life reputation, mixing notions of her establishment status with those of her questionable association with both suffrage and fascism. Margaret Damer Dawson, with whom she lived for six years until Dawson's death, is mentioned, but afforded no more status than that of co-worker. Miss Taggart, with whom she later lived, is not mentioned. Reference to her police rank implies fascism rather than professional success, and description of her dress has suggestions of a sexual power game.

Accordingly, the *Daily Telegraph* (18 December 1964, FL) obituary headline records 'Commandant Mary Sophia Allen, Britain's first uniformed police-woman'. It offers criticism of her fascism in the 1940s, notes she was a one-time suffragette who was imprisoned, and who tried to become elected to the House of Commons. The sense is of an establishment infiltrator. *The Times* (18 December 1964, FL) records in its heading her OBE, and recounts that 'with Miss Margaret Damer Dawson, Miss Allen, daughter of a former manager of the Great Western Railway, was a co-founder of the women's police service in 1914'. It, too, records her three prison terms as a suffragette, her reception into the Catholic church in 1953, and criticises her fascism and meeting with the Nazi leadership.

Obituaries of Edy Craig (1869–1947) do associate her with her women cohabitees, but in reference to her achievements, and especially in relation to her famous mother. *The Times* (28 March 1947, FL) records Craig's death:

> daughter of Ellen Terry, sister of Gordon Craig, the artist ... Her devotion to her mother shone more brightly than the remarkable theatrical talent which never, perhaps, received its due recognition ... To her friend and housemate, Miss Christopher St John, she gave invaluable help in the writing of the life of Ellen Terry.

The link between Edy Craig and Christopher St John is here authorial, and both women are somewhat overshadowed by reference to other, brighter, stars. Craig's establishment credentials are secured: in 1938, Dame Sybil Thorndike presided over a Savoy dinner to celebrate her 50-year connection with the stage, and Queen Mary sent a congratulatory telegram. This over-shadowing is also the case with other Craig obituaries (*Daily Mail*, 28 March 1947; *Observer*, 30 March 1947, FL). The *Manchester Guardian* seems to be alone in referring to Clare (Tony) Atwood, Craig and St John's third cohabitee at Smallhythe:[6]

> Only a few hours before her death last night Miss Edy Craig, Ellen Terry's daughter, was talking gaily with her friend and companion, Miss Christopher St John, of her plans for her annual Shakespeare

production [at Smallhythe in memory of Terry] ... Miss St John – who with Miss Clare Atwood, the artist, will continue to care for the house and theatre on behalf of the National Trust ... (29 March 1947, FL)

Public service and establishment connection is also stressed in the obituary of Eva Gore-Booth (1870–1926). Of course, obituaries reflect family truth of these women's lives, yet it is as if invocation somehow neutralises same-sex affiliation, in this case with Esther Roper, with whom she lived for 30 years. You could almost wonder whose obituary is being written:

> [Eva Gore-Booth] will be mourned by many women who never heard of her poetry, nor of her pacifist activities, nor even of her part in the women's suffrage movement. ... In Manchester, she and Miss Roper were associated with Mrs Pankhust ... [She was] sister of Countess Markievicz and of Sir Joscelyn Gore-Booth whose work for the co-operative creameries in Ireland and as a good landlord is well known. (*Manchester Guardian*, 1 July 1926, FL)

Female companionship in heroic adversity, in the service of others, is also emphasised in the obituary of Ethel Dunbar, who died in 1930. It is as if same-sex relationships are explicable in lives of self-sacrifice, particularly where this is associated with social welfare or medicine. In *The Times* (7 January 1930, FL) Miss Ethel Gordon Dunbar is recorded as one who 'rendered exceptional service as a nurse during and after the War'. A correspondent writes of her, the third daughter of Lieutenant Colonel Arbuthnott Dunbar of Morayshire, that she went to France in 1914 to nurse in a military hospital, then working with French refugees before 'She and a friend came forward as volunteers in a desperate cause' to work in a Polish prison camp. The obituary then quotes an American Red Cross authority record:

> Two, a Miss Leigh and a Miss Dunbar, decided they would undertake work in the prison camp ... These two women moved into a small building connected with the camp and worked day and night to relieve the situation. Both Miss Leigh and Miss Dunbar are reported ill with typhus, December 4 [1919; when they saw the need of refugees in Salonika, they] ... went out together as independent workers ... Miss Leigh died some years ago, and Miss Dunbar also contracted TB ... She fought gallantly through nine years of failing health, working between each breakdown, and the last two years of

invalid existence, spent in peace and surrounded in affection as they were, perhaps called for an even greater pluck.

At least such obituaries do record personal relationships. Others fly in the face of available evidence and ignore personal sources. Agnes Hunt (1876–1948) wrote autobiographical pieces in 1935 and in 1938, which both recorded her life and work with Emily Selina Goodford. Though this was a publicly known relationship, therefore, by dint of publication, *The Times* obituarist does not record any 'personal' life at all. Her death is noted, and her foundation 'of a hospital for cripples' (26 July 1948, FL). She was herself disabled, and 'It may well have been her disability which obscured her lesbianism from public view: the desexualisation of people with disabilities is not an uncommon phenomenon. Not even her Eton crop has raised much posthumous comment' (Hamer 1996, p. 33).

This is not the only explanation, however. Sophia Jex-Blake's relationship with Octavia Hill, and later with Margaret Todd, is not mentioned in her obituary in *Common Cause*. This 'pioneering doctor, daughter of Thomas Jex-Blake and Maria Cubitt' had 'great mental force'; 'learning that many women greatly prefer to be treated by one of their own sex' she studied medicine under Dr Lucy Sewall 'who became a life-long friend' (18 January 1912, FL). Sexualisation is subsumed within, or diverted by language into, public service where women's companionship is safe.

Lilian Barker is represented similarly as a dedicated public servant who operated in a personal vacuum. Though she lived with Florence Francis for 40 years, her obituaries do not mention this fact. Rather, they stress her good works as prison governor and one writer compares her work as a prison reformer with that of Elizabeth Fry (*Daily Telegraph*, 23 May 1955, FL). *The Times* (same date and source) describes her work in suffrage, the Red Cross and in girls' borstals from 1923.

> Clearly even then she had proved she was no ordinary woman, but those were the days of womens' suffrage agitation ... Her square-cut figure, usually severely dressed in tweeds and with her hair in the close Eton crop of 30 or more years ago, became a welcome and heartening sight to her charges ... 'I have laughed more people into being good than if I had preached to them for hours'.

The *Manchester Guardian* has a remarkably similar statement. Presumably both papers are truthful in their representation of Barker's physical appearance (photographs and drawings attest to this: *The Times*, 23 May 1955; *Time and Tide*, 9 October 1925; *Christian Science Monitor*, 5 June 1935; all FL). But their reference to the nature of her appearance suggests that this is used as a shorthand to reflect signifying aspects of her personality. Yet this emphasis is muted by its containment within statements which stress her recognition and maintenance of heterosexual standards. She was kindly, firm, a friend of the girls, with no sense of indecorum. Her relationships stress her respect for familial rites of passage:

> ... Lilian Barker could be shatteringly brusque at times, and would rap out commands in a stern deep voice. But equally she was known for her humour and understanding ... [She gave the borstal girls] prettily painted bedrooms [and said] ' ... they have stolen frocks and trinkets in order to attract young men, which is perfectly natural.' ... She would smoke a cigarette with [the girls in the her nightly talks] and encourage them to talk ... She went to weddings and christenings of ex-Borstal girls ... (*Manchester Guardian*, 23 May 1955, FL).

The *Daily Herald* (23 May 1955, FL), under the headline 'The Naughty Girls Loved Dame Lilian' opened its obituary with an incident which illustrated her masculine-feminine nature, shorthand signifier of her well-balanced persona: 'The woman with the Eton-crop and tweed suit faced a group of sullen-faced borstal girls. Suddenly she brought out a bag of peardrops, and handed them round. The tension eased ... The woman who beat toughness with kindness ...' Barker gave the girls 'gay dresses instead of jail garb', opened a swimming pool and hairdressers in the institution. Barker is quoted: 'Murderesses – some of the nicest women I've met' and ends with her words 'I have the makings of the worst possible Borstal girl. I could have led the governors a rare dance.' So, the obituary mythologises both the fallen and the saved woman who could have been embodied in the same figure: there before the grace of God goes Lilian.

Even the *Women's Bulletin* emphasised establishment and family credentials of *Dame* Lilian Barker, and it ends with one of the familiar platitudes of obituary: 'The world is poorer for her passing, but how much richer for her having lived, it is impossible to estimate' (3 June 1955, FL).

The language of the lesbian gaze, evident in the life interviews of Lilian Barker (see p. 95) and in descriptions of Christine Murrell (see p. 87) and Octavia Hill (see p. 89), features in obituaries of Cicely

Hamilton (1872–1952). *The Times* obituarist writes of this 'Actress and Authoress', 'an ardent feminist': 'Pale and expressive of face, with intelligent eyes, a witty and frequently acid conversationalist – she was not always a good listener ... a genuine individualist' (8 December 1952, FL).

> She was an extremely good actress. There was beauty in her grey eyes and tawny orange hair. But it was above all her personality and the power of her performance that shone through. (Lady Rhondda, *Time and Tide*, 13 December 1952, FL)

> Quiet, still, almost mono-syllabic, with now and again a questioning look from those wonderfully grey blue eyes ... (Elizabeth Abbott, *Women's Freedom League Newsletter*, December 1952, FL)

Whilst the obituaries, like Hamilton herself (Whitelaw 1990, p. 110), were sometimes reticent about her relationships with women, clues appear in records associated with her demise. Her death was recorded (*The Times*, 9 December 1952, FL) and the funeral itself was reported, with a list of those present (*The Times*, 13 December 1952, FL).[7] From this catalogue can be construed a sense of her relationships with a network of women, including Lady Rhondda. This sense is echoed in Elizabeth Abbott's piece in the *WFL Bulletin* (9 January 1953, FL).[8] Headed 'A Noble Woman and Friend', the writer gives an account of meeting Hamilton in 1919, from which time 'there existed between us an unshadowed and unbroken friendship'. She records 'How good it is to think that in these last months of illness champagne (or any other wine) was never wanting ... to the very end she was surrounded in that dear Bohemian quarter of Old Chelsea, by friends and neighbours ... '

Such obituaries refuse to obscure the centrality of women's relationships with each other. They are in rare contrast to others. Octavia Hill (1838–1912) is obituarised for her work with the poor (*Westminster Gazette*, 15 August 1912; *Occasional Paper*, March 1913, FL). Like Lilian Barker, it is as if Hill worked with no interpersonal relationships. Reginald Rowe wrote only of male influences upon her, and recalled 'a smallish, nice-looking woman, completely unpretentious ... She had steady brown eyes that seemed to look right into you but with kindly penetration' (*The Times*, 3 December 1938, FL). Note the 'but'; her masculine potential, even in 'penetration' was feminised.

Similar family ascendancy is reflected in the 1916 obituaries of Mabel Batten, Radclyffe Hall's lover from 1907. In published lists of mourners at the memorial service in Westminster Cathedral, Hall was placed below relations and friends.[9]

Family claim is common in obituaries, of course. Its association with notions of lineage, through heraldic display of medieval tombs for example, has a long-standing place in the history of the English art of death. In obituaries of lesbians, when this replaces or displaces reference to a lover, the effect can be a particularly distorting one. However, this was by no means inevitable in the period, even after *The Well of Loneliness* trial, which is repeatedly said to have frightened lesbians off. This is shown in the memorials to Katharine Courtauld (1856–1935) whom I identify as having a long-standing relationship with a woman because of the very existence of obituaries, one in particular.

'Miss KM [wrongly given as Kathleen] Courtauld, who farmed 500 acres, was a past president of the Essex Agricultural Show, died on 5 June 1935', records the *Daily Telegraph* (6 June 1935, FL). She was the eldest daughter of George Courtauld, son of the founder of the silk firm. *The Times* (8 June 1935, FL) adds other details, that she was a member of Essex County Council for 20 years, and a chief fruit farmer of the county, 'her apples had taken prizes in national competitions'. Neither newspaper mentions any personal relationship.

In striking contrast, Caroline Grosvenor celebrated the achievements of Katharine Mina Courtauld in the *Women's Farm and Garden Association, Quarterly Leaflet* of September 1935 (FL). The obituary included a photography of Courtauld, showing her wearing a collar and tie, and with short hair. It mentions that the Association renamed its headquarters 'Courtauld Hall' in 1933, in her honour. Personal details are provided. Born in 1856, Katharine Courtauld left home in 1888, when her father married for the third time, to 'a woman scarcely older than herself ... to live with her friend of school days, Miss Mary Gladstone, an arrangement which lasted with unbroken success until her death ... '. This may suggest a let-out, that there was family (un)reason for Courtauld's living arrangements, but it at least records their life-long devotion.

Some of the Grosvenor's language is apologist (for Courtauld's dress, and note in the quotation below the repeated use of 'but'). She also reflects a contemporary fixation on the combination of masculine and feminine qualities, as if the balance was necessary to explain a character. None the less, for the most part the obituarist is positive about aspects of life which others deny or obscure. Katharine Courtauld's family association is extolled in its own right, on her terms. Moreover, and uniquely for the obituaries I have searched of this period, it is Mary

Gladstone who is afforded the special place in the obituary, that of chief mourner, mentioned last, with the full weight that this gives her:

> No one who had the privilege of knowing [Katharine Courtauld] could fail to realize that she was a very remarkable woman. That she had enormous vitality and energy was shown by the many activities in which she took part [farming, orchards, sailing, shooting] … It was doubtless her entire sincerity and absence of pretence which influenced her outward appearance. She condescended to no feminine devices of adornment. With short hair, her masculine type of dress, her strong but very fine features, she could, but for her skirt, have easily been mistaken for a man. But in spite of the austerity of her appearance, she had a deep fund of warm-hearted sympathy which, combined with her sound judgement and unflinching honesty, made her a person of great importance to her own family and adored by its younger members. To Miss Gladstone, her life long comrade and friend, we can only offer our heartfelt sympathy in her irreparable loss.

4
Historicised Contexts: 'The Lesbian' and Late Twentieth-Century Discourse

The Discourse of Disclosure

Legal debate frames the politics of lesbian representation in the twentieth century. In 1921, parliament discussed whether or not to introduce provisions against lesbians; and in 1988 the Tory government contained a section in its Local Government Act forbidding 'promotion' of homosexuality by local councils:

> You are going to tell the whole world that there is such an offence, to bring it to the notice of women who have never heard of it, never thought of it, never dreamt of it. I think that is a very great mischief. (Lord Desart, 1921, in Weeks 1981, p. 105)

> I would be bold enough to say that of every thousand women, taken as a whole, 999 have never heard a whisper of these practices. Among all these, in the homes of this country ... the taint of this noxious and horrible suspicion is to be imparted. (Lord Birkenhead, the Lord Chancellor, 1921, in Weeks 1981, p. 105)

> (1) A local authority shall not (a) intentionally promote homosexuality or publish material with the intention of promoting homosexuality; (b) promote the teaching in any maintained school of the acceptability of homosexuality as a pretended family relationship;

> (2) Nothing in subsection (1) above shall be taken to prohibit the doing of anything for the purpose of treating or preventing the spread of disease. (Section 28, Local Government Act 1987/1988).

Promoters of the legal process at both ends of the century claimed that sexual law was designed to protect its citizens. Homosexuality is 'never heard of', while heterosexuality is treated as a said. Language is of concealment, attributed by the 'threatened' to the 'threatener', and it operates within a constructed aural/oral and visual discourse.

Sotto Voce or *Fortissimo?*

Legal language is here '"structured in dominance" because it skews and restricts its audience's possibilities for interpreting the material it claims to present without bias' (During, using Stuart Hall's phrase, 1993, p. 9). The audience is led to conceptualise homosexuals as secretive because the legislative discourse suggests that lesbianism is an unheard 'whisper', which its promoters wish to amplify. The image of the legislator is thus created simultaneously, as somehow reasonable, quietly spoken, amidst a potential lesbian cacophony. By invoking ideas of the sexual-sensual, the language appeals to the most basic principles, that corruption occurs through the senses: hear no evil, see no evil leading to speak no evil, an ingrained cultural idea(l).

This is reflected in discussion of sexuality in the early twentieth century, of which the later century makes use. Havelock Ellis's eugenic philosophy is based on 'sexual selection' as an idea: it is the title of part one of his *Studies in the Psychology of Sex* (1910), of which the second part is 'Sexual Inversion'. He argues that sexual choice is exclusively governed through the senses, of which touch and smell to humans are of 'comparatively less importance'. He notes:

> the very great part played by vision in life generally as well as in art, it is the most important of all the senses from the human sexual point of view. Hearing ... is the most remote of all the senses in its appeal to the sexual impulse, and on that account, it is, when it intervenes, among the first to make its influence felt (1910, vol. II, pt 1, p. 2).

Eyes and ears are thus the most vulnerable orifices. Given this primacy, protecting them from sexual corruption is therefore of great cultural importance.

The oppression of lesbians has, accordingly, been figured around sight (Jagose 1994, pp. 1, 165) as well as silence (Zimmerman 1992b, p. 2). Lesbians themselves describe self-recognition: 'veils were falling from eyes at a great rate' (Shulman in Ainley 1995, p. 30); 'It is like being blind, and then you see and you can't be blind again' (in Groocock 1995, p. 78). The thing and the thing obscured become synonymous: the veil, Eve Kosofsky Sedgwick has argued, represents not simply concealment but also concealed, 'a metonymy for the system of prohibitions by which sexual desire is enhanced and specified' (1986, p. 143). By this process, it is inferred that the lesbian is somehow a dissembler, who has sought to disguise her dangerous physicality.

The intellect controlled the senses, according to ideas of modernity which are said to have their origins in Western rationality and a Judaistic prohibition against making images of God. Here 'a sensory perception was given second place to what may be called an abstract idea – a triumph of intellectuality over sensuality' (Lyotard 1989, pp. 71–2). This has an effect on the visualised, and on lesbian iconography (discussed in Chapter 7) since, in the development of modernity 'there is a trajectory which moves steadily from the acceptance of the visual as the source of legitimation towards the visual or self-evident as precisely that which is dubious' (Docherty 1996, p. 157). This may be a triumph, too, of a Protestant-capitalist ethic which values the notion of consubstantiation, where the thing represents but does not become (as in transubstantiation) the other it signifies. Within such ideas of modernity, the lesbian is suspected of being transfigured (or as aspiring to that), and lesbian visual codes thus operate as (self-) evidence against her.

Here, twentieth-century determining discourse of lesbian, as other representation of the sexually dubious, operates within an educational paradigm. There is good knowledge and bad knowledge. Sexual knowledge, especially of an undesirable kind, is construed as secret knowledge. Good knowledge is open; yet the means to it is controlled. This paradigm is at the heart of sexual representation.

Views about 1921 are apposite, too, to legislative changes of 1988:

> It would seem to be precisely when the threat of lesbianism became an area of concern for white middle-class European men that lesbianism was construed as a *secret* that must be withheld from its potential practitioners ... when the objects of concern became white middle and upper-class women, lesbianism became *foreclosed*. (Hart 1994, p. 4)

In literature, through the twentieth century, notions of secrecy surround the representation of deviant or questionable practice.

Rebecca (1938), for example, contains several scenes which have a lesbian reading, where sexuality and secrecy are controlled by the father-figure, and in which knowledge is presented as penetrating via ear or eye: in one, the narrator tells of Mrs Danvers' insistence on taking her to Rebecca's rooms, which

> ... *struck a chord in my memory*, reminding me of a visit to a friend's house, as a child, when the daughter of the house, older than me, took my arm and *whispered in my ear*, 'I know where there is a book, locked up in a cupboard, in my mother's bedroom. Shall we go and look at it?' I remembered her white, excited face, and her small, beady eyes, and the way she kept pinching my arm. (p. 97, my emphasis)

The physical attributes of the friend are lesbianly, similar to those of Mrs Danvers herself. In another scene, her husband asks the narrator:

> 'When you were a little girl, were you ever forbidden to *read* certain books, and did your father put those books under lock and key? ... there is a certain type of knowledge I prefer you not to have. It's best kept under lock and key'. (p. 211, my emphasis)[1]

The 'type of knowledge' is left unstated. The context of the scenes suggests a clear sexual component, one into which the narrator, in her childlike state, is too young to be initiated, though she senses it; and one which deviates from the heterosexual pre-eminence of the plot.

Within sexological discussion, the notion of secrecy was associated with both masturbation and with lesbianism. Havelock Ellis, for example, agreed with earlier writers (e.g. Talmey 1904, p. 123) when he wrote: 'I am certainly inclined to believe that an early and excessive indulgence in masturbation, though not an adequate cause, is a favoring condition for the development of inversion, and that this is especially so in women ...' (1910, vol. II, pt 2, p. 277). Masturbation gives way to looking within: lesbians are said to have an early fixation on the mother-figure, followed by 'an internal censure inhibiting this incestuous impulse ... taking refuge in Narcissism, the self becoming the sexual object' (Ellis 1910, vol. II, pt 2, p. 304).

The 1988 discourse in Section 28 has embedded within it this notion of the lesbian as non-procreative, at definitional odds with the family in the real/pretend dichotomy. It attaches the idea to the presumption of non-social, non-ideal citizenry, based on an adumbrated selfishness or wish to corrupt. It also has a logic of the educational paradigm, that sexuality is something which can be learned rather than is essential. Hence, the public can be protected from it.

This is a philosophy based on the principle that sexuality had a cause, the truth of which was capable of transmission or suppression. Late twentieth-century discussion of sexuality operates within that belief, and also within parameters of the postmodern. The dominant political paradigm of real/pretend: revealed/secret, encased in legalistic frameworks, cohabits with postmodern notions of the fluidity of all boundaries between the real and the fictive world. Queer theory arose in the general philosophical mêlée. It propounds ideas of erotic diversity, and challenges those established by heterosexual hegemony. As such, it resists 'regimes of the normal' (Warner 1993, p. xxxvi) and privileges the personal. Here, it has been associated with 'the increasing individualism promoted under a capitalist system that continually diversifies markets by appealing to specialized tastes' (Bristow 1997, p. 222).

Thatcherite politicians proposing Section 28 appealed to their party belief in individual freedom. The wording of of the Act pluralises deviant sexual practice: 'homosexuality' is a group activity. The legal framework thus disguises its control of personal freedom within a language which frames itself as individual, '*a* local authority' versus group.

Furthermore, it poses as a compassionate 'I' who seeks to protect. Subsection (2) was added to enable education on HIV/Aids, and, (in)advertently, it links ideas of homosexuality with deadly infection. Under the auspices of caring, both individual and corporate good is said to be protected, with the nation and its individual citizen being presented as a bodily whole. Unity is posited as sacrosanct in a period in which there is said to be danger from inside and out:

> a homogeneous image of national culture is celebrated and enforced to counter the dangers posed by the increasingly global nature of economic exchanges and widening national, economic divisions. The new right image of a monoculture and hard-working family life, organized through traditional gender roles, requires a devaluation not just of other nations and their cultural identities but of 'enemies within': those who are 'other' racially, sexually, intellectually. (During 1993, pp. 13, 14)

Accordingly, the Tory government sought, in ostensibly separate measures, to identify racial immigrants and to educate its nation's young: in 1995 the Home Secretary launched a scheme to train head teachers, hospital administrators and social security officials to identify illegal immigrants, on the same day as the government chief adviser on school curriculum called for the development of 'a British cultural identity in all schoolchildren regardless of their ethnic backgrounds', advocating teaching subjects 'at the heart of our common culture and our national identity' (*Guardian*, 19 July 1995, p. 3). The nation was epitomised as white (non-raced), with non-white (raced), like the sexually deviant, identified as an outsider culture which needed to be 'nation-ed'.

Supporters of Section 28 'effectively equated the nation with the heterosexual "normal" space' (Smith 1994, p. 25). Real 'family relationship' is not defined by the Act, but is inferred by contrast to the pretend which is defined, by a heterotopic extension:

> The heterotopia is capable of juxtaposing in a single real place several spaces, several sites that are in themselves incompatible ... their role is to create a space that is other, another real space, as perfect, as meticulous, as well arranged as ours is messy, ill constructed, and jumbled. The latter type would be the heterotopia, not of illusion, but of compensation ... (Foucault 1986, pp. 25, 27)

Heterosexual family life is constructed, by its absence, as normalised. We are offered both a spatial and a value-laden dichotomy: The Family (in its ideal and fictive space to which we can make return) in contrast to the pretend family's subcultural significance, the style of which is evidenced by its impermanence and its association with disease:

> Style in subculture is, then, pregnant with significance. Its transformations go 'against nature', interrupting the process of 'normalization'. As such, they are gestures, movements towards a speech which offends the 'silent majority', which challenges the principle of unity and cohesion, which contradicts the myth of consensus. (Hebdige 1993, p. 367)

Never Thought, Never Dreamt

Sarah Hoagland has argued that there is an advantage for the lesbian in being beyond thought: 'it affords her a certain freedom from constraints of the conceptual system' (quoted in Frye 1983, p. 152). Having been thought, however, determining discourse needs to make sense of the lesbian, and does so as an infiltrator, within a Cold War episteme.

The language of the British New Right in the 1980s, and of New Labour in the late 1990s, promotes the idea of imminent collapse of identity, in order that it can promise salvation on its own terms. It writes a myth of modernity

> identified both with the making and the unmaking of the self. One story about modernity would identify it with the apprehension of the self's autonomous self-grounding ... according to the other story, the absence or impotence of God, the Church, the king, tradition, makes the modern subject more liable to come apart at the seams than ever before (Connor 1997, p. 203)

The myth of disintegration is based on a supposed vulnerability of the 'majority' who must be defended against the insidiously invisible enemy within. The Green Paper published by New Labour, 'Supporting Families' (launched on 4 November 1998) embodies notions of the need to protect the institution. The Home Secretary, Jack Straw, was quoted as being in opposition to lesbian IVF treatment, and saying 'that children are best brought up where you have two natural parents and it is more likely to be a stable family if they are married' (*Guardian*, 5 November 1998, p. 4). A National Family and Parenting Institute was announced within these measures, to provide advice, together with a freephone helpline. Crisis is suggested by the need for urgent action, at the same time that salvation is indicated: the Family, in danger of disintegration and taking Nationhood with it, is being saved.

Hegemonic collapse is conceived in emotive and bodily terms. Promoters of the Section 28 legislation associated wrong education with spread of disease, via an undefined conduit, homosexual shaped: 'Some of that which is being taught to children in our schools will undoubtedly lead to a great spread of AIDS' (Jill Knight, quoted in Durham 1991, p. 122). Though Allan Roberts MP claimed of homosexuality that 'It is not a disease to be caught' (Wilton 1995, p. 45), other, and powerfully popular, discourse continued to use suggestion of illness. Important differentials were created between the male and female homosexual, to demonise the male: '[Lesbians] do not molest little girls. They do not indulge in disgusting and unnatural acts like buggery. They are not wildly promiscuous and do not spread venereal disease' (Lord Halsbury, Official report, House of Lords, 18 December 1986, cited in Smith 1991, p. 132).

None the less, lesbianism was construed as a highly personal threat, 'As if you let a lesbian into your room, you would be contaminated – she sat on your bed, you might catch it!' (quoted in Markowe 1996, p. 160). Around two-thirds of respondents to the *British Social Attitudes Survey* (Jowell *et al.* 1990, cited in Markowe 1996, p. 45) perceived lesbians as at risk from Aids, despite the fact that they are actually a relatively low-risk group. Accordingly, lesbian sexuality became associated with the anti-homosexual censoriousness around Aids and 'old fears that sexual activity, homosexuality, and promiscuity led to disease and death' (Rubin 1993, p. 26).

To some extent the connection between death and sex can be attributed to Freud who linked 'the likeness of the condition that follows complete sexual satisfaction to dying … ' (*Standard Edition,* vol. 19, p. 47). This was taken up by writers such as Bataille in his study *Eroticism* (1957) who wrote of 'contagious impulses', based upon a Hegelian dialectic between 'continuity and discontinuity' (Bristow 1997, p. 123). In conditions where a dominant political group wishes to promote ideals of unity, for economic or other reasons of power, focus on individuals whose sexuality can be associated with fragmentation is clearly useful. The Idea of the Homosexual becomes in this situation a means of 'excusing, explaining, ignoring or propitiating whatever we do not understand about the world and whatever we most fear and despise in our own natures, just as we have used the concept of "the heterosexual" as an image of clarity, progress and social and cosmic harmony' (Rivers 1980, p. 311).

The Good, the Bad, the Ugly

Both notions, of the heterosexual and the homosexual, are predicated on an idea of the visualisable, the possibility of holding of a prototypical image in the mind: but whereas it is actually difficult to image an heterosexual by typology, a lesbian almost readily springs to mind:

> I think I always thought of lesbians as being old – ladies in sort of baggy trousers, thick shoes, probably walking dogs,[2] short hair, anoraks, unattractive.

> Well, frequently lesbians fall in my mind into two parts – one the female part and the other the male part … the adoption of part of male dress: ties, severe haircuts and flat-heeled shoes, the striding steps, and plaid skirts. (quoted in Markowe 1996, pp. 16, 98)

Here, as in 1920s and 1930s images, the lesbian is envisaged as active and masculinised, 'readable signs to fix the invert in the visual field' (Hart 1994, p. 10). Partly she is desexualised (old, unattractive), and partly she is associated with activity which contrasts to female passivity: 'One may be born a woman or a man, but one can only desire as a man' (de Lauretis 1991, p. 254).

The relative ease of visualisation is part of the success of the New Right promotion of the Idea of the Lesbian, and its ascendancy in making use of a cultural dominance of 'the epistemological regime of the eye':

> a visual enframing of the world, as a separated object of knowledge. Visualism signifies distance, differentiation and domination; the control which modernity exercises over nature depends upon that experience of the world as separate from myself, and my self-definition in the act of separation, which vision seems to promote. (Connor 1997, pp. 203–4).

Since 1988, with the introduction of Section 28, there has been an increased presence of images, which has been welcomed by many gay men and lesbians: 'the contemptible section 28 has strengthened our insistence that we will never let ourselves be invisible again'; 'lesbians and gay men have far greater visibility than before' (quoted in Healey and Mason, 1994, pp. 40–1, 65). Visibility has been, to a large extent, on the terms chosen by the determiner: however much lesbians can turn it to advantage, shorthand images have become culturally signed. These group, for the most part, around ideas of the good (chic, lipstick, pretend) and the bad (gauche, authentic) lesbian. Both had been established in early twentieth-century imagery (in the reputations of Lilian Barker and Radclyffe Hall, for example, see p. 95). In the later century, the distinction has been continued, with the good lesbian assuming a 'self-disciplining, self-limiting, fixed subject status, an otherness which knows her proper place' (Smith 1994, p. 205). Hence, in Foucault's terms, lesbians self-police, are guarded in both senses of the word.

The bad lesbian of the 1980s carries the values of her 1930s sister who walked 'shamelessly' through the corridors (see Chapter 1, note 15). Again she walks alone, this time in a sportive setting, invading heterosexualised space:

> No pretty young player is safe when the butch battalions are prowling the locker rooms [of the professional tennis clubs] ... The lonely nights and lack of male company make inexperienced girls

easy prey for the randy predators of the women's circuit ... Barricaded doors are often the only way of keeping the amorous amazons at bay. (*People*, 22 June 1986, in Hamer 1994, p. 64)

Corruption and Deception

As in the early part of the century, particular anger is expressed for lesbians in authority, especially teachers. In January 1994, the media treatment of Hackney headteacher Jane Brown, and her lampooning for refusal to take her pupils to see *Romeo and Juliet* because it was 'too heterosexual' suggests the strength of feeling to which the introduction of Section 28 ostensibly gave legitimacy. The Idea of the Lesbian is one who seduces, via education: 1988 legislation claims to prevent this happening, thereby inferring it did happen, without evidence that this is so. In Jane Brown's case, discussion centred around association with left-wing local councils, accused of misguided public policy, erosion of family values and waste of funds. This connection predated the Jane Brown events. In the debate around the 1988 legislation, supporters based their arguments on a conspiracy theory, that local councils did seek to corrupt the young, so that eventually 'the simple act of speaking the names of five local authorities ... [was] deemed sufficient to evoke the figure of the "promoter" of homosexuality' (Smith 1994, p. 193).

This has been powerfully pervasive. Hence, when a story was published in 1997 about lesbian ex-MP Maureen Colquhoun she is named as an ex-Hackney Borough councillor, as if that is enough said (*Independent on Sunday*, 13 July 1997, p. 6).

Similarly, the debate around an educational group for bullied lesbian and gay students in Manchester had all the overtones of eroded family values in the face of questionable political use of public money. A homework club for victimised teenagers was criticised for 'promoting homosexuality'. Part funded by the National Youth Agency and the Department of Education and Employment, the project was criticised by Conservative MP Nicholas Winterton since it 'could expose emotionally vulnerable teenagers to a most inappropriate environment'. The group Family and Youth Concern claimed it set gay teenagers apart: 'It makes it seem being gay is more important than study itself' (*Guardian*, 1 October 1997, p. 12).

Behind such tales is the whole idea of the Lesbian as a social truth. Reporting 'Sappho rising', A.N. Wilson associated two separate tales of lesbians, one of a TV portrayal of a 'secretly lesbian military officer', the other of a dismissed case of indecent assault heard in Cardiff Crown Court against a gym mistress:

> It was a ridiculous case, which should never have been brought. She had simply had an affair with one of her pupils. Most of us tend to assume, unless told otherwise, that gym teachers, officers in the WRNS, prison wardresses and novice mistresses are of homosexual proclivity. So what? The news which would have been worth reporting would be of a gym mistress who did not fancy her pupils, but perhaps it has been impossible to trace such a woman. (*London Evening Standard*, 14 March 1997, p. 11)

Wilson proceeds to contrast this with what he describes as the Victorian's wisdom on such matters, that lesbianism did not really exist: 'They also decided (most of the intelligent Victorians) that God did not exist either, so the lesbians were in quite good company.' Such connection between lesbianism and inflated ideas of self, albeit in a jokey framework, is a feature familiar in later twentieth-century discussion around motherhood (p. 116). It links with ideas of The Lesbian as somehow illusory yet very real and threatening in her duplicity. Indignation at her deception is similar to that heaped on pretend-males more generally (Faderman 1981, pp. 47–60; and see p. 55). In the later twentieth century, deception via the Internet gives a particular dimension to the artificial. Under the headline 'My hubby's an E-male', it was reported that,

> Bride Margaret Hunter has started a £350,000 fraud claim after the husband she met through the Internet turned out to be a woman.
> American 'groom' Holly Groves, 26, avoided sex by claiming to have AIDS and had bandages on her chest, allegedly from a car crash. (*Daily Mirror*, 20 December 1996, p. 11)

The bride is real, the 'groom' figmentary, as the punctuation signifies. Lesbianism and Aids are linked. We are offered here the nightmarish spectre of the virtual male, with another layer of cunning disguise offered by technology.

Lesbian Marriage

'Brief encounters. Where are all the long-term lesbian couples?', queried a headline in *Guardian Women* alongside a photograph of Gertrude Stein and Alice B. Toklas:

Rumours abound of all the Fredas and Marys running tea shops in pockets of Devon and Cumbria who have lived as discreet but committed couples for 30-odd years now. But have you ever met any of them? Nor have I ... despite a decade out of the closet, I know only one couple who have been together longer than seven years. (11 April 1994, p. 11)

By using the reference to the archetypal heterosexual and doomed, adulterous romance in the film *Brief Encounter*, the sense is of lesbian relationships failing in a framework of enduring, marital love. The paradigm of marriage as a fictive space, constantly threatened by lesbians, is one that has endured over the twentieth century, stimulated especially in the later period within Thatcherite political philosophy.

Hence there is the paradox of lesbians both desiring (and so buying into the notion of heterosexual marriage as desirable) and being rebuffed from the institution. A British headline, 'Gays Inch Up The Aisle', reported the battle within the United States to legalise same-sex marriages, the decision on which 'hangs on a few Hawaiian judges'. On the page (*Guardian*, 16 April 1996, p. 13), the story sits opposite a photograph of two men kissing, and an unrelated article on 'the killer suburbs' and city crime. Subediting thus arranges the text to reinforce the sense of threat, and by an outsider minority (judges, homosexuals). The discussion of the same issue later in the year suggests that gay marriage is 'a prospect that splits [the US] between happiness and horror':

'It strikes at the very heart of who we are as people' says [a spokesman of] the legal arm of the Christian Coalition ... Others ask where reform will lead. To legal unions of fathers and daughters? Polygamous marriages? Bisexual weddings with one groom and two brides, one a man, the other a woman?' (*Guardian*, 4 June 1996, p. 2)

This strikingly echoes an article in the *Sunday Times* which links the story to Britain where it could happen too:

despite successive Conservative victories, liberals and lefties are more entrenched than ever. In America they rely on unelected, unrepresentative judges – products of the leftist law schools – to do their dirty work for them. In Europe, they rely on Brussels bureaucrats and the Strasbourg court. ... What I would like to know is if some fool judge approves of paedophilia in, say, California, will that give the right to sickos to abuse children? ... [Rights of homosexuals to marry are being violated] as much as those of siblings who wish to marry one another, or of fathers who wish to marry their daughters, or of men who wish to take for themselves more than one wife – like me, for example – or of two men who wish to marry one woman. (2 June 1996)

This article makes use of notions of nationalism, being threatened by unreasoned and legislating outsiders. It also invokes the 'unreasoning I' of the author in order to contain him: we see the wishful polygamist, ('like me') who has desires which he accepts should be controlled by the 'reasoning you' of the British legal code as it stands now, as opposed to what it might be if we let outsiders legislate for us. The *Guardian* and the *Sunday Times* are extremely close in their language and approach. Intertextual repetition, with no evidence to support it, establishes a myth which links male and female homosexuality to abuse of the innocent, to incest, to the spectre of non-normal procreation, and to an iconography of kin- or self-twinning narcissism which is a common feature of visualisation.

Lesbian Motherhood

Closely associated with such later twentieth-century ideas of unnaturalness, which become established by repetition in the guise of objectivity, is that of lesbian motherhood. It is consistently presented in opposition to 'real' motherhood or family relationships. There is a hierarchy of aberrations, with lesbianism at its base. So, 'the perfect image of Nazi motherhood was seduced by the remarkable Felice', announced the *Radio Times* about a 'love affair between a German housewife and a Jewish lesbian' (22–28 February, pp. 76, 78). 'Virgin births' were described on the BBC news (11 March 1991), whilst the *Today* and *Daily Mirror* newspapers had front pages concerning 'the virgin mother'. It is as if the lesbian is saying these things of herself, making blasphemous claims about her affinity with the god-head.

In contrast, notions of earth-bound naturalness surround 'normal' maternity. 'The champion of natural childbirth', Sheila Kitzinger, was interviewed, for example, about her book *On Becoming A Grandmother:*

> In the preface she mentions that only one of her daughters is a mother, while some of the others are lesbians. ... she said 'some' meant three, and that they were all wonderful people, so she must have done something right. [Other newspapers] put this shock-

horror revelation into screaming banners and headlines. Which is very odd, because in the sacred spaces where wimmin go to read articles by and about wimmin, it was all very old news. Even people who are far too sophisticated to read big themes into the lesbian quotient have been saying how ironic it is that a childbirth guru with five daughters has only been able to get one of them to follow in her footsteps. (*Guardian*, 22 January 1997, p. 8)

'Mother' and lesbian are thus directly oppositional, as are 'sophisticated' and 'wimmin', and all are themselves below grandmother in a hierarchical normalcy.

'Granny loses child to lesbian' proclaims the same message: 'A devoted grandmother has lost a custody battle over her young grand-daughter to the lesbian ex-lover of the child's mother'. Moreover, the grandmother is 'a part-time legal secretary and a former parish councillor', while 'Miss Adams is on State benefits' (*Mail on Sunday*, 12 April 1998). Liberal legislators are thus chastised for letting down the majority of right-thinking citizens. This is a theme pursued elsewhere: 'I lost my girls to lesbian ex-wife. Heartbreak dad's rage at judge', proclaimed the *Sun* (9 September 1994) on its front page:

A devoted dad told last night how his life was wrecked by a judge who took away his two little girls and gave them to his ex-wife and her lesbian lover ... ' ... The children were thriving with me, but the judge decided to uproot them ... [and] went against what everyone wanted ... It's heartbreaking being a helpless victim of a legal system that is happy to put my two little girls into such a situation' ... How are they going to explain the weird set up they have been tossed into and that the dad in their house is really a woman?

In its editorial, the paper rhetorically asks its constructed reader: 'How can two women sleeping together be normal in the eyes of two little girls? Every parent will be scared by the implications of this disturbing case.'

'Everyone' and 'Every parent' are in creative opposition to the lesbians who are not quoted at all in the article. We must simply construe one of them as assuming a role of pretend male, even though claims of fatherhood are not their own words. They are also portrayed as outside the process which has judged in their favour, to whom a ball has been fortuitously but wildly tossed and who are now its lucky holders, against all rational choice.

'No need for a man about the house' (*Guardian Outlook*, 2 July 1994, front page) and the caption 'All-female family' (*Observer*, 3 July 1994, p. 25) reported the newly verified lesbian legal right to be joint parents. Both articles play on the notion that legal ruling has 'opened the way for us to become a nation of man-hating, all-female families' (*Observer*).

When the 'Church backs lesbian mothers' in a 'surprise admission' at a General Synod Church of England debate, and 'Lesbians have baby on NHS' (*Yorkshire Post*, 17 April 1997),[3] we should know that all institutions had sold out to destructive liberalism. Yet when the Child Support Agency tries to track down sperm donors of a lesbian couple with a 'virgin birth', living on social services family support (*Guardian*, front page, 14 May 1997) we can be assured that there is some sanity left. One arm of the state reaches out to try to save the rest from drowning.

Institutional Schism: The Church

The representation of lesbians, characterised by the good/bad dichotomy, is manifested in the setting of one institution against another, or when the loony subset is contrasted to the rational mainstream. Here another duality is exposed, where it is lesbianism, lumped together with male homosexuality as though it is the same thing, which leads to fragmentation, rather than the attitude towards it. We have here an image of negative procreation: the family of God terminally self-divided. 'First church to ordain gays faces split threat', 'The danger is that ordinary members will just leach away', stated the *Guardian*: the United Reformed Church (note the word 'United') 'is in danger of splitting over the issue' (note the passive verb, as though this is something being done to it). Homosexuality is frequently linguistically connected to evil: 'a bedevilled debate' describes the church's discussion on homosexuality (*Guardian*, 28 September 1994, p. 3).

The church family is threatened at its maternal heart. A vicar banned the Mothers' Union in his parish after one member, the mother of a gay man, condoned homosexuality in the organisation's international magazine, *Home and Family* (*Guardian*, 6 August 1997, p. 5). 'Double standards of the Church that allows gay priests to live a lie' (*Observer*, 2 October 1994, p. 8);[4] 'Hume highlights divisions over homosexuality' (*Guardian*, 8 March 1995, p. 3); 'Church split on gays looks for a miracle' (*Guardian*, 14 July 1997, pp. 2, 12) – these are just some of the reports on the self-schism of the church. Sin and sexuality came together on the day that the Lesbian and Gay Christian movement celebrated its twentieth anniversary with a service in Southwark

Cathedral. Homosexuals were presented as terminally plague-like yet mockable:

> Gomorrah and Gomorrah and Gomorrah, creeps in this petty pace. To many angry Christians, the thousands who filled Southwark Cathedral yesterday were a modern equivalent of a host of locusts, harbingers of fire and brimstone – the bearers of the worst plague of all, the sin of homosexuality … [Inside the church] despite the satanic predictions of their opponents, they all looked rather harmless; the devil may have the best tunes, but also the worst dress sense – there were a lot of bobbled jumpers in evidence. (*Observer*, 17 November 1996, p. 2)

Alternatively, the threat is from outside extremists. 'Mayhem in the cathedral as gay thugs hijack Easter', claimed the *Daily Mail* after Outrage! members protested in Canterbury Cathedral on Easter Sunday 1998, 'the holiest day in the Christian calendar'. The subheading alleged that 'They have disrupted a sacred place'. The Archbishop is reported as saying, 'There is a dialogue going on between the Church and serious-minded homosexuals' (13 April 1998), thereby invoking the familiar good/bad dichotomy. Outrage!, meanwhile, are said to have 'invaded' the pulpit (*Guardian*, 13 April 1998, p. 4): it is said to be 'colleagues in Asia and Africa' who find the idea of ordination of homosexuals to be 'morally repugnant'. The unreformed originators of sexual corruption in the early twentieth century are the ones now maintaining moral standards.

Institutional Schism: The Forces[5]

The robust attitude of the armed forces in Britain, too, is framed around the idea that homosexuals as a whole weaken the organization by being there. Frequently, this is expressed in terms of piety or of heresy: the Ministry of Defence maintains a 'lesbian's index' to aid in 'witchhunts', the index in religious terms being a list of written passages condemned to be expunged as heretical. Investigations of lesbians were described in terms of an inquisition: 'It was never enough for somebody to confess – we had to prove that they were gay … If their name was on the index the investigator could use it to bully the woman – it might intimidate somebody into confessing.' Another story, side-by-side on the page, headlines 'MoD unrepentant over sacked gays' (*Guardian*, 6 August 1994, p. 3).

One report indicated that, pending a legal judgment, several homo-sexuals were suspended from work. A solicitor acting for a lesbian former-RAF nurse said: 'They have been left completely in limbo' (*Observer*, front page, 14 May 1995). Another lesbian, dismissed from the military intelligence, inverted the paradigm, spoke in same-sex hagiographic terms and gave the nation female identity: 'I appeal to you to recognise the service and sacrifice of all the lesbian and gay people who have served this country ... I ask you to lift the threat of dismissal from my life and theirs. I am proud of my country and the service I have given her ... ' (*Guardian*, 1 July 1995, p. 8).

A further feature of language about lesbians in the forces relates to climatic disaster, one part of nature rebelling against another: 'a rising tide of anger and a growing body of legal criticism' described lesbian and gay opposition to the military ban (*Guardian*, 6 August 1994, p. 3); 'the tide of history' was turning against the Ministry of Defence, stated two separate stories in the *Guardian* (8 June 1995, p. 2 and Leader, p. 16); 'opening the floodgates' was used to describe a legal ruling in South Africa which gave same-sex partners access to health insurance (*Guardian*, 27 January 1998).

Institutional Schism: The Law[6]

'Can the church observe employment law as well as serving God?' set up the God/Wordly divide underpinned by an Employment Protection Act ruling, in a *Guardian* editorial, which went on to report the General Synod debate on homosexuality (14 July 1997). 'Sacked lesbian to sue RAF' was the headline, abutting a story on the church split about sexu-ality, when a lesbian took her employment challenge to the High Court (*Guardian*, 8 March 1995, p. 3).

When Cherie Booth QC acted as Counsel for the case of a lesbian railworker claiming travel rights for her partner, ideas of division stretched to innuendoes about matrimonial difference (or, conversely, suggestive of conspiracy to subvert). Newspaper coverage focused on Booth 'as lesbians' champion against Government', while 'Ms Booth's husband [Tony Blair, the British Prime Minister] has signed up to the [EU] treaty ... which will outlaw discrimination on grounds of sexual orientation' (*Guardian*, 10 July 1997, p. 4). When the legal action failed at the European Court of Justice, it was noted that the European Commission of Human Rights 'considered that stable homosexual rela-tionships did not fall within the scope of the right to respect family life ...' (*IDS Brief*, 608, March 1998, pp. 2–3).

Similarly, reports on changes to Immigration law uphold the distinction between Family and Lesbian: announcing that same-sex couples may be given entry to the UK, a spokesman stated that, despite this, government would still maintain 'primacy to the family' (Peter Sissons, reporting on the BBC's *Nine O'Clock News*, 10 October 1997).

Lesbians and Violence

The idea of the lesbian as destructive is embedded in her treatment under the law and in general discussion where she has 'almost always been depicted as predatory, dangerous, and pathological ... the shadow of the lesbian is laminated to the representation of women's violence ... ' (Hart 1994, p. x).

Reports of women's crimes frequently associate one kind of deviancy with another: Louise Woodward, the British au pair convicted of killing a baby in her care in the US, was described as pretending to be a man during an on-line cyber sex session (*Guardian*, 28 October 1997, p. 5). Other stories include reports of 'Lovers in for the kill or the thrill?' (*Guardian*, 21 December 1996, p. 5); 'The boyfriend', who turned out to be a girl (20 February 1996, p. 6).

We are frequently faced with a paradox in representation, between the crazed lone lesbian and those who engage with real or mythic lesbians elsewhere, sometimes in a *délire-à-deux*. Accordingly, British media depiction of US murderer Aileen Wournos described her lover with whom she had an inseparable bond (Hart 1994, p. 185), and other coverage suggests that women together are prone to inexplicable and hysterical behaviour, in a form of 'contagious folly' (Castle 1995, pp. 190–252). So, the conviction of two nurses in Saudi Arabia for the murder of another was covered with accusations that they were lesbians operating in a 'hothouse atmosphere' (*Guardian*, 12 August 1997, p. 3; 24 September 1997, p. 7); and when writer Anne Perry was revealed to be Juliet Hulme, convicted as a youth of murder with her best friend, coverage of their 'lesbian' relationship featured typical psycho-sexual language of the early twentieth century:

She is both like a child and like an adult, but the two parts seem not to connect ... [Her partner in crime] insisted on being called 'Paul', and her dark, curly hair was cut short like a boy's ... 'They were absolute opposites in every way' ... Who was the leader and who the follower? ... (*Guardian Weekend*, 29 June 1996).

Given that 'situational homosexuality' (in Havelock Ellis's terms) placed lesbians atypically within prisons, or crowded working-class conditions, amidst criminally deviant women, it should have been no surprise that Myra Hindley, imprisoned child-murderer whose crimes 'horrified the nation', hit the front pages with her lesbian lover (*Sun*, 7 October 1994).

Body, Science and Community

The same notion of individual versus group, with the lesbian affiliated by inference with selfishly focused sexual behaviour of a destructive kind, was embedded in the discussion on TV Channel 4's *Right to Reply* (14 January 1995): the sole two items for discussion were a *Horizon* documentary on autoeroticism, including necrophilia and mutilation, and the 'censorship' of the lesbian kiss on the Channel 4 soap, *Brookside*. The viewer was left to make a self-evident connection between the items, as though all deviancies can be explained or situated bodily and together.

There has been an essentialist response to such views, by both lesbian and anti-homosexual: 'I think it's part of your nature, you can't change the way you're born ... It's like deciding what colour you want to be born, or something' (quoted in Markowe 1996, p. 161). Such assertion forms part of an internalised resistance to scientific discussion, which has repeatedly focused on the idea of a physical or a genetic cause for homosexuality. In 1995, for example, the UK lecture tour of New York psychiatrist Charles Socarides received much press coverage for his views that it was a treatable disease: 'homosexuality cannot make a society or keep one going for very long. It operates against the cohesive elements in society' (*Guardian*, 25 April 1995).

So-called breakthroughs in genetic medicine, again, were widely reported. Dean Hamer, an American molecular biologist, announced he had discovered the markers of a gay gene (*Guardian 2*, 25 April 1995, p. 2); and Jim McKnight claimed that homosexuals are 'evolutionary by-products', and, that as a Darwinian, he grappled to explain 'the survival of a homosexual gene in the face of diminished reproduction' (*Times Higher*, 29 August 1997, p. 18). Both researchers, and the reports of them, focus on bodily 'cause': doctors, armed with genetic blueprints, might be able in future 'to predict a foetus's propensity to violence, crime and, possibly, homosexuality too' (*Guardian 2*, 21 October 1997, p. 6).

Conversely, Dorothy Nelkin, a sociologist of science, contextualised the quest for genetic explanation in the political situation: *The DNA*

Mystique, her book (with Susan Lindee) investigates 'the gene as a cultural icon', in the belief that 'Behavioural genetics shifts the blame on to the individual, and appears to legitimate the argument that no matter how much money we put into social services, it is not going to do much good' (*Times Higher*, 21 November 1997, p. 19).

In a period of political emphasis on individual freedom under late twentieth-century British Thatcherism, and its consequent excuse for erosion of funding for social services, we can understand why there might be a scientific emphasis on cause at the most centrally individual and peculiarly intimate level of gene. And, accordingly, why a lesbian might express her experiences of constraint in bodily terms: 'I was going around with a large part of myself amputated really' (in Ainley 1995, p. 37).

Responsibility is thus said to rest at personal level, within a network from which the lesbian is axiomatically excluded: 'There is no such thing as society: there are individual men and women, and there are families' (Margaret Thatcher, Prime Minister, *Woman's Own*, 31 October 1987). Lesbian self-perception in such a political situation suggests a sense of singularity:

> Growing up, we generally perceived ourselves as different from our families and friends ... (quoted in Curb and Manahan, 1985, p. xiv)

> I always had a sense of myself as not really fitting in. (quoted in Markowe 1996, p. 13)

> I felt strange thinking that there was nobody else in the world who felt like I did. (in Markowe 1996, p. 14)

In Thatcherite discussion, there is a Cold War and post-Cold War bearing: the lesbian conspiracy promoted by hostile outsiders gives way to ideas of the threat from within. She is everywhere, and a threat to society; she is nowhere, and to be mocked and pitied as an aberration. Popular discussion swings between the two: Myra Hindley is both laughable ('with her floral knickers round her knees as she romped ... ') and a threat, one part of a dark deviant relationship ('me and my shadow') with co-murderer, Ian Brady (*Sun*, 7 October 1994, pp. 4–5).

Under the headline 'Lesbian doc is reinstated', the *Sheffield Star* described a psychiatrist who had been struck off because of (consensual) sexual relations with a patient. The doctor attributes her own action to loneliness: 'I do not think I would be vulnerable again because

I am not in the same danger of isolation in a very small community that I was at that time' (11 September 1996, p. 2).

The notion of 'community' has been increasingly invoked in late twentieth-century determining language, ascribing a 'community' identity to minorities, partly to suggest members of the group are indecipherable and their differences inconsequential, and partly to suggest that this subculture (a mass) may be a threat. Here, '"communities" are not seen as naturally existing, but as created and developed in specific and concrete ways' (Hughes 1987, p. xii). There is complex interplay between ideas of nationhood and unity, and the posited opposition of the lesser grouping, 'community': both 'sides' chart territory, make 'ideological resistance, when efforts are made to reconstitute a "shattered community, to save or restore the sense and fact of community against all the pressures of the colonial system"' (Said 1993, pp. 252–3, quoting Davidson 1978, p. 155). The heterosexual constructs an idea (so a reality) of a homosexual community, in order to restore its own sense of cohesion, thus setting up an Hegelian heterosexual/homosexual dialectic. Lesbians respond (or perhaps they started it all?) by claiming a group sense.

Lesbians may, or may not, feel as if they do live in a 'community', and if they do it is likely to be different from that of heterosexual creation, designed as fictive-real space, itself to counter notions of a threatening Lesbian Nation. Sometimes the 'homosexual community' is a threat (with 'formidable organisational powers', *Guardian*, 16 April 1995, p. 13); sometimes it is weak, and self-destructive: 'Marriage made in hell', as gay 'brothers in arms' show a 'backlash against the bull-dykes' (*Guardian Weekend*, 17 December 1994, p. 31), or 'Lesbian militants target gay men' (*Guardian*, 2 February 1995, p. 6).

Ideas of fragmentation, and self-policing, have been particularly effective in dividing the women's movement through 'that whole ethos which wanted to pander to the straight press by saying "No, no, we're *not* lesbians ..."' (Goldwag in Groocock 1995, p. 118). And it also effects the self-alienation of women's detaching themselves from the stigma of 'community' via out-of-body/dysmorphic metaphor, where 'lesbian' is destructive of family at language level:

> when I opened my mouth and 'lesbian' came out ... I feared the blow. As if my word might vaporize my children, my mother ... might obliterate me and my lover in a public place. The power of my own word turned against me. (Minnie Bruce Pratt in Warland 1991, p. 27)

'Lesbian' is a word written in invisible ink, readable when held up to a flame[7] and self-consuming, a disappearing trick before my eyes where the letters appear and fade into the paper on which they are written, like the field which inscribes them. (Meese 1990, p. 83)

When I first came out, I didn't like the word 'lesbian' ... in fact I couldn't even write it down ... I couldn't watch myself writing [it]. (in Markowe 1996, p. 126)

Thus discourses of the postmodern operate within a (self-) divide-and-rule paradigm, shifting definitional axes to unsettle observers and listeners, according to political imperatives.

5
Lesbian Lives in the Later Twentieth Century

Alone in a Crowd

When Maureen Duffy was interviewed for a newspaper about her novel *The Microcosm* (1966), her writing was said to have brought her 'into contact with many lonely women who live outside London, whom she sadly feels are trapped by their environment, unable to help themselves'. Duffy herself was said to have 'forged a place for herself in society, still keeping outside consumer units ... ' (Stott 1969). The artist Gluck was described in a biography as having 'set herself apart from society' (Souhami 1988, p. 11). Thus the lesbian is represented as beyond the fringes, the pale, of collectivity and of society.

Others, when they live in it, disrupt: 'a neighbours row shattering Lakeland's quiet' reported the dispute involving Maureen Colquhoun in Ambleside, the town which has 'been riveted by the bitter feud involving the Labour party's first openly lesbian MP' (*Independent on Sunday*, 13 July 1997, p. 6). 'Forging', 'shattering' and 'riveting' are violent verbs to describe domestic life.

Jeanette Winterson, on the other hand, interviewed in her own domestic setting, has 'woven' her own life story, but her home with other women is called 'a coven', a 'ménage' (Turner 1994, pp. 18, 22). Another writer says of Winterson, 'Not only has she excised men from her quotidian world ... the household revolves around her needs as the planets around the sun.' It is as if Winterson has usurped, put her humanity (moreover woman, moreover lesbian) in the central place within the natural order of daily life. Her home 'consists of a small coterie of admiring women: when I suggest a comparison to the 1920s Paris salon of writer Natalie Barney, Winterson seems pleased' (Messud 1992, p. 5). Meanwhile, Barney's is the very home, shared with Romaine

Brooks for some 50 years, which Germaine Greer described as lacking calm domestic routine, full of 'frenetic emotional life' (1979, p. 60).

There are two possibilities about lesbian households: they are either threatening communities of witch-like ('coven') potential, or they are places for withdrawal. Natalie Barney lived in both: in 'a colony of women poets', 'her stronghold and her sanctuary' (obituary, *Observer*, 4 February 1972). Elizabeth Robins 'rejected the demands of heterosexual life and turned to a network of women writers in Boston for solace and strength ... ' (Marcus, in Robins 1980, p. vi). Maureen Colquhoun accordingly 'seems to find refuge among a circle of trusted friends' (*Sunday Times*, 16 November 1980), whereas she describes herself in positive spatial terms (see pp. 138, 153).

Outside/Inside

Going in and coming out, are of course, one of the principle paradigms describing lesbian lives (Sedgwick 1990). Its language permeates even the most seemingly innocuous descriptions. Greta Garbo, for example, has an image 'like a moon breaking through darkness' (Souhami 1994, p. 1), but it is night all the same. Lesbianism is often under wraps: Gertrude Stein and Alice B. Toklas are described, confusingly, as being in 'the very fabric of this union, wrapping Alice's central importance to Stein's private life in the shroud of her public demeanour' (Benstock 1986, p. 165). Benstock expands the mixed metaphor: Stein 'made style – that never-to-be-trusted garment that clothes linguistic operations – serve as a mask for her lesbian subject matter, an "envelope" ... that hid her real self' (p. 187). Here seizure of biographically justified metonymic images has implications for literary, as well as life, interpretation.

Authors appropriate the metaphor of secrecy, even when lesbians have not necessarily used such descriptions of themselves. Rose Collis chose as her subtitle of lesbian portraits, 'Historic Lesbian Lives Unveiled' (1994) though many of the subjects were not themselves secretive. Martina Navratilova's 'little girl public mask' (*Observer*, 3 July 1994, p. 23) and Nancy Spain's 'veils of mystery' (Collis 1997, p. 181, quoting a friend of Spain's) suggest an urge to conceal which may, or may not, have been their subject's own. Indeed, another life commentator says of Navratilova, 'Martina never wanted to hide it. She was always honest and upfront ... She never had any problems dealing with it or admitting it' (Chris Lloyd, TV tribute 1994). Even in denial, the biographer perpetuates the uses of negative discourse.

The writer Rosemary Manning, on the other hand, does use the notion of inside/outside in her own text: 'To come out at the age of seventy ... to come out of what, I ask myself? A cave? ... An outworn carapace?', she begins her chapter, 'Truth Will Out'. She says her lesbianism had been kept 'under covers':

> The habit of secrecy ... The years of dishonesty had formed a hard shell and I continually found myself moving back under its protection, as a prisoner sometimes comes to love his gaoler. Or perhaps I was playing a game, like a child crying out to her companions or to the grown-ups around her: 'I'm invisible! You can't see me!' (1987, pp. 1, 2, 4)

Unseen, Unsexed, Unhinged

Invisibility, then, in the 1980s and 1990s, has been an enduring image of lesbianism, as earlier in the century. Lesbian relationships continue to be described as ghost-like, other-worldly, to reduce their political significance. Violet Martin is thus the 'soul-mate' of Edith Somerville, with whom she co-wrote (Montgomery-Massingberd 1991). Use of ethereal imagery can be intended more positively, but still has the effect of suggesting an unearthly, and hence insubstantially threatening, assembly:

> By incorporating allusions to *The Well of Loneliness* in *A Room of One's Own*, Virginia Woolf ... brings Radclyffe Hall, her novel and the trial into literature forever in a narrative strategy calculated to emphasise the privacy of the woman writer's room is in fact collective and not private at all, since the company she keeps there include the ghosts of all the women writers before her ... (Marcus 1990, p. 178)

The effect of ghosting lesbian lives is that the nature of sexuality becomes murky, and removed, as it were, from bodily possibilities. 'It is doubtful whether their relationship, although highly emotional, was actually sexual', it has been written about Louise Abbema and her partner (Greer 1979, p. 60). Similarly, Rosa Bonheur and Nathalie Micas are said to have been 'sexless'; Gluck showed 'intense virginal fastidiousness' and Gwen John had a 'passionate love for another woman' but her feelings were 'pure' (pp. 59, 60, 64). Ivy Compton-Burnett was described as 'standing at the asexual extreme of lesbian sensibility'

(Rule 1975, p. 105), while Eva Gore-Booth and Esther Roper are said to have 'put aside sexuality from their lives as an irrelevance' (Lewis 1988, p. 6).

Accordingly, Eve Balfour's 50-year cohabitation is called 'friendship' (*Country Living*, 1989, quoted in Collis 1994, p. 154) as is the relationship between Natalie Barney and Romaine Brooks (*Observer*, 5 September 1971). So, lesbian relationships merge with other, less significant others, in a broad-brush phrase.

The language of kinship, likewise, displaces. Leonard Woolf, for example, described the relationship of Octavia Wilberforce (a doctor who treated Virginia Woolf) with the writer Elizabeth Robins, with whom she lived from 1908–40, as 'that of a devoted daughter' (1970, p. 84). Shari Benstock describes Adrienne Monnier as a 'mother and sister' to Sylvia Beach (1986, pp. 209, 210), whilst Edith Somerville and Violet Martin were said to be 'devoted spinster cousins' (Montgomery-Massingberd 1991).

This notion of celibacy perpetuates the idea of 'spinster', with its 'bulling heifer' connotation, where women lovers only suffice when males are absent:

> That Dorothy [L. Sayers] should still have been a virgin at 28 is not so extraordinary. A whole generation of young men of her age had gone to France in the First World War and never come back. England was full of young women, widowed or unwed, who were to grow into maiden aunts ... (Brabazon 1988)

> Real boys, after all, were in short supply – so many had died on the battlefields of Europe ... Women, having had to take up their work during the war, now took up their image. (Summerscale 1997, p. 89)

Radclyffe Hall's biographer, Michael Baker, states that 'The sight of women dancing together was not unusual, a hangover from the war kept alive by the continuing scarcity of eligible men' (1985, p. 134).

The cliché of frustration or low abundancy is often repeated. Sylvia Beach's headaches may have 'been the result of her efforts to repress certain aspects of her personality ... apprehensions about physical love-making or puritan guilt concerning love between women' (Benstock 1986, pp. 209–10). This reiterates earlier ideas of frigidity and neurosis (Meagher 1929).

Some biographers link illness and sexuality, with classism to boot:

For many years Violet [her lover] dealt as bravely with the shame of syphilis, which at that time was incurable and devastating to a woman of her background and upbringing, as Marguerite [Radclyffe Hall] dealt with the stigma of lesbianism. (Cline 1997, p. 57)

Others transform the language, and challenge detractors: Harvey Fruish, a former Northampton Labour councillor, wrote to Maureen Colquhoun after she had been sacked by the constituency:

It has taken me a while to overcome the nausea and disgust I felt when the decision went against you ... I have never seen such a persistent display of sustained hatred by the few infecting the good sense of the many in the party as a whole. As in life, it is the first disease that is infectious, not good health ... I am left with a mixed feeling of sorrow and shame ... that some of our members allowed themselves to succumb to the appeals of their baser nature ... (Colquhoun 1980, pp. 147–8).

A biographer wrote of Katherine Mansfield's 'two short love-affairs with girls' that they 'occurred now under the direct influence of her reading Oscar Wilde' (Alpers 1980, p. 46). Such things are clearly catching from the page.

Race

Bodily associations of lesbianism and race continue in the later twentieth century. Sometimes this has bizarre manifestations, as when Katherine Mansfield is quoted about a lesbian relationship: 'My mind is like a Russian novel.' This, writes her biographer, 'is the earliest thing in [her writings] which might be interpreted as showing she was acquainted with Russian authors' (Alpers 1980, p. 50). Maata Mahupuku, her lover, is described in racist terms as 'dark-skinned and exotically beautiful' (Tomalin 1987, p. 15). Janet Flanner, similarly, met the 'sloe-eyed exotically named Solita Solano [who] ... had things to hide' (Castle 1993, p. 189). Elsewhere, 'The clumsy Miss Moberley [fell] for the airs and graces of "French" Miss Jourdain' (Iremonger 1957, p. 94).

Smith (1994) analyses two key moments in determining the connections between anti-homosexual and racist statements, in the speeches of Tory politicians Enoch Powell and Margaret Thatcher. She argues that the language of the later century takes an 'hegemony-as-normalization approach' (p. 242). Her observations can be applied to attitudes to self and body (in Daphne du Maurier, discussed on p. 61) and in the political life of Maureen Colquhoun, both of whom refer to Powell at crucial moments of crisis around sexuality. Colquhoun's deselection as an MP was associated by her constituency party with her views on immigration. When asked for a view on Enoch Powell's speech in January 1977, she was construed to be in his support and was discredited by her opponents. 'It seems clear that her own avowed sexual attitudes and practices were the real basis of their disapproval' (Vallance 1982, p. 203). At this point, it was said of Colquhoun that 'Some people think her image has been blackened' (quoted in Colquhoun 1980, p. 155).[1]

Animals

It should not be unexpected, therefore, in this philosophy of supremacy flowing from Darwinian rationality, that lesbians should be seen as lower life forms (Sibley 1995). The language of biography is peppered with analogies, seemingly innocuously throw-away, of lesbians to creatures, plants, even fruit. Derogatory terms are not only directed at homosexual women, of course. As with misogyny in general, which seeks to distance the Other, even ridiculous images signify deeper opinions.

Radclyffe Hall has been described as 'the coltish creature wearing diamond studs and a tailor-made jacket' (Cline 1997, p. 60) rather as Christine Murrell 'looked like a young colt' to her lover (St John 1935, p. 36) 60 years before. This suggests the immaturity and social gaucherie of the subjects, both common lesbian descriptions. Jeanette Winterson is 'like a queen bee, surrounded by willing drones' (Turner 1994, p. 19). Vita Sackville-West was 'Like one of her own plants, she grew not according to the rulebook but according to the dictates of her own complex nature' (Glendinning 1983). Perhaps more bizarre is the idea of Dorothy L. Sayers (whose representation is discussed pp. 157, 167) being 'ripe for the plucking' by a man, having been just described as 'aware of female sexuality' in the context of man-less women after 1918 (see p. 129) (Brabazon 1988) and Martina Navratilova being seen by the press 'as a big juicy plum' (TV tribute, 1994).

Whilst such images are, of course, not only confined to the derision of lesbians, but appear, too, in reference to heterosexual women, they have especial weight when the other is both woman and deviant woman, being abject or over-active, employing her wily sexuality for dubious means. In this context 1997 media coverage of issues around fox hunting suggest more than idle reference. Woman as fox is a common enough analogy, as is the fox hunt to describe sexual pursuit.

Vixens are cunning, and the animal, in the American slang at least, has become synonymous with sexual attraction.

The fox in the context of lesbian action has appeared in various literary forms, from D.H. Lawrence's *The Fox* (1923), to Penny Casdagli: 'This fox is dangerous, predatory, transgressive, hunted, hunting, haunting, bringing Nature unnaturally into an artificially constructed environment: a stunning and unusual sight ... this fox is lesbian ... ' (1995, p. 263; and see Manning 1987, pp. 64–76).

Newspapers made links between homosexuality and parliamentary debate about a proposed ban on fox hunting, around a Countryside Rally in London (July 1997). The occasion allowed anti-homosexual statements to be 'legitimised' within discussion of something even less acceptable.

'Hunted to extinction, the hated country cousin', said A.A. Gill's headline, in a column which also covered nuns and other 'endangered minorities' (*The Times*, 14 July 1997). Other writers used the same images. Lesbians and gay men, we might say, are tarred with the same brush: 'The attempt to outlaw fox-hunting is all tied in with sado-masochism. Not to mention Gay Pride ... ' (Melanie Phillips, *Observer*, 13 July 1997, p. 2);

> Gay day for the fox. The countryside rally ... put me in mind of Gay Pride ... it's not just that fox-hunters and gays both tend to be fond of fancy dress, of bright colours and leather gear ... There was a familiar feeling in the crowd at last week's rally: that of a minority discovering strength in numbers ... both claim the right to enjoy a range of sensual pleasures that most people do not wish to take part in ... Same-sex sex and ritualised violence towards animals are both, moreover, human universals, though their manifestations may vary from culture to culture and over historical time. (John Ryle, *Guardian*, 14 July 1997, p. 5)

Against or For Nature?

Foxes, of course, are natural predators. We can claim not to blame them for their urges. Similarly, commentators on lesbian lives invite toler-ance by invoking the 'natural'. 'This was a fact of life ... this was Martina', said fellow tennis player Christine Lloyd of Navratilova (TV tribute, 1994); 'I just never thought there was anything strange about being gay', said Navratilova of herself (*Observer*, 3 July 1994, p. 23). 'To me it seemed the most natural thing in the world. But then it was a pretty weird world', said Nick Laurie about his mother's relationship with Nancy Spain (Collis 1997, p. 210).

There is a hidden agent here, a reasoning 'I' who, by her/his presence, enforces the (anti-lesbian) rationality of the majority. In unspoken parenthesis is the phrase 'I don't care what anyone else thinks, to me you are OK'. The dissenting/confirming voice in the wilderness is shown to be just that, endorsing a minority view. '[Our friends] understood that we were normal people entitled to the same rights as everyone else', said Pam St Clement, an actor, about the hostility of the press (Healey and Mason, 1994, p. 52) thereby enforcing the paradigm of reasoned antagonism. This is reflected, too, in Claire Harman's biography of Sylvia Townsend Warner. Writing of the reactions of their friends to the news of the relationship of her subject with Valentine Ackland, Harman writes that one, 'a worldly and unshockable man, had given them his blessing' and others 'thought no ill of them for several years, only opining that Valentine might be improved by a little make-up ... ' (1989, p. 114).

Immaturity

The explanation of lesbians as immature smacks of similar treatment, and suggests, again, a complexity in the place lesbians occupy on the cultural nature/against nature divide. Aspersion of childishness is commonplace in biographies of lesbians in the later twentieth century, as in the earlier work. Hence, Charlotte Brontë is said to have had 'an adolescent crush' on Ellen Nussey which died at the appearance of Constantin Heger (Foster 1958, p. 130); Ivy Compton-Burnett had 'crushes' even in old age (King 1993, p. 229); and Virginia Woolf 'when she was twenty and still affected by many of her adolescent needs' was attracted to Violet Dickinson (Trautmann 1973, p. 17). Daphne du Maurier's feelings for a man, even at 14, in contrast to her emotions for women, had 'little to do with schoolgirl crushes' (Forster 1993, p. 17).

Biographers give a sense of curtailed development: ' ... she saw herself as a creature of the water rather as Peter Pan was a creature of the air', wrote Kate Summerscale of Joe Carstairs (1997, p. 210). The same image[2] is used by Margaret Forster of Daphne du Maurier's enchantment with Gertrude Lawrence (1993, p. 266), and, of herself, by Nancy Spain (Collis 1997, p.250). Stevie Smith was described as if in a never-land between unsexualised ages: 'At first sight I took her for a schoolgirl, because of the pre-adolescent figure ... Then I saw the old-maiden sorrow and non-experience' (Mackworth 1987, pp. 111–12).

Man and Boy Dominatrix

As in the 1920s and 1930s works, lesbians are often represented by biographers as boys (e.g. Souhami 1994, p. 20; Summerscale 1997, pp. 24, 67, 96). Moreover, these are boys who play games:

> In the great tradition of little tomboys who grow up into big tomboys, Mercedes [de Acosta, a lover of Greta Garbo] did not play with dolls. Instead her favourite toy was a white rocking horse in whose stirrups she used to stand and 'lasso everything in sight' – no great surprise, really, given how effectively she hauled in lovers in later years. (Collis 1994, p. 33)

The 'lasso' quotation is from de Acosta herself (1960, p. 31). The transfer of inference, while playful, suggests an inequality within de Acosta's subsequent same-sex relationships, with her lovers as objects/animals, whom she captures. When other lesbians are referred to as 'Don Juan', a prototypically male seducer (e.g. Chalon 1979, p. 66), we presumably infer that their affection was based on principles of oppression. Other descriptions infer similar bravado: 'piratical trousers' for Maureen Duffy (Stott 1969); 'amazon' for Natalie Barney (Jay 1988).

Some lesbians do describe themselves as playing a role. Rosemary Manning tells how she 'dressed up' in her brother's naval uniform ('Reach for your Freud') (1987, pp. 3, 228). Biographers use their subjects' dress as a basis to claim hierarchical roles. 'In photographs [Stein and Toklas] look like a double act of pontiff and acolyte, or little and large, or a mountain and its shadow' (Souhami,1991, p. 17); 'the other one's maid', said a hotelier of the same pair (quoted, Stendhal 1995, p. ix). Both Stendhal and Wineapple (1996, p. 296) speculate on who was the 'aggressor' in the relationship, seeking identification within a male/female codification. In the same way, Benstock speculates about Sylvia Beach and Adrienne Monnier:

> Like Gertrude Stein, Sylvia loved to work outdoors chopping wood; although she referred to herself as 'he', she did not play the male in her relationship with Adrienne. She was the pursued object of Adrienne's affections, not the pursuing lover. (1986, p. 210)

This shows a paradigm within a paradigm. In the later twentieth century, Stein and Toklas have become a shorthand term for married couple in lesbian biography (see pp. 114–15). Invoking their names is a crisp way of suggesting male/female parts within a relationship: 'the journalists got it all a bit confused. They could never decide which of us was Gertrude and which was Alice' (Pam St Clement, in Healey and Mason, 1994, p. 52).

The shorthand has a knock-on effect. Mention of female assertiveness, axiomatic of maleness, seems sufficient to justify a label of potential lesbian. Lilian Baylis was often assumed to be a lesbian, for example, because she was 'a dominating unmarried woman whose closest friends (monks and clergymen aside) were mostly women (most of them unmarried); and because those who did not know her believed her, quite wrongly, to be mannish and butch' (Findlater 1975, p. 241).

Weapon-carrying in itself suggests sexual force: 'When she was not brandishing her umbrella at policemen, Dame Ethel [Smyth] found time to compose 5 operas and countless orchestral pieces', reported the *Daily Telegraph* (15 February 1993) in jokey style, invoking the common device of making fun of lesbian creativity. 'Alice [B. Toklas] is always carrying bags and umbrellas', wrote a biographer (Souhami 1991, p. 17), as though this bound her to subservience or ridicule. Edith Somerville's writerly assertion over interpretation of her own work is dispatched with 'the old girl cracked her riding crop, so to speak, at the publishers' (Montgomery-Massingberd 1991).[3] Lesbians are scary. When Salman Rushdie was asked to comment on 'infamous novelist' Jeanette Winterson, he is reported saying: 'I've got enough trouble. I don't need any more. What do you think? That I want a second fatwa?' (*Observer Review*, 8 January 1995, p. 3), thereby linking lesbianism and religious extremism.[4]

Such representation endorses prototypes of the lesbian which are based on constructed male, and heterosexual, gaze. Germaine Greer, when she writes of women artists who were lesbians, calls upon this view: 'There was nothing titillating about the full trousers and painters' smocks that Bonheur wore' (1979, p. 59). She uses the same gaze-point when writing of Romaine Brooks: 'the cross-dressing that [she] and her lesbian friends went in for was titillating, like the lipstick and pearl earrings that Una, Lady Troubridge, wore for her portrait by Brooks' (p. 60).

Heterosexual typology is called upon, too, by other writers who may claim to be feminist. Edy Craig, we are told, was 'tall, dark and handsome ... [with] a slight lisp. Chris [St John] herself had rather bulbous features, a slight limp and also had to contend with a cleft palate with [sic] gave her a speech impediment. *However*, it was the start of a lifelong, *if not beautiful*, relationship' (Collis 1994, pp. 56–7, my emphasis).

Hence, we may read that because trade-unionist Alice Franklin 'looked so like a man with her short-cropped hair' (Stott 1978, p. 13) she must have acted like one sexually, whatever that means. Biographical descriptions lead their readers to read off roles, with little sense that gender is itself constructed and relates in complex ways to a configuration of identity. Such judgements transfer across media, so that visualisation of the lesbian can receive aural representation. It is understandable, therefore, why, in a BBC Radio 4 profile (18 January 1997) of 'pioneer doctor' Sophia Jex-Blake, her 'female companion' was played by a deep-voiced actor.

Female Parts

And yet, in the same way as biographers of the early twentieth century showed the 'acceptable lesbian' as combining parts, writers of the later period likewise include female qualities in their depiction, as if to convey image coherence. It was said of Nancy Spain that 'She was one of those very few people who had very feminine and masculine parts in her. She had an equal quantity of both'; 'There was tremendous sensitivity; she was very female despite her, what we'd call now, very butch image' (quoted in Collis 1997, pp. 250, 206).

'Octavia [Hill] could be dauntingly brusque, sharp, immovably obstinate and implacably firm. But she was also invincibly modest, generous, self-aware, and on occasion unexpectedly frivolous' (Spurling 1990). It seems to surprise another writer that Ethel Smyth had feelings:

> a firm-jawed Amazon apparently, soft collar and tie, a turned down felt hat, and thick flat-heeled shoes. I was all the more touched at the evidence of so much surface masculinity, to remember that here was the same sensitive being, the same heart beating, which had long ago nearly broken for love, in one of the saddest romances of literary history. (Cardus 1967)

Marriage

Lesbians, like Smyth in this context of failed heterosexual romance, are measured by the gauge of matrimony, and found lacking. Definitions of lesbian appear under 'extramarital', along with concubinary, incestuous and adulterous (*Roget's Thesaurus* 1994). A lesbian is a loose woman. This is a model which seems hardly to have changed since Renaissance times. 'All [women] are understood either married, or to be married … ', stated a legal clerk's definition of 1632 (Graham *et al.* 1989, p. 7). Thereby is encapsulated the heterosexualisation of 'woman' as a term. Not to want to be married is a definitional impossibility. The bewilderment about lesbians as women or not-women has its origins in such codifications; just as the confusion about the status of lesbian relationships has its basis in the very heterosexualisation of marriage as an institution.

As in the 1920s and 1930s biography, descriptions, thus definitions, of lesbians operate in relationship to marriage. Hence, Charlotte Brontë's relationship with Ellen Nussey was said by a biographer to have been 'in some ways as close to a marriage' (Fraser 1988, p. 456). 'They were together 14 years which, in this day and age, is quite a chunk of marriage', said Nick Laurie of his mother's relationship with Nancy Spain (Collis 1997, p. 107). Similarly, the relationship of Stein and Toklas 'fulfilled the codes and expectations of conventional romantic love' (Souhami 1991, p. 20). Such codes are treated as if they are self-evident, and heteronormality is preserved within lesbian biography.

Within a lesbian family, one partner is invariably described as the 'father-figure'. This is said to be the case of Nancy Spain (Collis 1997, pp. 176–7); Jeanette Winterson, 'breadwinner and "father" of the family' (Messud 1992); and Martina Navratilova: '[Her] relationship with [her lover] Judy's sons is strong. "She plays football and basketball with them" said [Judy's mother]. "It's absolutely fantastic, she's more like a father to my grandsons"' (*People*, 21 June 1987).

Family and Home

The representation of Navratilova at this point is heterosexually located (Hamer 1994, p.69) and hence endorsed, though simultaneously interrogated for its usurpation of natural boundaries. Oppositional discourse plays an in-the-river-on-the-bank game: the anti-lesbian can jump (or push the lesbian) either way as exigency suits. Whilst the 'family' is an appropriate motif for Navratilova's relationship when her lesbianism is treated in a (relatively) positive fashion, at other times she is outside its contours. Navratilova herself observes, for example, that sponsorship 'is going to be controversial if they sign me for some good home product, or whatever' (TV tribute, 1994). Interestingly, in the same interview, she says of her own self-recognition, 'I knew I had feelings for women ... I really felt at home, I felt comfortable with a woman.' Home is clearly where the heart is, and can shift depending on the approbation, or otherwise, given by external endorsers.

Other commentators on lesbian lives invoke the family to exclude, or to scrutinise, lesbian occupation. Maureen Colquhoun lives within an (in quotes) 'extended family' and was previously a member of Gingerbread, a single parents' support agency (*Independent on Sunday*, 13 July 1997).[5] It is not mentioned that, while she was an MP, she proposed an early-day motion in parliament which called for 'family friendly' working hours (Collis 1994, p. 160). Reference to Colquhoun's pretend or dislocated family serves to underline her perversity. Otherwise, family mention underscores (retrieved) normality: when Gillian Boddy interviewed an early lover of Katherine Mansfield, she is referred to as 75 'and a great grandmother' (1988, p. 17), as though age and reproduction can prove that neither woman could have been serious/authentic lesbians.

Elemental Imagery: Earth, Space and Air

As in the early twentieth century (see pp. 64–74), lesbians use a range of images from the elements to self-describe. Language of home is used to signify earthing, stability, grounding. Earth and space are recovered by lesbians who have been spatially constrained.[6]

Prior to her self-recognition as a lesbian, Maureen Colquhoun said she had 'led a sheltered life … I saw my move in living with Barbara [Todd] as a freedom' (1980, p. 89), taking off 'into the orbit of love' (*Woman's Own*, quoted in *Gay Times*, 21 September 1978). The image suggests a new spatial location within the element, though one still with a gravity.

After she had, in her own words, 'come out' on a TV programme, Rosemary Manning felt at once liberated and aware of her imprisonment, 'I felt an enormous load fall from my back … freedom from the past does not come all that easily. Shall I ever be liberated from its shackles?' That it was a partly self-imposed incarceration is reflected in her Foucaultian self-description, as 'a butch prison officer' (1987, p. 4). Another lesbian writes about coming out at work: 'I felt that I had expanded to fill the space that had been allocated to me all the time but I'd been too shrunk and crouched to take it all up' (in Ainley 1995, p. 37); and another describes an earthly shift when recognising aspects of sexuality. 'It was very tilting – things shifted on an axis when you saw her [Nancy Spain on TV] … ' (Alison Hennegan in Collis 1997, pp. 218–19).

Biographers take up the imagery. 'She felt a sense of freedom in the unencumbered rooms', wrote Diana Souhami of Gluck at the start of her relationship with Nesta Obermer (1989, p. 140). Describing the day after Sylvia Townsend Warner and Valentine Ackland had become lovers, Claire Harman wrote, 'The cool autumn morning into which Sylvia woke was unlike any other … part of the new landscape in which Sylvia moved' (1989, p. 100). This recalls something of Sylvia Townsend Warner's own imagery of that day, which itself echoed several facets of lesbian imagery:

> My last day, and our first. It was a bridal of earth and sky, and we spent the morning lying in the hollow tump … listening to the wind blowing over our happiness, and talking about torpedoes, and starting up at footsteps. It is so natural to be hunted, and intuitive. (diary entry, 12 October 1930, in Harman 1995, p. 70)

There is a sense here of imminent threat to a newfound identity. Friendly elements are capable of turning.

Elemental Imagery: Water

Same-sex analogy of home and harbour has a long history, it seems:

> She took me in her arms, hung around my neck, and cried; and I sympathised with her and told her, if she would confide in me for her pilot, I would soon steer her into a safe harbour, in which she might lie snug and secure from the dangers of the stormy world. (Elizabethe Hughes and Sophie Snow, c. 1787; cited in Donaghue 1993, p. 173)

Such analogy is used by twentieth-century lesbians in both the earlier and later periods. Joan Werner Laurie was as 'like an anchor to Nancy [Spain]' (Jackie Forster in Collis 1997, p. 286). Joe Carstairs and her lover 'seem to have lost their bearings, but [the lover with nothing] to anchor her, more dangerously so' (Summerscale 1997, p. 121). Gluck's biographer similarly stretched the reference: 'In her last years, when she was beached, lost and lonely, that was what her painting showed: a lone bird flying into the sunset, waves washing in on a deserted shore, an iridescent fish head washed up by the tide (1988, p. 14). Later, Gluck painted 'the river at a point where it changes course, as she felt she was herself changing course, and flows to the open sea' (p. 148).

Rosemary Manning (1987) used the water analogy of her own depression about sexuality, ultimately overcome. The 'fat, slow fish lurking in muddy waters' (p. 5) is caught. Her final image is of 'the fishing party, our rugs and picnic baskets on the green bank. In this especial rural scene, my friends and I, in a final gesture, toast our loves and toss our champagne corks into the river at our feet' (p. 234).

Elemental Imagery: Fire and Light

Biographers, as in the earlier period, use the element with heterosexual, and pejorative, overtones: Radclyffe Hall's 'may have been an unholy love, but it had some element which survived the white heat of passion and the cold deadness, the non-feeling which is so often the conse-quence of unnatural union' (Dickson 1975, pp. 22–3). 'These memoirs were not recalled in tranquillity, there is still a whiff of gunpowder about them' (Introduction, Ida Baker's memoirs of Katherine Mansfield, L.M. 1985, p. ix). Violet Trefusis's correspondence with Vita Sackville-West is prefaced thus:

> Violet's passion for Vita [was] an all-consuming passion which all but destroyed her. In a sense, it did destroy her: the youthful Violet whose idealism burned with a pure bright flame was transformed into a *femme de lettres* … there remained in the shadows glimmer-ings of the 'other Violet' an ephemeral, fanciful creature. (Jullian and Phillips 1976, pp. 149–50)

Lesbians and darkness remain linked: 'Menaced by "night terrors" since infancy, [Katherine Mansfield] instinctively and consciously explored her darker side. At such times these strangely morbid elements of suicide, fulfilment through death, were to haunt her all her life' (Boddy 1988, p. 17).

Rosemary Manning seems to challenge such negative connotation: 'I have moved into a world of warmth and understanding in the common-ality of women, a world I have looked for all my life' (1987, p. 234).

Metamorphosis

Many lesbians express their transitions in terms of enlightenment or of rebirth: 'That was the beginning of my proper life', and, 'it dawned on me that I was a lesbian' (in Ainley 1995, pp. 36, 40); 'Lesbianism is a total way of life in the sense that it's like being born again. I mean that's how I feel' (in Ettorre 1980, p. 33); 'it *is* me. And to change it you would have to completely kill me off and start me all over again' (in Ponse 1978, p. 178).

Such language of self-description can be seen to endure through the twentieth century, giving enforcement to both positive and negative typology. Later twentieth-century self-expression, likewise, engages with earlier auto/biographical models. Ideas within modernism recur and are reinscribed by lesbians who write and are written within the so-called postmodern of the twentieth century.

6
Lesbian Auto/biography in the Later Twentieth Century

The State of the Art: Theories of Auto/biography

Selfhood[1]

'The mosquito has no status in our culture until it bites you.'
'The death of my son was the first thing that happened to me.'
'I had no biography before I arrived in Paris.'

Thus the mayfly arriving after its chrysalised sojourn knows
 only who
it is not, a maggot any more when it emerges from the coffined
 burrow to see,
flies in the new confines of the air what now it is.

Conversely, a lesbian writes of her life after the death of her mother: 'What has happened since is but a postscriptum. It really doesn't count' (Trefusis 1952, p. 232). These are points of redirection, making the future change, either into something which happened next, or making the past the new future.

The recognition of the difference between self and other forms the pivot of auto/biography, and the means of writing. The autobiographer is 'surrounded and isolated by his [sic] own consciousness, an awareness grown out of a unique heredity and unique experience ... Separate selfhood is the very motive of creation' (Olney 1972, pp. 22–3).

Schism from others may cause one type of self-awareness. Otherwise, it is claimed that *self*-fragmentation serves as the inspiration: 'there is no such thing as the ego on its own, since the ego exists, comes into being, only as difference from itself ' (Rose 1991, p. 146). Self-consciousness may enable re-engagement with historical conditions that brought about individuation:

In acquiring one's conception of the world one always belongs to a particular grouping which is that of all the social elements which share the same mode of thinking and acting ... The starting-point of critical elaboration is the consciousness of what one really is, and is 'knowing thyself' as a product of the historical process to date which has deposited in you an infinity of traces, without leaving an inventory. (Gramsci 1985, p. 423)

Women's auto/biography has been analysed increasingly to establish such an 'inventory', and to indicate that it has distinctive traces which set it apart from male traditions of the genre. Women write

out of a need to differentiate the self from others, only to show that its constitution and individuation predicated reference and relatedness to others ... The female 'I' was thus not simply a texture woven from various selves; its threads, its life-lines, came from and extended to others. (Stanton 1984, p. 16)[2]

Patterns of self-recognition in slave narratives suggest parallels with lesbian lives.[3] Whether in isolation, fissure or reunification, with self and/or others, auto/biography is predicated on a sense of personal epistemology, even, or because, it has been transfixed, transcended or transfigured by the ontology of others. This definitional centring on one person leads to a paradox of the genre: for one person 'to tell the truth' about themselves might seem a straightforward act, for who better to recite the tale truthfully? And yet, it has been claimed that autobiography 'is the least reliable of genres – one person in relation to one world of that person's manufacture' (Rosenblatt, in Olney 1972, p. 169). All autobiography dithers around the coincidence of the writing I and the written I, the distinction between enunciation and utterance (Marcus 1994, p. 190). If the confusion around personal fluidities within the postmodern is added to this, then the genre may seem to dissolve still further.

Within the postmodern, 'The one world which the modernists sought to know is replaced by a plurality of autonomous worlds that can be described and the relations between which we can explore, but that can never be the objects of true knowledge' (Bertens 1995, p. 78). Auto/biography may appear thus to be a theoretical impossibility as self gives way to self like a flipping electronic timetable on a railway station: only the latest matters for the others have already gone. The authentic self is overhauled or superseded in this 'academic version of the consumerist ethic whereby the latest, despite – or rather because of – being little different from the last, renders the latter obsolete' (Dollimore 1991, p. 22).

Theorists of the postmodern aver there has been a dissolution of the knowable and authenticated self, including the Authorial One who has the (non-)specificity assigned to literary characterisation which

> advances an attack on the notion of identity, or of an essential Selfhood which is not traduced by a temporal dimension which threatens that Self with heterogeneity. In short, it leads to an elaboration of 'characters' (if they can be called such, given their confusing ontological status) whose existence (rather than essence) is characterised by *difference* (rather than identity). Postmodern figures are always differing, not just from other characters, but also from their putative 'selves'. (Docherty 1996, p. 60)

Stability of interpretation accordingly cannot be found in even the character of the author, and the shifting text is the only, if questionable, source of authority. Philosophers have argued for a separation of author and text, for the recognition of an impersonal writer, who did not precede the written (Barthes 1968). The author, it is argued, has been introduced as a fallacy, a distraction to limit meaning: in reply to his own rhetorical question 'What is an Author?', Foucault (1972, p. 114) replied, 'the author is the principle of thrift in the proliferation of meaning'. Readerly focus consequently should transfer from the writer to signifiers within the text, and readers should cast off the shackles of a belief which restricts the possibility of new meanings (Sprinker 1980, pp. 322–44). Auto/biography, likewise, is devoid of authorial stance, and offers only an illusion of reference (de Man 1979). Both author and genre are thus deconstructed.

For autobiography, of course, the dissolution is of subject as well as of author. Deconstructionist statements have especial significance for genres in which author/self identification appears paramount:

> the text takes on a life of its own, and the self that was not really in existence in the beginning is in the end merely a matter of text and has nothing whatever to do with an authorizing author. The self, then, is a fiction and so is the life, and behind the text of an autobiography lies the text of an 'autobiography' ... Having dissolved the self into the text and then out of the text into thin air, several critics ... have announced the end of autobiography. (Olney 1980, p. 22)

This might seem something of a relief, given the rumpus. But lesbian autobiographers are driven by a different imperative, and value personal writing in association with a lesbian-feminist politics of self. They are caught in the double cross-fire of the exchange about both 'authorial' identity about sexual 'identity'. It is as if patriarchal theorists have taken their scissors to the already hole-y, but otherwise useful, string bag which holds the lesbian self together. If some theoretical traditions express ennui with their author, therefore, in women's writing, like lesbian and black writing, she has just been named, and her experience, and that of her reader, has been invested with nascent critical importance:

> The death of the subject and of the author may accurately reflect the perceived crisis of western culture and the bottomless anxieties of its most privileged subjects ... There remain plenty of subjects and authors who, never having had much opportunity to write in their own names or the names of their kind, much less in the name of culture as a whole, are eager to seize the abandoned podium. (Fox-Genovese 1988, p. 67)

Lesbian auto/biography sits in a particularly complex relationship to theory of the postmodern. Amidst the furore, lesbian writers, and readers, wish to form, or attest to, an authenticated self across time and history, *and* to a reshifting self, relocating according to experience, and recognising sexuality at change-points in a life. Hence, many writers claim to be (re)born to a new self when they identify as lesbian, and hence they assert an essential ('it is me', in Ponse 1978, p. 178) and a constructed self: they are a still point in their own turning world. In that sense, such auto/biography is almost an embodiment of post-modern flux, the epigone of its theory.

Ideas of origins of the self may refuse a teleological connection of past and present. As of things, so of people: 'What is found at the historical beginning of things is not the inviolable identity of their origin; it is the dissension of other things. It is disparity' (Foucault 1977, p. 142). Chronological self-beginnings may not be the origin of identity. The art of self-writing is a re-enactment of the drama of identity formation where we can see autobiography as not only 'the passive, transparent record of an already completed self but rather as an integral and often decisive phase in the drama of self-definition' (Eakin 1985, p. 226). Having become recognised, and thereby fixed at a moment of lesbian self ('This is me'), that self then becomes the antithesis of fixity. It both is and is not at the same time. The authenticated lesbian self is that which has been defined by the difference between what it is now and heterosexual others ('I always had a sense of myself as not really fitting in'; see p. 123), and/or the difference between what it is now and discarded selves ('it's like being born again'; p. 140). It has been shaped out in the space of theoretical mêlée.

It is no coincidence, therefore, that there is said to be a crisis of selfhood at a time when lesbians are claiming to have found themselves. 'For many women, access to autobiography means access to the identity it constructs' (Gilmore 1994, p. xiv): denial, therefore, is not just whipping away one rug from beneath women, but exposing a whole void where the floorboards might have been. Where the prefix or descriptor 'autobiographical' is allowed, 'it had negative connotations when imposed on women's texts ... women could not transcend, but only record, the concerns of the private self; thus [naming this as a genre] had effectively served to devalue their writing ... ' and the label 'autobiographical' was 'wielded as a weapon to denigrate female texts and exclude them from the canon' (Stanton 1984, pp. 6–7; Jelinek 1980, p. 10).

Women, and lesbians, are caught in the pitchfork of desire. Both to name and not to name this as a distinctive genre, therefore, has its dangers. 'Writing that works the borders of definitional boundaries bears witness both to repressive inscription under the law of genre and to the freedom and dispossession of existence outside the law' (Benstock 1988, p. 2). To claim a genre based on notions of the objectified concedes to misogynistic claims about the value(lessness) of experience in pedagogy and in literature, whilst not to name fails to validate a literary language of lesbians' own experience.

There are other problems, too, with claiming this to be a genre. Biddy Martin has rightly pointed out that the very title 'lesbian auto/biography' suggests 'that there is something coherently different about lesbians' lives', and that 'lesbianism becomes the central moment around which women's lives are reconstructed'. She considers that a reading community is posited by the label, with narratives assuming 'a mimetic relationship between experience and writing and a relationship of identification between the reader and the autobiographical subject' (1988, pp. 78, 83–4). Rather it may be the case that several factors simultaneously, or sequentially, or independently and far apart, create what may be styled 'identity', with sexuality being one of a range of possibles, including race, class, age, (dis)ability, culture or serendipity.

There is also a danger, in claiming genre status, of silencing some lesbian utterances, and giving a primacy to the articulate, or of seeming to endorse particular life-narratives as authentic, while dismissing others. Then, authors may effectively 'rewrite' themselves in advance, not to fabricate their experience, but to use words which will render their identity decipherable. The keepers of genre, then, act as protectionists, a hound which guards the gates. To do this, of course, is to do patriarchal dirty work, barking for someone who already has a pack of dogs.

It may be that such theoretical conditions have resulted in there being a relatively limited number of lesbian autobiographies, if we are to count only single-author publications. Many later twentieth-century lesbian life-narratives are encased in a series of personal testimonies with other writers:[4] sexuality may be there as an organising principle, but sole authorship is avoided, with arrangement on the basis of a 'women like us' principle (the title of a collection by Neild and Pearson 1992). This may reflect an impulse towards authentication through mass, a theoretical positioning to emphasise collective, if individualised, space.

There is another, similar, manifestation of lesbian autobiography, in which individual personal account is contained within theorised narrative. Liz Stanley, for example, enters her own text as an autobiographical I, and intersperses her discussion with personal material and photographs of herself (1992, pp. 45–55). From this, she probes the idea of individuality as construct even within its own theory, a double disappearing/reappearing act with self 'as a fictive textual construction even if not a fictional one' (p. 54). Similarly, Valerie Walkerdine (1990) interweaves personal material within methodological discussions, showing that social structures and individual life intersect in complex ways. Auto/biography and theory mutually validate.

Such an approach has its attractions (in confirming the status of the personal), but also inherent dangers. Whilst it seems to bridge the alleged chasm between theory and life, and thus endorse experience, it actually

> advertises the status of *theory* as a superior kind of writing ... the suggestion is that only a theoretical criticism of autobiography can justify *analysis* of autobiographical texts ... it assumes that autobiographical writings can only be taken seriously when they are taken theoretically to mean something more than a critical practice can elucidate (Benstock 1988, p.3).

Linking experience with theory does suggest a lack of confidence in the intellectual status of the personal as well as in the genre of auto/biography and the principle of self-authentication outside and beyond theory. Feminists engaging in this (albeit enthralling) process seem to be in danger of privileging the articulate once more, implying that untheorised accounts of self are invalid.

Lesbian feminists in this mode of corporate autobiography have developed another double-edged dilemma. They seem to challenge a male autobiographical hegemony which privileges the 'conscious awareness of the singularity of each individual life' (Gusdorf 1980, p. 29), and thus to have challenged a tenet of New Right philosophy embedded in individualistic manifesto where 'the secret of selfhood is commonly seen to lie in authenticity and individuality, and its history is presented as a biography of progress towards that goal, overcoming great obstacles in the process' (Porter 1997, p. 1). This nicely echoes male procreative models: 'Nearly every writer on male fertility indulges in a panegyric on the sperm's qualities, its supposed capacity for independent, purposeful existence' (Pfeffer 1985, p. 27). The act of unlocking of this 'secret selfhood' suggests, paradoxically, a closure, a completion, that the act is sufficient unto itself: and it has rightly been asked how this kind of narrative can 'represent a subjectivity whose construction is by definition never complete?' (Raitt 1993, p. 63). Lesbian-feminist emphasis in theorized life-narrative upon the personal-within-the-group accordingly challenges ideas of strident individualism being paramount.

> The fundamental inapplicability of individualistic models of the self to women and minorities is twofold. First, the emphasis on individualism does not take into account the importance of culturally imposed group identity for women and minorities. Second, the emphasis on separateness ignores the differences in socialization in the construction of male and female gender identity. From both an ideological and psychological perspective, in other words, individualistic paradigms of the self ignore the role of collective and relational identities in the individuation process of women and minorities. (Friedman 1988, pp. 34–5)

Some lesbians may thus experience a particular shakiness of the ontology of self, which a notion of 'group' may alleviate. On the other hand, and this is the dilemma, some lesbians may experience the converse, and feel a fierce sense of I-ness ('it *is* me') which is denied significance by theorists who may have blunted the sharpness of the lesbian 'I'.

Having said that, there is no doubt that feminist theorists of women's and lesbian auto/biography have engaged with, and thus drawn attention to, the intersection of I and We. Accordingly they have created space in the theoretical discord to enable both individualised and 'group' autobiographics to be conceptualised. This has been manifested in several ways.

Leigh Gilmore, for example, has explored the ways in which Gertrude Stein 'used autobiography to inscribe the lesbian couple as the "subject" of *The Autobiography of Alice B. Toklas* … [and] resists the notion that autobiography is a discursive site for shoring up the self' (1994, pp. 202, 204). Similarly, Monique Wittig has explored the idea of the coupled female subject, rather than the individuated 'I' (1975, pp. 63–73).

In auto/biographical practice, some writers have disclosed the community and women's friendships within which lesbian lives intersected, to reveal networks of female relationships (Whitelaw 1990; Morley with Stanley 1988). This has enlarged the view of the canvas upon which women's lives are portrayed. Further extensions of the idea of inter-relation emerge with discussion of the reader of lesbian auto/biography, the effect on her of the text and its facilitation in 'writing' her own life. A recognition that there is a complexity in the reception enables a systematic self-referentialisation to occur, where lesbians consider the effect on their personal epistemology of reading another Life (Hallett 1998).

An additional facet of this comes with the idea of role-model, not in the most obvious sense, but in terms of invisibilised enablement, through the life interview, the obituary, the representation, within the compass of the genre. In a review of a book of Robert Mapplethorpe's work, for example, Ingrid Sischy used the occasion to come out herself in print, stating that she had been empowered by Mapplethorpe's photography and relieved to find homosexuality represented 'in an unqueasy, honest and often beautiful way' (Sischy 1989, p. 145). That this is powerful as a communicative means is attested in the urge to police such possibilities of transfer, presumably behind the mooted prosecution in 1998 of a British university for keeping a copy of Mapplethorpe's photographs in its library (*Guardian*, 20 March 1998, p. 6; Nead 1998).

Lesbian Autobiography: the Practice

Lesbian autobiography, in its most formal definition of a written account of her life, by a lesbian, which is organised around the principle of her sexuality, remains the clearest manifestation of the genre. Study of two examples (by Rosemary Manning and by Maureen Colquhoun) reveals that these lesbians express themselves in ways that echo feminist theoretical models, and which are antithetical to male prototypes of autobiography as an expression of overriding individuality.

Manning's *A Corridor of Mirrors* (1987) balances on the lesbian fulcrum of peculiar sameness: 'I am not of course unique. I am one of many' (p. 4). She writes of her life unfolding in a situation in which models of homosexuality are imbued with notions of disease from which she acquired a negative sense of self even before she read theorised accounts:

> I don't think I had even heard of these sexologists when I was growing up ... A strong whiff of these malodorous views hung in the air ... Ignorant as I was of [these] writings, I grew up with unexpressed fears derived from them. (pp. 2–3)

Descriptions of her emerging self-identity are framed in terms of such secret/open binaries, rather as Vita Sackville-West did almost exactly seventy years before (see pp. 83–4). 'I had not even spoken of [my lesbianism] to more than one or two close friends, though it must have been known to most of my circle': it is an open, if confined, secret, around which there was 'an active unwritten law', 'unexpressed fears' (pp. 1, 3). Manning found empowerment through breaking a silence. Here we can see an emerging and refining lesbian logos at work. Manning had moved from her earlier autobiographical piece, *A Time and a Time* (1971) which she considered semi-fictional and selective, towards an increasing honesty, yet tinged with doubts about the authenticity of words which are 'awkward customers. Intractable creatures ... [with] their double meanings and their capacity to convey specious lies ... I have used words to conceal or obfuscate ... And this despite my intentions to tell my own truth clearly' (p. 163).

For Manning, language and sexuality run together within a framework of fore- and disclosure. 'Why do I share these private things with you, the reader? Partly because communication is my trade, but more importantly, because they are the essence of me' (p. 165). At the heart of her thesis is the idea that personal identity and the words that describe it are one, so failure of words is failure to be true. This is (implicitly or consciously) based on an idea of knowledge contained in language, a paradigm which has endured through the twentieth century, indeed it is a culturally ensconced tenet of Judaeo-Christian foundation within the Word as both a source of lies and of truth, contained from the beginning. 'I have neglected to create myself' (p. 178): Manning's text is her self-recreation, in just such a language of sin/redemption within a vernant garden context in which 'one has to cut away a forest of misapprehension and downright untruths' (p. 26):

> And I resist the old temptation to dress it up in metaphor. I know my dangerous tendency to use words as a barrier or throw them into the air before me like a smokescreen. So I strip off the verbiage and write ... (p. 179)

> I was like a tree with three main branches, each growing malformed, each blown from its true growing course by the ill-rooted condition of its parent trunk. These branches were love, creativity and music. (p. 112)

Words are both the means to the thing, and the thing itself. Manning charts her own entry into language and her relationship to an order of things, making tacit use of Jacques Lacan's idea of the 'mirror stage', a crucial juncture of subjectivity. She is in (her title) a corridor of mirrors, and enacts as she walks it her transformation of perspective. Initially, she writes of herself as an outsider 'peering in' (p. 29). Gradually, the object and subject come together as, over the course of the writing, the parallax shifts: the object (lesbian) is unchanged but the lesbian observer changes position. In her younger mirrors she sees 'as it were a double image, myself as lover and writer' (p. 134). This marks, in Lacanian terms, the early mirror stage when the immature woman sees her image as another, though it has the appearance (illusion) of cohesiveness: the moment of recognition of the self/other is the moment when the divided subject is born, with the splitting of the 'I'. This marks an entry into language. For the lesbian subject, words are especially elusory since language of her has been formulated within constructions of difference between male/female and (for her) especially fraught relationships with Lacan's Law of the Father and the male dominance of the symbolic realm. Whereas self-homing for the lesbian is always difficult, because the split 'I' cannot be rejoined, Manning makes use of other theories of the self associated with mirrors in formulating her lesbian subjectivity. She challenges the idea of the unknow-able by relating her experiential sense of self to other women like her, so that the singular (albeit made up of diffusion) gives way to the plural (made out of singularity): 'And what then is reflected in the last mirror of the corridor? Not the solitary figure of myself, but ... my friends and I' (p. 234).

The autobiographical process allows Manning to disengage from herself and to analyse moments of transition in her sexualised identity. She looks on, as if disembodied, at the refracted image constructed by the language of the other (in both senses: of other people and of herself as an outsider). Within the course of the narrative, she is able to look beyond herself and see that 'The mirror does not reflect back a unique, individual identity to each living woman ... Isolate individualism is an illusion' (Friedman 1988, pp. 38–9). Here language and experience (derived from the senses) come together, intellectualism does not alto-gether triumph (see p. 106): 'The prevailing social order stands as a great and resplendent hall of mirrors. It owns and occupies the world as it is and the world as it is *seen and heard*' (Rowbotham 1973a, p. 27; my emphasis). Manning's entry into a Lacanian alien or antagonistic symbolic order is thus modified by the recognition that in her own self-image other women look back too, not only her lost lesbian self. This marks a coming to maturity, in Simone de Beauvoir's terms, *The Coming of Age* (1972) where we are made finally self-aware 'by seeing ourselves in the mirror as though through the eyes of a stranger' (Woodward 1988, p. 91).[5]

Manning describes in just such terms her process of review and reconciliation:

> Its truth must derive from my ability to capture as faithfully as I can and interpret the lives I have lived, and I, the writer who looks back upon those earlier selves, am a multiple personality created by them, incorporating their essences, often metamorphosed and, in some cases, long suppressed. I am not painting a static portrait. I am, rather, walking along a corridor of mirrors in which I observe myself at different stages of my life.
>
> The book is a dialectic between old and present selves. When I have finished it, I shall expect to have changed still further. The present self who writes this page cannot stand still. (1987, p. 9)

The self is many in one. Multiple selves shift, move, and the lesbian tries to halt the process and the settled self for a moment in order to describe its essence, before it moves on again. Manning attests to a protean identity, personal lesbianism on an axis of essentialism and self- and other-construction. The lesbian is, and is not, at once: 'You are of course never yourself' (Gertrude Stein, quoted in Manning 1987, frontispiece).

Manning seeks autobiographical wholeness after her 'piecemeal' revelation in her novels. Her coming together is expressed in spatial terms: 'These years have been a voyage of self-discovery, in some ways of *re*discovery ... ' (p. 179). She quotes John Donne, 'O my America my new-found land!', a poem about 'a woman whose body expands to encompass a whole new world' (Docherty 1996, p. 100). Her process of self-occupation has been brought about, paradoxically, by the recognition that other people occupy her space, and that there are threads to other women, literary[6] and real.

Her book was inspired, she tells us, by the loss of a lover, 'and the formation of a new and redemptive relationship with her' (p. 178). It is dedicated at the outset to that lover ('For Jan'); and the work, like so many autobiographies, is circular: writing it enables her to begin again.

In a similar way, the opening announcement of Maureen Colquhoun's autobiography, *A Woman in the House* (1980) suggests a lover as a jumping-off point, and destination, for her writing: it opens 'Dedication – for B.T.', Barbara Todd. Though the abbreviation of the name to initials may suggest concealment, Colquhoun had been public in her love, and Todd was already named as her partner in *Who's Who*.

The wordplay of the title (concerned with her time as an MP and her lesbian self-emergence) leads into the heart of the representation of Colquhoun, who is repeatedly shown to be at the intersection of ideas about lesbians and the house/home. She appropriates space and normalises its woman-centredness, in describing her self-awareness in spatial and temporal terms:

> When I parted from Keith Colquhoun [her husband] (for Babs) I suddenly, for the first time in my life, knew I was in control of my own space in the world, had my own time-scale, and was living my life in the way I wanted it ... (p. 82)

Colquhoun was outed in the press because of her housewarming invitation, the cartoon on which, by Barbara Todd's daughter, showed a double-headed women's sign, with the two women's faces on it. The *Daily Mail* gossip column reported this as 'depicting two intertwined females' (15 April 1976). It was as if the invitation to a lesbian home was simply too much.

In representing herself in her house in the autobiography, Colquhoun is suggesting a self-homing. This is in contrast to the ways in which she was treated at the time when her relationship with Barbara Todd became publicly discussed. Other people separated the idea of the Lesbian from her, couching this in the language of speech when 'my friends in the House, could hardly bring themselves to discuss homosexuality, although one or two did say that they had "never met a homosexual, what were they really like?". As if I wasn't homosexual at all' (p. 83). In addition, there is a sense from others of an alienation from the very word and the signing of it: another woman MP complained, 'Now we won't be able to have our hair short or wear trousers in public for fear of being labelled ... lesbian' (p. 92). Lesbian appears to be a name given to you by others. Colquhoun claims it as her own by writing the book in which she contains a sense of being which is in determined contrast to press treatment of her. Papers such as the *Daily Mirror*, for example, ran a front-page editorial peppered with words like 'normal' and 'confess' (29 September 1977).

Biography of Lesbians: The Life Interview

Subsequent biographical writing about Colquhoun appears to rise to the bait of her metaphors with a counter-counterdiscourse, framed in the same language (for example, in Elizabeth Vallance's *Women in the House: A Study of Women MPs*, 1982). Colquhoun is frequently placed at a point of tension with notions of the home.

The cover of Colquhoun's autobiography is itself biographical in the same style: it refers to her as 'a radical in British politics ... [who] insisted that the Speaker of the House should designate her 'Ms' – an uncompromising frontal assault upon the very fabric of the age old traditions of the British Parliamentary system ... ' (1980, front cover notes). It endorses the idea of a lesbian as attacking the centre of maleness ('frontal assault'), and it invites surprise, admiration and pity at her being 'a warm-hearted and courageous woman without a shred of hypocrisy'.

This conjures up a picture of a lesbian in defiant battle against an antagonistic world. An interview with Colquhoun creates the same idea, with its headline 'The brave truths of an awkward woman', 'mother, feminist, lesbian, radical [the same words as the autobiography's cover]: embarrassing and needling the House' (*Sunday Times*, 16 November 1980, FL). The article, by Jennifer Monaghan, opens with Colquhoun quoted as saying those same words. Thus does quotation within quotation without attribution obfuscate who says what about whom, including oneself.

The writer comments on 'The unfortunate photo on the dust jacket [of the autobiography] which makes the author look a cheery, butch battleaxe. ... To meet she is neither a battleaxe nor butch, but an ordinary woman ... '. She thus sets up and reinforces a whole set of assumptions by appearing to demolish them.[7] Colquhoun suffered an 'inquisition into her private life', she 'admitted' her lesbianism; a fallen woman, she experienced 'naïve surprise', 'idealistic optimism', at the 'nightmare', and takes 'refuge' from a lost world. She is represented in oppositional terms to the maternal, via denial: 'Ms Colquhoun sees no incompatibility between lesbianism and motherhood.'

Such tension between life forces is inherent, too, in an interview with Maureen Duffy which suggests the unnaturalness of non-procreative desire. She is quoted: 'Marriage was more wrong for me than almost anybody. The prospect of having children never attracted me ... the whole sort of physiological business revolted me ... ' (*Guardian*, 30 January 1969, FL). Duffy (like Colquhoun) is described as a child of a single mother. 'She lives with her dog ... surrounded by a vast collection of blank staring heads which are really wig-blocks.' The article does go on the explain that Duffy is working on a visual art project with Brigid Brophy which makes use of these heads, but the enduring sense, endorsed by a photograph, is of a withdrawn and eccentric lesbian.

Another writer, Jeanette Winterson, was interviewed in her home about her book, *Art and Lies* (1994). The interviewer transfers the fictive to the real in describing Winterson's life in terms suggesting reification. She 'lives in a fantasy world'. The article ends 'can Winterson in her writing make a fantasy [of being man-womanly, and woman-manly in Woolf's terms] like this one real?'. Throughout, she is represented as insincere, self-deluded, a 'Preacher Woman' (as the headline says), and with terms suggesting demonic derangement, in tacit cross-reference to Winterson's own semi-autobiographical novel, *Oranges Are Not the Only Fruit*:

> As she talks, she seems to see the image she is describing ... It is as if she is both writing and reading her own private autocue ... This is a preacher's trick ... [She] can throw words and images round her parlour ... controlling and manipulative, a consummate practitioner ... practised raconteuse ... courteous to a fault ... (Turner 1994, pp. 18, 19, 25)

The interviewer presents herself, on the other hand, as honest by unstated contrast. She has gone to 'reveal' Winterson, about whom 'A nation gawped'. Her language displays a salaciousness: 'The minute I got home from the Jeanette Winterson job, heads started poking round my door and the phone started ringing from old pals. So what was she like? Was she as mad as they say she is? ... Hadn't I allowed myself to be charmed? ... Did she flirt with me?' (p. 25). The heterosexual female is passive, sane, sincere, the lesbian active, deranged, pretend.

The suggestion of lesbian trickery or deceit is set up, too, in an interview with Martina Navratilova. Newspaper 'delvings' are mentioned; commas are given significance of pregnant pauses: 'Everyone would know, eventually' about her lesbian lovers (*Observer*, 3 July 1994, p. 23). This interview establishes an imaginary dichotomy between Navratilova and the shockable public with is both respectable and repressed: 'Outside, Middle England was hot and bothered. The agitated gent in the blazer and the pink-cheeked matron ... could not decide which was the greater issue of the day: Prince Charles compounding his infidelity with candour – or Navratilova's contemplating motherhood in a terminal state of lesbianism.' The passage is a structuralist's delight, with opposition between public and secret, normalised and contentious, momentary and enduring, life and death.

Elsewhere in the interview, the writer sets up more imaginary binary dilemmas. Navratilova has become an establishment figure, 'the *grande dame* of Wimbledon ... just one more title before she abdicated'; in the *Observer Sport* section she is 'the equivalent of the Queen Mother'; yet she challenges the bastions of respectability, set side-by-side with an errant prince. Her potential childbearing is referred to as resulting in 'a specimen to behold'. Communistic aspersion is made in Cold War rhetoric: 'It has been an epic journey by the velvet-soft romantic from Prague on one of the most cherished diversions of the bourgeoisie.' Ostensibly, the narrative suggests that Navratilova's defection has led to an opening out, a freeing, but the interview ends, 'it is a world infested with as many vipers as the one she left behind'.

Biography of Lesbians

In entitling this section 'Biography of Lesbians', in contrast to the next on 'Lesbian Biography', I suggest here the differentiation to be made between works that either deny or obscure the importance of sexuality to their subject, and those that organise around that very principle (see Whitelaw 1995, p. 108, who makes a similar separation). This distinction leads to the question of a decision that has been made on the authenticity of the lesbian life, for who is to say what constitutes a 'real' lesbian or, indeed, a non-lesbian? None the less, there is a relatively uncontentious distinction in narrative terms to be made between Lives which do not, and do, assert the centrality of sexuality. Some subjects, of course, are treated in both ways, by different writers, and these will be discussed as in a hinterland between the two forms of lesbian biographical writing.

Some biographers of subjects who might have a toe in the lesbian sea do not mention the idea, the ultimate censorship and one which avoids debate. This is the case with a biography of Enid Blyton (Mullan 1987) despite suggestions that she might have been 'a closet lesbian' (Brooks 1997, p. 10; Banks-Smith 1996, p. 9). Some biographers at least enter the debate, to deny the lesbianism of their subject, and accordingly the reader is flummoxed by what is actually meant by 'lesbian' in such works. Tallulah Bankhead 'was not a lesbian, [though] by her own admission she had had love affairs with women as well as men, having a penchant, it seems for boyish females' (Gill 1972, p. 37). Note 'admission' and 'penchant' which give a negative and a trivial aspersion; so what does constitute 'lesbian' if it is not this?

Berry and Bostridge (1995) claim that a postwar vogue for 'deviant literature' led to the 'myth' of the alleged lesbian relationship between Vera Brittain and Winifred Holtby. Of Dorothy L. Sayers it has been stated that she 'knew all about lesbianism. Mary Whittaker [in *Unnatural Death* 1927] is quite the nastiest of her villains and is obviously a lesbian':

> in spite of [Sayer's] masculine style of dress, which became more pronounced as she grew older, there is no evidence that she was ever in love with a woman. Indeed, had she noticed such tendencies in herself she would have fought against them, for any kind of homosexuality was the 'unmentionable' sin in the circle to which she had been raised. However broadminded she was to become later, as a young girl the only permissible love was that between members of opposite sexes. (Hitchman 1979, pp. 43–4)

This confines the idea of even a possible lesbian inclination to Sayers's youth and masculinity. Similarly, maleness is raised in a biography written specifically with the aim of 'scotching of the lesbian insinuations' about Edith Somerville and Violet Martin: 'That Edith was a lesbian has gained general acceptance through an unlovely combination of affected liberalism, ignorant salaciousness and the sad assumption that huge vitality and strength in a woman implies masculinity' (Lewis 1985, p. 208).

Denial is frequently couched in terms of masculine versus feminine parts, ironically in a style which is highly reminiscent of Havelock Ellis's descriptions *of* lesbians (see p. 25), of around seventy years before:

> There was a good deal that was masculine both in [Elizabeth Bowen's] physical self and in her mentality ... her manner – in discussion ... or in 'knocking back the drinks' – could be, and were, described as those of a 'gentleman' as easily as those of a 'lady'. Her responsiveness to place, people, atmosphere, mood, on the other hand, were of the order that is pre-eminently considered feminine ... Her fondness for cosmetics, her concern for her appearance, were almost anxiously feminine. If ... she was ever worried about herself as a woman, it was because she very much wanted to be one. (Glendinning 1977, pp. 189–90)

The vehemence of the biographer's stance does raise a question about just whose anxiety this is. She continues: 'She was a man's woman' as if this precludes attraction to women. The frameworks are categorical and the biographer shows none of the blurring of the postmodern: 'For a heterosexual woman, a close friendship with another woman is just that, and no more. For a lesbian, nearly all relationships with women must be coloured by the possibility of love ... ' (p. 190).

This distinction is maintained by other biographers: 'Like other people, she had female friends: that seems to be the gist of it ... May Sarton, who fell in love with her, was not left in any doubt about Elizabeth's feelings for *her*: mild friendship, nothing more ...' (Craig 1986, pp. 128–9). Sarton herself had used similar terminology. Her words seem to have been picked up by Glendinning, though they are not attributed:

> Elizabeth, so sensitized to atmosphere, to place, to the total content of the moment, responded to my passionate feelings for her. We slept together in my big bed after an exchange that had great tenderness in it ... For me that romantic night meant not the beginning of a love affair, but the seal set on a friendship. (1977, p. 197)

Other writers do allude to their subjects' sexuality, in order to distance themselves:

grotesquely masculine in appearance ... the aggressively uniformed Mary Allen ... seems never to have taken her uniform off ... She had the utmost aversion from dresses ... [Her uniform], complete with peaked hat, navy-blue breeches ... knee-high shiny black boots and monocle, caused a sensation. (Lock 1979, pp. 128, 150)

The most common strategy, however, is side-stepping the issue, or not naming the possible. Lilian Barker's relationship with her lover's family 'was never close for there were certain things about Lily that they would never accept' (Gore 1965, p. 61). The relationship between Angela Burdett-Coutts and Hannah Brown with whom she lived for 52 years is blatantly dismissed: 'The pursuit of this theme ... is best left to the psychologists ... Of such ideas Miss Coutts and Mrs Brown, like Queen Victoria, were happily unaware' (Healey 1978, pp. 75–6).

Others side-step to stand behind their subject's ostensible behaviour. Nancy Cunard's relationships 'with several women friends often contained a touch of romantic intensity; but her life remained full of attachments to men'; 'Nancy was linked to her homosexual friends by something more subtle. She shared with them a feeling of being different, of living outside the herd' (Chisholm 1979, pp. 96, 163). The lesbianism of her friend, Janet Flanner, is likewise obfuscated, as if by Flanner herself: 'That Flanner was a lesbian is carefully hidden behind her professional role as a journalist ... It is evident that [she] was part of the Paris community of lesbian writers ... she maintained friendships with heterosexual women as well' (Benstock 1986, pp. 115–16). Flanner used the journalistic pen-name 'Genêt', and impersonating her 'may well have robbed [Flanner] of her own voice' (Wineapple 1989, p. 208; who tellingly entitles her biography, *Genêt*, with Flanner's name as subtitle).

Hermione Lee invokes Virginia Woolf's own distrust of naming: 'she did not define herself as a Sapphist. She could not bear to categorise herself as belonging to a group defined by its sexual behaviour ... She wanted to avoid all categories' (1996, p. 490). In her writing on Elizabeth Bowen, too, Lee is reticent about her subject's sexuality, leading another critic to write of her approach that 'the lesbophobia inspiring such negations [results] in serious critical oversights' (Hoogland 1994b, p. 342).

Biographers thus conceal lesbian lives in the ways that Adrienne Rich described:

Whatever is unnamed, undepicted in images, whatever is omitted from biography, censored in collections of letters, whatever is misnamed as something else, made difficult-to-come-by, whatever is buried in the memory by the collapse of meaning under an inadequate or lying language – this will become, not merely unspoken, but *unspeakable*. (1979, p. 199)

Lesbian Biography: The Land Between

Some women are consigned to a lesbian hinterland by their biographers, buried indeed by what is alleged to be too hard to come by.

'My loves were Adrienne Monnier and James Joyce and Shakespeare and Company' proclaims Sylvia Beach. This ... is the story of these three loves. The first is the story of the love between two women. The details were and still are little known. (Fitch 1983, p. 1)

Fitch appears to consign lesbianism to sexual acts. Of the affection, and cohabitation, of Monnier and Beach there is ample evidence upon which to draw conclusions about their woman-centredness, yet Fitch is cagey because he believes that 'Sex can be overemphasised in modern biography' and in any case, sources of information show a 'sense of privacy [which] was typical of the time' (p. 61; and see Fitch 1990). Hence, he does not probe the details that do exist, which document lesbian existence, with or without bodily acts.

Shari Benstock, on the other hand, does name, but collapses her meaning in displaced terms. Adrienne Monnier was 'Playing both wife and mother to Sylvia, she cooked for her, looked after her health, protected her interests' (1986, p. 209). A page later she 'served as both mother and sister to her lover, she did not play the "wife" in any traditional way with Sylvia' (p. 210).

Lesbian Biography

Some Lesbian biographies grudgingly note a lesbian component in their subjects' lives, though this is frequently 'misnamed'. Katherine Mansfield had 'early bisexual relationships' (Boddy 1988, p.113), or went through an 'adolescent lesbianism' (Alpers 1980, p. 46). Edie Brendall, an early love of Mansfield, had 'a sweet and simple nature ... [a] Colonial Kate Greenway' (p. 49).[8] Lesbianism is literary:

the feelings, at the time, were genuine enough, no doubt. But it is clear as well that some part of [Mansfield's] mind was capable of

standing off and seeing them as 'copy', even in the midst of loving
– as though her account of them was a way of emulating her
favourite writers. (p. 49)

Claire Tomalin, likewise, displaces lesbian affection not once (to
maternal) but twice (to literary-maternal): when she interviewed Edith
Bendall,

> she said she thought Katherine had simply misinterpreted her
> motherly gestures. No one can say with any certainty now whether
> Katherine was working up the incidents ... dramatising them to
> make literature; or recording true experience ... (1987, p. 36)

Vita Sackville-West's sexuality is likewise displaced, firmly
ensconced in a heterosexual identity by Nigel Nicolson when he edited
his mother's autobiography, having found the manuscript in a locked
bag after her death. The title, *Portrait of a Marriage*, is his, and it reveals
his thrust. He interweaves his own biographical narrative with his
mother's own, and refers to the work as 'a panegyric of marriage'
(Sackville-West 1973, p. 3). The outcome of the drama with Trefusis
shows that 'love triumphed over infatuation', and Sackville-West's
narrative is framed in a corrective context, of his parents' 49-year
marriage. Nicolson acknowledges the importance of other women in
her life, including Virginia Woolf, though these are peripheral to the
enduring marriage.

Biographies of Woolf (e.g. Gordon 1984) likewise minimise the
strength of the intimacy between Virginia Woolf and Vita Sackville-
West. It is as if heterosexual longevity, even with infidelity and lack of
marital sexual activity, outweighs shorter-term lesbian relationships
which may have had as little, or more, physical activity attached (Bell
1972, p. 119).

Similarly heterosexist is Victoria Glendinning's life of Sackville-West
(1983). Glendinning's views were clear in an interview (1983) she gave
about the life: 'I began to believe that all lasting marriages are sustained
by an equally intricate, if less bizarre system of checks and balances ... '.
It as if lesbian love somehow serves as a sail-trimming system within a
marital yacht voyage.

Glendinning's biography is not just of one lesbian, but of many who
had relationships with Sackville-West. Ideas of lesbians are not historicised to give a sense of the contemporary conditions of lesbian
expressiveness. With 'childlike' Mary Campbell, for them both there

was a 'fusing of mother and lover' (p. 180). Though dates are significant in lesbian history and formation, that is not apparent: 'women like [Hilda Matheson] in 1928, were often too clever, serious or ambitious for the middle-class professional men who might otherwise have married them' (p. 210).

Glendinning frequently links illness, primitivity and sexuality: 'one real difficulty was that Evelyn [Irons] was not free; she lived with another young woman, Olive Rinder, who had tuberculosis and was inclined to be hysterical' (p. 240),

> Women continued to fall in love with Vita, and declare their love, notwithstanding her age [she was 55] and arthritis ... [She had a] spell-binding quality, touching a nerve in women of little sexual sophistication who had never before been attracted to other women. Her conventional, upper-middle class friends in Kent were, in their simplicity, more susceptible than might have been women with greater self-knowledge and experience of sexual complexity. (pp. 348–9)[9]

Such links are made, too, by biographers of Sylvia Townsend Warner and Valentine Ackland: Wendy Mulford (1988) and Claire Harman (1989) both 'set up an antithesis between Townsend Warner's strength and Ackland's neurosis', and this, like Diana Souhami's biography of the painter Gluck (1988) 'reinforces the stereotype of the lesbian artist, as helpless neurotic' (Whitelaw 1995, pp. 116, 113).

'Who in his right mind would court a woman in a man's suit?', asks Souhami (p. 12), who notes Gluck's 'severance from gender, family and religion' (p. 17). There appears to be no sense that Gluck's lesbianism and/or Jewishness might have contributed to her enduring creativity and sense of self. Souhami repeats, without problematising it, another truism of lesbian representation when she writes about Gluck's 1937 portrait, 'Medallion', of herself with her lover: it reveals Gluck's 'uncertainty as to where the boundaries between herself and others lay. Despite the defiant gaze she melts into another woman' (p. 126).

In her biographies, Souhami herself frequently does the melting: she threads together the words of her subjects to form a narrative. This can be effective, and would seem an empathetic way of writing, but it can lead to a distortion, with the biographer standing so closely behind the subject that we cannot tell 'fact' from interpretation. She forms a seamless quilt of quotes. When she writes about Violet Keppel her intertextuality is blatant, though unacknowledged. She echoes Vita

Sackville-West's words about her time with Violet ('it is a morass, my life, a bog, a swamp, a deceitful country', see p. 85) to reflect instead Violet's situation at that time 'shaping into a quagmire of confusion, lies, deception and sham' (1996, p. 151). This is flagrantly unhistoricised when Souhami cites words from the House of Lords 1921 debate on lesbianism. Its authority is used at face value, and attributed as an attitude to Violet's husband, with no justification cited. This leads both to personal misrepresentation and historical inaccuracy. 'Lesbianism was not a subject for discussion, the word was not used' (p. 151). Denys Trefusis 'was like those 999 out of every thousand women who, in Lord Birkenhead's view, had "never heard a whisper of these practices" of lesbianism. He was straight from the killing fields and not acquainted or tainted with "horrible and noxious suspicions"' (p. 153).

This tendency in biography for the writer to use her subject's own vocabulary, with the pitfalls it opens, is shown, too, in Margaret Forster's *Daphne du Maurier* (1993). She uses her subject's self-description about lesbianism without any contextual discussion, and it is hard to know, therefore, whether it is her own or du Maurier's negativity which has seeped into commentary:

> She and [her sister] wore boys' shorts and shirts and ties and thick schoolboy socks and shoes – they liked to dress *exactly* as boys in an era when young girls did not wear trousers ... even clad in the most boyish of clothes and doing the most boyish of things Daphne looked indisputably and very fetchingly feminine ... What her family did not realise, and this was much more serious, was that Daphne actually convinced herself she *was* a boy. (p. 14)

This is 'much more serious' to whom? Forster does not name her subject as a lesbian, ostensibly it might seem because du Maurier herself emphatically rejected that label. Instead, she uses du Maurier's own code, 'Venetian'. Forster also colludes with du Maurier's definitions of sexuality, echoing her racism and association of lesbianism with foreigners: the French teacher 'had an allure lacking in the down-to-earth English governess' (p. 30). Relationships with women are designated as maternal substitutes (pp. 56, 239). The word 'woman' is heterosexually inscribed, and hence differentiated from 'lesbian' by definition: 'She was a woman and must live as a woman and that, to her, meant suppressing her attraction to [another woman]' (p. 64). Again, there is an osmosis between Forster's and du Maurier's attitudes: 'Daphne reflected on her own past love-affair, the only one in her married life, or at least the only one with a man' (p. 292). Biographical empathy can thus lead to misplacing the lesbian in the text.

Similar losses, this time at sea, occur in Kate Summerscale's biography of Joe Carstairs (1997), though she cannot be accused of empathy. Sexual significance disappears in a fuzz of eccentricity: 'Joe Carstairs was too singular and strange to be representative of anything other than herself' (p. 6). Carstairs is treated as a fantastic figure of the sea, with her passion for boats and her purchase of an island used to explain her identity:

> To survive, Joe constructed a fantasy of private power around herself, as if building a raft on the waves; this fantasy was to manifest itself throughout her life in her desire for walled, moated worlds – for boats and islands. (p. 20; and see pp. 99, 100, 120)

Descriptions do not acknowledge lesbian traditions in which 'Sappho's island resonates in our dreams and fantasies, and is recreated imaginatively in lesbian feminist literature' (Zimmerman 1992a, p. 124).[10] Though the metaphor has lesbian roots, therefore, it is used to suggest an eccentricity beyond sexuality: 'she saw herself as a creature of the water rather as Peter Pan was a creature of the air' (p. 21), an analogy that has already been noted (p. 206). For Summerscale, this justifies description of Carstairs's 'childlike spirit' (p. 81), and her island home of Whale Cay as 'Neverland' (p. 185).

Lesbian identity disappears too, as the biographer's 'well-fed schoolboy' (p. 67) 'mannish woman' (p. 27) 'in the guise of a man' (p. 59) who 'loved to dress up as a woman' (p. 143) is accused, with no sense of irony, of being confused: 'Her desire of visibility was equalled by her desire for concealment, and in order to obscure herself she played "in the modern spirit" with the idea of fixed identity' (p. 109). The biographer, and her lesbian subject, disappear in the whirlpool of her own mixed metaphor.

(Mis)appropriation of images is also a feature of Rose Collis's biography, *A Trouser-wearing Character*, of Nancy Spain (1997), a work for which I am otherwise personally indebted (Hallett 1998). Though Collis never goes to Summerscale's convoluted lengths, neither does she provide an historicised context for the attitudes of contemporary commentators. So, when Spain's friends and acquaintances refer to her as transvestite or a boy (p. 251), two people (p. 125), masculine and feminine (p. 250), though these are clichés of identity, they receive no explanatory placing.

Though Nancy Spain's lesbianism is seen to be central to her personality and life, she is also shown somehow to be larger than that. The title of the text, albeit using Spain's own words, has a suggestion of either eccentricity or role play, or both, about it. The biography opens, 'Trouser-wearing characters are mostly born, not made', presumably indicating a manifesto of the 'born lesbian':

> The appearance of 'square-peg' children in families is often initially greeted with acknowledgement and protective nurturing only to be replaced by attempts to force them into round holes once adulthood beckons ... This particular pirate [a word used of Spain by a friend] waged war against a predetermined destiny. (p. 1)[11]

This gives the sense that Spain's difference and personality were her drive, and that is reinforced later, when a publisher's view of Spain is transmuted into a biographical truth about 'her increasingly infamous eccentric style and image' (p. 108). That Nancy Spain carved for herself a career as a 'personality' is somehow converted into an essence.

Here we have an acute dilemma: 'To justify an unorthodox life by writing about it is to ... reviolate masculine turf', and furthermore, locating lesbianism within, or outside, 'normalised' models of human behaviour, uses only 'the available fiction of female becoming' (Nancy K. Miller 1991, quoting Heilbrun 1989, pp. 11, 18). The problems of Collis's biography go to the heart of Lesbian biography more widely. Nancy Spain is depicted as a one-off, like Carstairs, so that sexuality cannot be treated as a feature of their subjectivity which gives 'traces' to others. Neither biographer attends to the specificity of the moment, of the register of their individualised sexuality at the time, how this affected their creativity in particular ways. We are left with a sense of charm, of personality, but no idea of the problematics of identity ascription, the interiorisation of sexuality, the wider lesbian milieu or, conversely, the heterosexual hegemony, which also (in)formed their lives.

Similar criticisms may be made of the Lives of Radclyffe Hall which do not give an idea of the range, or limit, of choices available to their subject. Michael Baker's title, *Our Three Selves* (1985), ostensibly a quotation from Hall herself, carries innuendo from sexological definition of lesbianism as a 'third sex'; and Sally Cline's *A Woman Called John* (1997), again uses Hall's own name, but gives no explanation about masculinisation in the styling.[12] Both works fail to reconstruct the historical moment of the formation of lesbian expressiveness.

Some lesbian biographies do just this. Ann Morley and Liz Stanley's *The Life and Death of Emily Wilding Davison* (1988) and Lis Whitelaw's *The Life and Rebellious Times of Cicely Hamilton* (1990) reconstruct more than an individual biography. They locate their subject, and her potential lesbianism, in a lived community of women friends, neighbours, colleagues. Whitelaw is particularly explicit in her approach: 'I am not at all concerned about what they did in bed but I am very much concerned with all the other choices that they made about other women' (p. 109). Thus, Hamilton can be individualised amongst similarity, and recognised to be intentionally resistant rather than merely eccentric.

Lesbian biography, according to Lis Whitelaw (1995, p. 108), is generally written by a lesbian. *Edith Craig (1869–1947) Dramatic Lives* (Cockin 1998) may not have been. Its author locates lesbian life in a framework of lesbian ownership, which inadvertently criticises Whitelaw's identification of author/subject sexuality: 'The assumption that, because the subject of my research was a lesbian, I must be a lesbian as well as a feminist, has raised some important political issues about overlapping and mutually exclusive identities and categories, about appropriation and advocacy' (p. 3).

Cockin effectively wipes out previous attempts (e.g. Manvell 1968, p. 306) to explain Edy Craig's lesbianism as refuge from a failed heterosexual affair. Instead, she locates her relationships within a range of choices open to the New Woman, where Craig, St John and their cohabitee Tony (Clare) Atwood do not imitate 'the nuclear family' (p. 4):

> In exploring the limits of gender, other boundaries were reassessed, tested, broken down or reinforced. The reassessment of the political and the extension of the political into the so-called 'private' gave rise to an awareness of cultural and sexual politics. (p. 61)

Cockin is able in this way to assess how the women constructed their own identity within prevalent conventions; and also to judge the effect of the centrality of their life-long women-centredness on the creativity of this group of individual lesbians. She locates the relative balances in Craig's life, where sexuality and professional activity intersect, to present Craig's pioneer suffragism, theatrical innovation and sexuality as part of a life fabric which Craig herself had woven. The work gives due weight to the mutually informing elements of Craig's 'dramatic lives'. It presents a lesbian Life and lives which extend in application beyond the specific to the particularly, and historically, generalised.

AfterLife: Critical Reviews of Lesbian Auto/biographies

Unlike Cockin, most reviewers fail to locate subject, text or author, or to recognise critical judgements as literary-political. A review (Lewis 1994) of Shirley Roberts's biography of Sophia Jex-Blake, though it mentions in passing a female companion, mentions no personal relationships at all, and so suggests by silence that Jex-Blake's life was determined by its professional success. In a similar way, Jenny Uglow (herself an erudite biographer) reviews Barbara Reynolds's Life of Dorothy L. Sayers (1993): 'Her lasting loves ... were of the mind as much as the heart' (Uglow 1993). This smacks of Carolyn Heilbrun's criticism of James Brabazon's biography of Sayers, which 'reads her life as a fall back on the intellect' (Heilbrun 1989, p. 52).

Some reviewers, however, do enlarge the art of lesbian biography by suggesting counterviews or wider theories. One review of David Nokes's *Jane Austen: A Life* (1997) calls Austen 'a shadowy silhouette ... [with] the pathos of her obscure, involuntary celibate and relatively penurious existence' (Neill 1997). Marilyn Butler (1998), on the other hand, criticises the idea that 'essentially solitary' Austen pours herself into her art as compensation. Butler mentions the loss of potential biographical material, possibly in censorship, and refers to Terry Castle's 1995 essay on Austen's intimacy with her sister and a possible lesbian interpretation of this. Reviews such as Butler's problematize and highlight gaps as well as reasons for them. This is unlike a review of Margaret Smith's edition of letters of Charlotte Brontë which tells us that Brontë's letters to Ellen Nussey were destroyed, but disingenuously proceeds to think it is a miracle that those to a loved male survived (Walter 1995). We have a sense of 'secrets', but only if we know which lines to read between.

Similar innuendo hovers around reviews of Katherine Mansfield biographies. Claire Tomalin's *Secret Life* invites 'Katherine unveiled' type headlines to Hermione Lee's (1987) review which adds another layer to the mystery of 'sexual ambiguities, her "dizzying" changes of face and heart'. She mentions, like Tomalin, with no sense of its stereotyping, 'schoolgirl lesbianism' and does not question Tomalin's idea of the 'race between work and death' as an organising principle of a Life.

Some twelve years later, headlines still say, though with aural/oral transposition, 'The true voice of Katherine Mansfield'. Ambition, sexual hunger, ruthlessness and 'her faithful friend Ida Baker' are mentioned in this review (Lowry 1998) of an edition of her notebooks, but Mansfield's often moving descriptions of her lesbian feelings are not alluded to, nor are other, creatively informative, moments. There is, accordingly, no enlargement of the frame. Likewise, Jan Montefiore's review of *Selected Letters of Sylvia Townsend Warner and Valentine Ackland* (1998) refers to the womens' 'happy if often difficult marriage'. It is as if the only adequate point of comparison is marriage, to convey an enduring, or sincere, lesbian pairing. This even undermines the unmarried heterosexual couple.

Truisms of lesbianism are unchallenged in a review of Souhami's *Greta and Cecil* (1994). The piece actually reiterates, and so strengthens the effect of, Souhami's views, as though they are uncontentious. 'Narcissistic Cecil' sees Garbo as 'mirror image', and Garbo was 'a mannish woman and he a womanly man': 'they were friends partly because their androgynous fantasies interlocked, but mostly because they were two miserable people who had the knack of cheering each other up' (Freely 1994).

A review of Sally Cline's biography of Radclyffe Hall endorses a stereotype too: the lesbian in a 'tragic situation'. The writer allows only that Hall had 'a much happier and more fulfilled life ... than she gave to any of her literary creations' (Walter 1997). Cline's book is more critically reviewed by DeLombard (1998), for its over-reliance on Hall's fiction for psychological insight, however the writer reiterates ideas of Una Troubridge as 'classic literary wife' and Hall as 'an insecure, domineering woman'. The photograph that accompanies the article, of Hall in dinner jacket, is cropped (unlike the same picture in Walter's article), to show only the upper part of Hall's body, in a dinner jacket, not revealing that she was also wearing a skirt, or that Troubridge was next to her in the scene. The sense is of an isolated, masculine figure.

This is borne out by a review of Souhami's *The Trials of Radclyffe Hall* (1998): 'Hall was as reactionary as most Edwardian men of her class.' There is an almost parodic explanation of lesbianism: 'Constantly uprooted, physically bullied by her mother and sexually molested by her "disgusting old step-father", she quickly acquired a revulsion towards men ... an unhappy girl desperate for a mother's affection' (Merritt 1998). Lucasta Miller (1998), on the same book, states that Hall 'has always been something of an embarrassment', repeating the causal connection between stepfather and lesbianism, since he 'could have put her off heterosexuality for good'. The review underscores the idea of the Lesbian as 'eccentric'.

Similar ideas are expressed about Kate Summerscale's biography of Joe Carstairs. Surprisingly, of these, one appears in the gay and lesbian *Pink Paper*, and the other is written by an lesbian academic. Neither problematises the biographic presentation of Carstairs as eccentric.

'Speed freak' headlines the account of the first of these (Butler 1997). No questions are asked about Summerscale's failure to give a political context to Carstairs's sexuality.

Terry Castle's review (1998) is even more striking, for a lesbian who has written analysis of 'ghosting' lesbian lives (1993), and who now refers to Carstairs as 'an optical illusion'. She locates Carstairs among 'people so monstrous, incandescent, or freakish themselves that only a quasi-supernatural description seems to do them justice ... singularity so tangible as to border on the uncanny'. Carstairs is described as 'voraciously homosexual ... pursued by a gaggle of female fans', an 'odd little homunculus', 'renegade', 'hallucinatory being'. Castle notes, but appears to endorse, Summerscale's lack of sociopolitical analysis: 'She is not concerned with rehabilitating Carstairs for potential groupies, feminist or lesbian or both'. Castle's collective phrases (gaggle, groupies, 'extraordinary Sapphic society') sound odd from the pen of a feminist, as does her 'wish to register Carstairs's audacious achievements as lesbian seductress'. She seems to value the Life for its revelation as a study in 'preposterousness': 'such luminescent creatures ... in their pathos'.

In general, then, and in some striking particular, the reviews of lesbian Lives do little to challenge or develop the genre. Rather, they seem to reinforce stereotypical assumptions. Because reviews are widely read, the perspectives they project are especially powerful and responsible for perpetuating ideas of lesbian sexuality.

Afterlife: Lesbian Obituaries

Obituaries, too, are widely read. They are characterised as a form, often by their third-person style and their normalisation of heterosexuality. The passage of time over this century has done little to assuage the impression of silences and gaps which characterise this form of writing in the early period, despite potential challenge: theories of the postmodern have not deconstructed their narrative of life, or the art of obituary would fall apart under the pressure, and whilst obituaries of male homosexuals appear, possibly because of the impact of Aids, to mention male partners more explicitly, this has not had a concomitant effect on lesbian death notices.

Lesbian obituaries fall into several groups, classically bearing out Adrienne Rich's statement: some are silent, some mis-name; some, however, say more than they write by cross-reference, outside the Life, in a new development of the genre.

Silences

Some references are determinedly silent, and infer only a professional life for their subject. The actor Noele Gordon may or may not have been a lesbian, though there was suggestion of this in her lifetime. Her obituaries say she was 'a household name' and 'national celebrity' and she is heterosexually located ('I was awfully good at playing tarts'). There is no mention of family, friends or any personal life (*The Times*, 15 April 1985). Julia Smith, TV producer, again, is lined up in counterpoint to lesbianism: the soap she produced 'dished out murder, teenage pregnancy, cot death, homosexuality, AIDS, drug addiction, racism, abortion and many other unpalatable facts of life' (*Independent*, 21 June 1997; *Guardian*, 20 June 1997, takes the same line exactly). *The Times* (20 June 1997) ends in classic style: her 'marriage ended in divorce. She had no children.'

The obituary to Joe Carstairs in the *Daily Telegraph* (26 January 1994), actually written by Kate Summerscale who was later to be her biographer, remarkably, does not mention her same-sex relationships at all. Carstairs's speedboat feats are recorded, and her family links. 'She promptly married Count Jacques de Pret, and left him at the church door ... '. The obituary ends, 'For the next 40 years she lived in Florida and Long Island, making occasional forays into New York in a Mercedes, equipped with a revolver.' Eccentricities are the hallmark of the *Telegraph* obituary, and Summerscale happily admits that preparing this piece whetted her appetite to write about Carstairs, 'to fill in the delicate gaps that characterise obituaries, name the oddities' (1997, p. 3). In some way, then, from the silence a language was born, and a Life came from a death.

Other obituaries are more blatantly censoring. Esmé Ross Langley, a very important figure in the lesbian movement in Britain, was transformed by her obituary (*Guardian*, 25 August 1992) into 'the kind of person whose death [the paper] might acknowledge – but without having to address her lesbianism' (Griffin 1993b, p. 159).

(Mis)naming

More oblique language consigns same-sex affection to 'friend and companion' (Ida Constance Baker, *The Times*, 25 July 1978). Whatever the sexual construction we place on these obituaries, the centredness of affection suggests one element, at least, of same-sex intimacy. Elizabeth Pennington, who worked at the BBC, 'whose modest exterior conceals life of unexpected richness ... found great consolation in the blossoming of her friendship with Margaret Aumonier, a friendship which comforted and sustained her, and enriched her life' (*Guardian*, 18 October 1986). Historian Veronica Wedgwood 'lived for nearly 70 years with her close friend Jacqueline Hope-Wallace' (*Guardian*, 11 March 1997). Anne Wood, opera singer, 'shared the latter part of her life with the mezzo and teacher Johanna Peters, who looked after her devotedly' (*Guardian*, 23 June 1998). Including such attestations in a list of lesbian obituaries is not to name the women as such, simply to suggest that the tenor of testimony endorses a woman-centred affection, and documents for posterity that these existed.

Other obituaries give only remote suggestion between the lines of the life, or obliterate traces of lesbian relationships. Eve Balfour, founder of the Soil Association and instigator of the organic movement in British farming, lived with Kathleen Carnley for 50 years, yet her obituaries do not commemorate this fact. Both *The Times* (17 January 1990) and the *Daily Telegraph* (16 January 1990) end with supreme irrelevance: 'She never married.' The latter's one inference is so oblique that a reader would have to be acutely attuned to the nuances of sexology to pick up the male-assertiveness/female-softness conjunction so familiar from Lives: 'Although … [she] held tenaciously to her own objectives, she had a flexibility of mind and understanding that made her always receptive to other points of view.' The *Guardian* (23 January 1990) says, 'She was a formidable and forthright woman, but she certainly knew how to enjoy herself. She was an expert sailor … '; and The *Independent* (27 January 1990) notes 'great determination of purpose [she] could undeviatingly pursue her ideals … '. Not one of these publications suggests a personal or intimate dimension to her life. Ginette Spanier's sexuality (*Daily Telegraph*, 21 April 1988) was marked by inference and the naming of her friends (Nancy Spain and 'the court of Noel Coward'). Her obituary records her marriage, separation, widowhood, with no mention of relationships with women.

Lesbian readers are left to read what they will into obituaries of other women. Elizabeth Bowen was described by Veronica Wedgwood:

> her outward appearance and way of speaking indicated her rare quality … punctuated by the occasional staccato flick of her hand, holding the inevitable cigarette … sense of freedom, frankness and shared pleasure in her company that lifted the spirit and left an afterglow of happiness. (*The Times*, 27 February 1973)

This compares with descriptions of Joe Carstairs (Summerscale 1997, p. 114), of Lilian Barker (see p. 100) and of Havelock Ellis's designation of lesbians. Indirectly, therefore, there are lesbian determinants in Bowen's obituary.

Margot Gore, a pilot, was commemorated in several newspapers (*Guardian*, 25 September 1993; *The Times*, 4 September 1993, *Daily Telegraph*, 15 September 1993), her name being associated with one Joan Hughes or Joan Nayler in each. The photographs of Gore are in pilot's uniform. The obituary to novelist Patricia Highsmith in the *Guardian* (6 February 1995) arouses expectation in its reader, then thwarts it by wordplay. She was established 'as a writer outside the mainstream of both "straight" and crime fiction'; 'The novel's lesbian theme, though decorously handled, prompted her to a pseudonym'; '[She] was taken more seriously in Europe than at home, where her amoral universe ... [was] never likely to curry favour.'

Alone at Home

An obituary (*Independent*, 25 April 1991) to P.L. Travers, creator of Mary Poppins, was intriguing: 'She never married, "but I have a family" she would say to deflect further probing – an adopted son and grandchildren whom she loved.'

There is another group of obituaries, with contrasting elements, referring to lesbians in groups/communities or as isolated. Of the former, Natalie Barney, 'an ornament of Parisian literary life ... colourful, truly legendary', is described in a community of women, yet 'She is survived by her younger sister.' No reference is made to Romaine Brooks with whom she shared her home for over 40 years (*The Times*, 4 February 1972), nor, elsewhere, to Clemence Dane's intimate relationships, though she 'kept open house for her friends ... The drama she did not write ... she found in daily living which she shared with innumerable friends' (*The Times*, 29 March 1965).

Another obituary attests to such living, an obituary to feminism at least: Esther Hodge, who wrote *A Woman-orientated Woman*, 'was happiest in a woman-centred society' (*Guardian*, 18 February 1995). This way women's spaces are marked as real.

In contrast, Djuna Barnes 'lived a retired life' (*The Times*, 21 June 1982); Garbo was in seclusion (Castle 1993, p. 2); and Daphne du Maurier was 'increasingly reclusive' (*The Times*, 20 April 1989; the same word is used in the *Daily Telegraph*, 20 April 1989, and the *Guardian*, same date). Presumably the obituaries are factually true, but the inference is interesting. In du Maurier's case so, too, there is an intriguing addition to the style of the obituary, the innovatory feature of the genre in the later twentieth century, where intertextuality widens the reference of the subject to fictive manifestations which bear upon their life.

Life Beyond

All of the broadsheet British obituaries mention *Rebecca* and its 'evil literary housekeeper'. The *Independent* piece has an extensive interpretation of the book, and shows a still from Hitchcock's film of *Rebecca* where Mrs de Winter faces Mrs Danvers, the lesbianly housekeeper, with Mr de Winter between them; Mrs de Winter's arm is extended to Mrs Danvers across a table, linking them spatially. The obituary notes that du Maurier cultivated a 'loyal following [of women readers] by embodying their desires and dreams in her novels', and the writer expands to give a lengthy reading of the film/novel on an Oedipal theme, revealing the Freudian subtext of

> violence, murder, a sinister villain, sexual passion ... a fascinating study of an obsessive personality, of sexual dominance, of human identity and of the liberation of the hidden self ... [millions identified with] the plain, nameless narrator ... a woman who defines her personality by overcoming the mother-figure of Rebecca to win the lasting love of her father-lover. (*Independent*, 21 April 1989)

This is a striking deviation from the normal thrust of the obituary as a form. There is double dissimulation going on, with a subtext to the obituary as well as to the reading of the novel/film. It is as if the interpretation of *Rebecca* can couch meaning itself in heterosexual psychoanalytical terms of displaced lesbianism, and that this can bear inadvertently on du Maurier's own life. There is no naming of sexuality, and two narratives sit alongside each other in innocent parallel.

This kind of cross-reference is found in obituaries to Beryl Reid, who has not been considered as a lesbian, with a film text serving as reference point. All of the broadsheet British newspapers refer in their obituaries to Reid's acting part in *The Killing of Sister George*, 'about lesbian power-play amongst the women of a radio soap opera' (*Guardian*, 14 October 1996). Searching for a serious play that suited her, 'from the moment she read the script of ... *George* she knew the quest was over ... Explicitly about lesbians, it shocked the provinces' (*The Times*, 14 October 1996); and, elsewhere in the same paper, 'Miss Reid devoted her life to her trade, choosing not to have children and seeing both her marriages fail through the demands of her job ... '. 'As the tough lesbian radio actress June Buckridge ... [Reid] became a household name and proved she could play straight roles' (*Independent*, 14 October 1996, carrying a photograph of Reid as George, in a still from the film).

It is as if the contours of the obituary as a form can only transmute suggestions by references to art. It may be that the lesbian eye is seeing too much here: after all, *Rebecca* and *Sister George* were possibly the two most successful works of these women. But it is interesting at least that the obituary expands here to allow new meanings to bear on the characters, the lives and/or their creators. If nothing else, we can see the potential of the obituary as a form to encompass subtexts which are capable of literary reading.

Naming

There is a final group of obituaries which can be read with less effort as clearly, and explicitly, lesbian, commemorating a same-sex emotional focus for lives. May Sarton was

> one of those writers who is loved, almost as a personal friend, by readers who fell under her spell ... To women she had a special relevance ... [she wrote about] the obligations, trials and necessary self-reliance of women, she also wrote from the point of view of a self-confessed lover of her own sex. (*Guardian*, 26 July 1995)

Sandy Horn was 'known to lesbian communities all over the world' Her lover is named, and her life experience as a lesbian, in personal and campaigning terms, is celebrated by the writer (*Guardian*, 10 November 1994). Jackie Forster, likewise, is commemorated, both *as* a lesbian and for her lesbian work. She was praised for using '*that* word' by which 'she made steps towards building a community in a world wracked by division'. 'Before Sappho, the organisation [she] and Babs Todd co-founded, there was nowhere to meet and no forum for discussion even in London' (*Guardian*, 27 October 1998, p. 22).

That word is not used of Gwynneth Thurburn, but her female companionship is given centrality in her life. Whilst the *Daily Telegraph*, with characteristic reticence, does not mention her partner (but says of Thurburn that 'Grey haired, immensely tall, she had a kindly gaze', 25 March 1993), the other broadsheets all name Vera Sargent as her 'lifelong companion' (*The Times*, 26 March 1993). The *Independent* (26 March 1993) obituarist was a friend and colleague of Thurburn, who had been Principal of the Central School of Speech and Drama. His piece is accordingly warm and personalised, and describes the life of the two companions 'of more than 50 years' with recognition of their centrality to each other's lives, though within a corrective and familial context:

> The two women, who had devoted their lives to young people, soon found themselves [in retirement] adopted by neighbours who had young children – as Thurbie said, 'It's as if they had been looking all their lives for two maiden aunts' … I realised Thurbie would never read [a book he had sent her]; but hoped Sarge would welcome it as a link with someone they had both loved.

As explicit is the piece by her work colleagues in the *Guardian* (24 March 1993). The piece ends: 'Our thoughts and gratitude go to Vera Sargent who gave her unstinting and selfless support for so many years.'

The obituary, then, can bear witness to same-sex centrality in a woman's life. As a form, whilst it continues to operate within normative frameworks, over the century its boundaries have been expanded. Partly this may be as a result of lesbian-feminist activism, so that certain figures are themselves commemorated precisely for creating lesbian space; partly, too, the obituary seems to have exploited the potential of the subtextual so that half-said (as well as silenced) can be taken to signify the existence of lesbian life. Lesbian configuration, it appears, has moved into the between-ground, formulated notions of identity from the fictionalised, from the semi-stated, moved the partially iterated into the speakable.

7
Visual Auto/biography: (Self-)Portraits and Lesbian Iconography Across the Twentieth Century

The Eye of the Beholder

Seeing is believing, particularly in white, patriarchal, Western culture which has given primacy to the eye and to the visual(isable) in terms of both recognition and memory. For the lesbian and for the anti-lesbian alike, for different reasons, being able to recognise and to image in her absence the Lesbian is equally important.[1]

The description of Christopher St John can be read either way: 'in old age she looks neither "heavy" nor "ugly" but rather like a lesbian' (Hamer 1996, p. 30, rebutting Baker 1985, p. 264). The question is, what *does* a lesbian look like? The statement, in a history of twentieth-century lesbians, gives no sense of the eye of the beholder, or of St John's projection of lesbian self, whether in endorsement or counter to the dominant modes of lesbian expressiveness. Instead, it plays to the idea that a lesbian *is* visualisable: we would know her if we saw her or were trying to avoid her, moreover we could image her in her absence and memorise this vision for future encounter or avoidance.

It seems that visual construction of the lesbian has changed little over the century. Simone de Beauvoir had written in 1949, 'We commonly think of the lesbian as a woman wearing a plain felt hat, short hair and a necktie' (p. 425). Over the period, the visualisable has been augmented, or challenged, by 'evidence' of the visually recorded, making use of various artistic media. Photography has an especial 'power of authentication' (Barthes 1981, pp. 88–9). This has been endorsed by Tessa Boffin, a lesbian photographer who noted 'its supposedly intimate connection with reality ... documentation of the "Real"' (1991, p. 49).[2] I have used the language of 'snapshot' in my introduction. In a sense, every auto/biography is that, and for lesbian

176

auto/biography the metaphor is especially apt, since there is always felt to be something exemplary in lesbian Lives. Each contains 'the burdens of scarcity' (Grover 1991, p. 187), and a responsibility which goes with that weight, to the beholding eye: if it is an antagonistic observer, and the Life is lesbian friendly, to appear 'respectable' or understandable in that observer's terms – and likewise, but on different terms, if a Life is revealed to a friendly eye. Playing to, and creation of, the audience has a particular meaning in writing or revealing a minoritized Life. Here the subject is felt, by all parties, to be reducible, readily visualised before and after observation, almost a caricatured visuality.

The advent of photography and of classification schemes was historically (and probably philosophically) contemporaneous: 'Through being photographed, something becomes part of a system of information, fitted into schemes of classification and storage' (Sontag 1977, p. 156). Susan Sontag argues that photography established a new relationship between life and representation: 'reality as such is redefined – as an item for exhibition ... an interminable dossier, thereby providing possibility of control' (p. 156). Early-century sexology essays and tracts (for example Broster *et al.* 1938) used photographic case study to reinforce and prove theory (or vice versa). Word and image mutually authenticated.

For Sontag, photography is felt to have revived 'something like the primitive status of images ... [A photograph] is part of, an extension of that subject' (1977, p. 155). Later nineteenth-century religious unbelief, she argues, 'strengthened the allegiance to images. The credence that could no longer be given to realities understood *in the form of* images was now being given to realities understood *to be* images, illusions' (p. 153). This happened historically when ideas of the Lesbian were formulated, around the notion of a visualisable object, standing for a whole life or lives. Though she does not apply it to this, Sontag's observation on image-duplicating is applicable to lesbian configuration: being able to visualise, mass reproduce as it were, and control the means of reproduction (with all its punning relevance) means 'we can acquire something as information (rather than experience)' (p. 156).

Such a view can be applied to lesbian auto/biography through portrait, whether actually visual or visualised, for which photography is a metaphor: the lesbian, because she is visualisable, has authenticity. It is, paradoxically, in the interests of the anti-lesbian to ensure the lesbian is *not* 'never thought of' (in the words of the 1921 debate) but is thought of in certain, controlled ways, given an authenticity which can be derided. The lesbian herself feels advantaged by being thinkable, having increased visibility, as later twentieth-century language puts it. For both, constructions of lesbianism depend on 'images of authenticity taken from the established order' (Dollimore 1986, p. 185). Hence, visualisation (by anti-lesbian and lesbian) and self-portraiture move in parallel, whilst also moving apart: the lesbian deviant group

> begins to speak on its own behalf, to forge its own identity and culture, *often in the self-same categories by which it has been produced and marginalized*, and eventually challenges the very power structures responsible for its 'creation' … There are many strategies of negotiation [including] the transformation of the dominant ideologies through (mis)appropriation, and their subversion through inversion. (pp. 180, 182; and see Elliott and Wallace 1994, p. 53)

This chapter will consider the iconography of lesbian visual representation, formulated within 'established' (heterosexual, structurally denigrated) identification, yet developing a strategy of such 'subversion through inversion', with its variations. Visuality is considered across the century, to test out (dis)continuities between the modern and the postmodern, and indicate (in 'Writing Ahead and Behind: Futuring the Lesbian Eye') the intertextuality between the two phases, to explore the dialectical effect within iconographic lesbian formulation.

One in the Eye

Accompanying an article on lesbian relationship longevity, or the lack of it, there appeared a photograph of Gertrude Stein and Alice B. Toklas (see p. 114). This was an effective shorthand to the archetypal lesbian couple, a cryptic marriage allusion, only manageable because lesbian and non-lesbian alike can image the pair, with all the affection/derision that their iconography contains.

The power of the visualisable is attested to by the hasty distancing that took place by women in the wake of lesbian events some 50 years apart: after the 1928 trial of *The Well of Loneliness*, Toupie Lowther changed her sartorial style (see p. 55), and after Maureen Colquhoun's sexuality became known in 1976, other women felt the need to do the same (p. 154). Writers reviewing Radclyffe Hall's work in 1924 claimed to, or did, confuse author and work (p. 93); and 60 years later actors playing lesbian roles distanced themselves from their parts. This suggests how strongly the seen and the thing are one in the eyes of the observer. So it came as little surprise when Ellen DeGeneres came out in both fiction *and* in life (on TV's *Ellen* in 1997 in the US and 1998 in the UK screening). And it came as no surprise, even to Joanna Trollope, the author of *A Village Affair*, when the actor Sophie Ward who had played a lesbian in the TV dramatisation of the book, herself turned out to be one: 'I write about things that really happen' (in Clark 1996, p. 9). In fact, she wrote about something that went on to happen, a kind of vindication of Carolyn Heilbrun's definition of women's autobiography (1989) where the writer writes her life ahead, but this time it was an actor who played out aspects of her sexuality in advance.

The power of this identification is shown in the fact that Anne Heche, another lesbian actor, having made her relationship with Ellen DeGeneres public, immediately afterwards found herself unemployable (*Guardian*, 8 May 1998); and in the commentary around the actor Anna Friel, who played lesbian Beth Jordache in British TV, Channel 4's soap, *Brookside:* 'Her role as "lipstick" lesbian[3] ... had already enveloped her in scandalous glamour, but she wanted more – credibility as a serious actress' (*Mail on Sunday Magazine*, 12 April 1998).

In interview, Friel flaunted her heterosexual credentials: '"I lived with my ex-boyfriend for two years" ... She revealed she slept with him on the first day they met ... and that she enjoyed really good lovemaking ... [They split up] "But it was for all the right reasons" ...' (Duncan 1998). Of the lesbian elements in *Brookside*, she said: 'I had to think how I could make the lesbian scene true when I felt uncomfortable doing it.' Similarly, Catherine Deneuve distanced herself from the reality of the play when she denied a lesbian magazine the right to use her name after she had the part of a lesbian vampire in a film: 'They tried to use the fact that I had played lesbian roles in films, but it was nothing to do with my life', and she also 'admitted' that body doubles had been used in lesbian sex scenes (Feinstein 1998, p. 2), thereby giving a cogent metaphor for lesbian identification and attempted separation of the signified and signifier.

This is testimony to the power of the Judaeo-Christian philosophy of the eye and of imaging as a cultural habit, ingrained by devotional (and postdevotional) typology. Identification of the actor and the part, and anxiety about it, are part of the twentieth-century mode of confounding the act and the action. This is a post-Reformation literalness, perhaps an embedding of the Protestant-capitalist ethic (see p. 106), a loss of the capacity to separate, a fear of imagery because it may be, or become, the same as the thing it represents. In lesbian representation, as with that of any denigrated group, this has especial association because of bodily aspersion, as if in becoming close to a lesbian one can catch the inclination or be suspected of having done so. This is particularly the case with acting a lesbian, or gay, part: after all, it is nonsensical, and seemingly unheard of therefore, for an actor playing across racial or gender lines to say, 'I am not really black/a woman', or for Deneuve to deny she is a vampire. Partly, if actors do take such a role, it is clear they are indeed playing a part, whereas sexuality is invisible; partly it is because of the social register of such acting, that it is indeed only playing a part, whereas lesbianism is construed as an essence, an added essence at that to a heterosexual staple. Twentieth-century construction of lesbian identity has all to do with (postulated) fear of non-recognition, hence of provision of conspicuous signifiers by both anti-lesbian and lesbian, in order to be noticed.

Revelation

Lesbian signs are often larger than life, part of an inflationary spiral of overstatement, whether this is sartorial or imaged. Dominant ideology administers lesbian visual signs in many media. 'If lesbianism is seen as a congenital condition, not a sexual-social relationship, then a single individual can quite well exhibit a lesbian identity in isolation. According to this view, the individual woman is almost an "example of" lesbianism' (Ruehl 1991, p. 34). Hence shorthand ascriptions appear in photographs or descriptions in obituaries where the text and the visual representation are in dialogue.

Obituaries of Naomi (Micky) Jacob, for example, headline 'The Rebel in Collar and Tie' and show a photograph of her with cropped hair: this obituarist only met her one month before when 'she was so violently alive. She wore the tweed skirt and jacket, the tie and shirt which were her trade-mark. Her hair was shingled, her jokes were scandalous. She answered to the name of Micki [sic] ... [and became a socialist] when it was not respectable for a man, let alone a woman, to be so' (*Daily Herald*, 28 August 1964). Most other obituaries carry a similar photograph with the subject's eyes meeting the observer (e.g. *The Times*, 28 August 1964), and a commentary which underlines her sexuality without naming it: one has a subheading 'Animal Lover' and records that 'Naomi was too feminine a name for so robust and dominating a personality ... memory of her crop-headed, cigar-smoking personality will not soon be forgotten' (*Daily Telegraph*, 28 August 1964).

If hair and physicality are visual shorthand, then hands too feature in photographs of Martina Navratilova (e.g. *Guardian*, 2 July 1994, captioned 'With these hands ... '). It is as if one part of a snapshot will suffice for understanding the whole, sexualised body, even when there is no overt mention of sexuality in the commentary.

Other lesbian obituaries use the art of photography to reinforce their words. Almost invariably, lesbians are active in these representations, not passive or reclining as in many women's obituaries. Joe Carstairs, for example, is shown at the wheel of a speedboat, in blazer and beret, her eyes meeting the camera (*Daily Telegraph*, 26 January 1994). Eve Balfour, similarly, meets her observer's gaze, wearing a beret, a cravat and in a uniform of some kind (*Daily Telegraph*, 16 January 1990); Margot Gore is in pilot's gear (*The Times*, 4 September 1993); and Daphne du Maurier is shown outside, frequently in some sort of physical activity, accompanied by her dog(s) (*The Times*; *Daily Telegraph*, 20 April 1989).

Action, and vigorous at that, serves as similar shorthand for understanding the assertiveness of the lesbian subject. So Ethel Smyth is envisaged as on the move, usually with a hat, 'brandishing her umbrella' (p. 135), or/and with a dog (*Guardian*, 11 October 1967; *Scilly-up-to-Date*, February/March 1992, a tourist promotion, FL). Octavia Hill, in a cartoon (with the headline 'Under-dressing') is shown striding along, in a huge hat with bags held firmly in each hand: 'She would call on the grandest in the land in her shabby rent-collecting clothes, muddy galoshes and frightful pen-wiper hat' (Spurling, FL, unlabelled, *Guardian*?, 1990). Such a picture, visual and visualised, is presumably what the writer is after when she appeals for public subscription for a sculpture to be erected to give 'a more entirely satisfactory record of her spiritual power than is shown in Sargant's otherwise fine portrait' (Margaret Shaen, letter to editor, *Manchester Guardian*, 26 July 1925, FL).

Descriptions work without the visual representation being to hand. Hence, when Maureen Colquhoun's photograph is described as being like a 'battle-axe' (p. 155), presumably we should be able to call her looks to mind. A biographer's reading of a picture is somehow used as evidence of objectively realised signs. So when Hall's biographer Michael Baker describes a photograph of 'John as a young woman', the strikingness of the gender-gap between name and personal pronoun is used to bear out the alleged meaning of the visual script: 'at the centre of a family group. No men are present ... all attention clearly focuses on John ... Like a royal prince flanked by his retainers ... the "man" of the family' (1985, pp. 21–2).

In life-associated media, such as reviews, likewise the photograph has particular status. In a review of *The Trials of Radclyffe Hall*, for example, a photograph shows her in collar and tie, with jacket, skirt and sturdy shoes. She holds a cigarette in one hand, and a dog from a lead in the other. The caption says: 'Radclyffe Hall: a man "cursed with a woman's body"' (*Guardian Weekly*, 23 August 1998). Quotation reinforces interpretative authority, and the photograph gives additional evidence of the authenticity it carries.

It is here that we can observe the ways in which some lesbians have appropriated and in some senses transformed dominant ideological configuration. Romaine Brooks's 1923/24 portrait of Gluck is entitled 'Peter (A Young English Girl)'. This uses, it has been noted, 'a strategy of visual dissonance ... where the title directs the viewer to look again and to look *differently*' (Elliott and Wallace 1994, p. 49, my emphasis). This is a similar *effect* to Baker's and to the review's creation of disharmony between visualisation and meaning, but these intended to create a negatively received disquiet, for us to look again at the picture having read the caption, and to look back *in the same way*. In other words, text and picture are used to mutually bear out a sense of oddness. Here we are directed to readings based on a *congruity* between what we think of Hall and what is said and seen (so proved) of her, a congruity of image/self/word which stimulates a notion of *in*congruity as Woman/femininity separate and as eccentric/pretend/masculine coagulate around understanding of Lesbian. In Romaine Brooks's portrait, on the other hand, title/text and picture raise questions not answers. The observer is invited to engage in the interpretation, and is not directed to a fixed meaning about appearance. We can read Brooks's strategy as being part of a reappraisal of ideas of lesbian identity manifested through physical appearance,

> *recycling* images, voices, and costumes in the interest of creating a newly visible and deviant sexuality – albeit within the confines of an élitist and unproblematized social position ... This [the Gluck portrait's] exploration of the visual confusions of cross-dressing upsets an essentialist understanding of gender and overturns the notions of 'origin' and 'imitation' as they are used to regulate gendered identity. (Elliott and Wallace 1994, p. 54)

This plays upon the already unsettling cross-dressing of Gluck herself. It is a similar idea which Brooks used in her portrait of Una Troubridge with dogs, when she depicted her in a monocle, with tie and jacket, a three-quarter view which (as in many deliberately foreshortened reproductions of portraits of Radclyffe Hall) Brooks often employs and which allows that the subject may be wearing a skirt on her lower body. In that portrait, Brooks played with the depiction of lesbians with dogs, a typology which runs through many representations (see Chapter 4, note 2). Again, as in her own self-portrait (1923) in riding gear and top hat, stereotypes which the lesbian subject herself already echoes by her real chosen dress and occupation are appropriated by the artist. She plays with the idea of the idea, portrays the lesbian use of the cliché. So, the fact that lesbians often did choose such sartorial style, wore particular types of hats, or were indeed Masters of Fox Hounds (as was Edith Somerville) is itself part of the subject, and the artistic play with ideas of self-realisation.

If we approach Brooks's pictures as portraits that only depict a physical reality then we might fail to see that the lesbian subject is already part of her own self-reference, that the portrait is a further extrication of other-reference to, and within, a cultural hegemony. When biographers (including obituarists and reviewers) use photographs as visual evidence of eccentricity or incongruity, they do not add the subject's own dimension, that, as an agent, she has already engaged with dominant modes of self-expression, and has chosen to appropriate them, subvert or ignore them. The visual anatomisation of lesbian identity in this way treats the lesbian doubly as an object. She is judged by how she looks in support of a verbal commentary about that; and as if she did not choose to look like she did in the first place, but happened to be wearing what she was.

Failure to engage in the double level of signification which does operate in lesbian portraits has led to misreading. Hence, Gluck's portrait 'Medallion' (1936) of herself and her lover, and her attribution of it as their wedding celebration, has been read by Souhami in a constative way (1988, p. 126). Because they say they are husband and wife, and the portrait proves it, then we lose any notion of portraiture as performative, as itself playing with the idea of heteronormality. Hence, lesbians are rather sad figures, aspiring to an institution they cannot actually inhabit, rather like would-be graduates having their photograph taken in academic dress.

Similarly, the photographs of Gertrude Stein and Alice B. Toklas in the summer of 1910 have been read as narrative, with the meaning in what we see, rather than in texts beyond, in our other visual and literary knowledge of the pair. The real/intended observer, and their response created by the text, is forgotten in this reading of the photographs, though they are mentioned as addressees:

Pleased with the photographs, they made one into postcards, which they sent to friends. The first public signature of their relationship, it hinted at the way they would, in their future together, enjoy constructing a double persona, one that hinted at their intimacy only in the most predictable terms ... They were married, they said, half parodying the form and half taking it seriously; and in a sense, they were. (Wineapple 1996, p. 320).

What we can see here is a heterosexualised (and retrospective) reading: it is perhaps the first visual signature in a narrative which gives marriage a central and photographically proven status as a midlife transition route, and which privileges the visual as a sign; it reads back-to-front, in the knowledge that they did stay together. This is only 'predictable' if marriage is an allowed statement of seriousness. The pose may be a counterdiscourse (Elliott and Wallace's phrase 1994, p. 52).[4]

Visual material is often treated, therefore, as evidence to bear out ideas of the Lesbian which have themselves been derived from the picture. Hence, in the circularity, the individuation, or, conversely, the intertextualisation of self, which is manifested visually, is frequently ignored.

When Stein and Toklas were photographed by Cecil Beaton in the mid-1930s (Cecil Beaton Archives, Sotheby's, London; rep. in Stendhal 1995, p. 199), they were arranged facing each other, some way apart, and looking at each other. It has been said that this double portrait 'conveys a sense of independence along with relationship':

The opposition of the figures ... certainly could be read as a masculine/feminine one, though that is not the only possible reading. That of famous author and admiring friend would be another.

What *is* clear is that this is a portrait of a pair of women each absorbed and focused on the other. (Ruehl 1991, p. 38)

The photograph could be read in a different way, as consciously engaging with a whole set of notions of lesbian identity, cross-referencing with heterosexual types and with lesbian imitation and parody of them. All our expectations of reading the relationship are both met and flouted.

With photography, beyond portraiture more generally, we have expectations of neutrality. The media's exponents are especially canny at appearing invisible, and we have come somehow to expect objectivity of them. Frequently we do not read the subjects of photographs as actively projecting their sense of self, and they are seen as passive; and the photograph can seem as if it is a statement simply of what is.

If we use Stein and Toklas by Beaton as an example, it is possible to recognise a number of ideas about same-sex love, drawn from contemporary and classical sources. These could be taken as straightforwardly authoritative. One reading might say that the photograph reflects the subjects' latent narcissism. They face each other as if in a mirror but they are not identical or even refracted likenesses that look back. In Freudian terms (Freud 1914), they are showing a desire not only for a reflection of themselves in each other, but also 'a desire to experience oneself being loved by others … a tendency to objectify that which reminds one of oneself or of the self as one would like to be/have been … an object that has some fantasized relation/similarity to the self' (Lewis and Rolley 1996, p. 182).

Havelock Ellis's views might be applied. These have been felt to have influenced visual representations of lesbians from the late nineteenth century, in ways which might appear helpful to reading such photographs:

> that tendency which is sometimes found, more especially perhaps in women, for the sexual emotions to be absorbed, and often entirely lost, in self-admiration. This Narcissus-like tendency, of which the normal germ in women is symbolised by the mirror, is found in minor degree in some feminine-minded men … (cited in Hart 1994, p. 50)

Culturally ancient notions of friendship may be referenced too. 'He who looks on a true friend looks as it were upon a kind of image of himself', 'a friend is a second self' (Cicero 1922, cited in Faderman 1981, p. 66). The Platonic view of friendship valorised same-sex (male) bonding, for which

> neither heterosexual nor female same-sex desire can claim the status of the original from which the other derives or departs, rather both are caught up in the kind of infinite doubling *of each other*, a doubling that was also associated with relations between lover and beloved in female same-sex desire. (Ballaster 1995, p. 26)

Alternatively, or as well, we could interpret the photographs as a visualisation of ideas of selfhood. The women might seem to be confrontational, and their stances might suggest, in Hegelian terms, a struggle between two participants towards knowledge and individuation:

> This presentation is a twofold action: action on the part of the other, and action on its own part. In so far as it is the action of the *other,* each seeks the death of the other ... Thus the relation of the two self-conscious individuals is such that they prove themselves and each other through a life-and-death struggle ... It is only through staking one's life that freedom is won. (1977, pp. 113–14, cited in Docherty 1996, pp. 4–5).

Whilst it would be neat to apply such readings of 'terrorism' to the way Stein and Toklas are posed in Beaton's photograph, this does not necessarily allow for their counterdiscourse, their elsewhere merger in 'coupling the signature, Gertrice/Altrude', which 'reveals Stein's ambivalence about the self as a unified figure ... [and] destabilizes the signature on which traditional interpretations of autobiography depend' (Gilmore 1994, p. 204): 'As an object, an autobiography, like a photograph, simulates the action of the eye in a way that obscures how the apparatus of representation works on and within the scene it depicts' (p. 200).

If we expose the apparatus, Beaton's work can be recognised as a possible collaboration with Stein and Toklas, a commentary on lesbian autobiography. We can see Beaton and his subjects as active participants in debates about selfhood, operating between Hegelian paradigms and a women's/lesbian philosophy of merger, where 'the individual does not oppose herself to all others ... but very much *with* others in an interdependent existence' (Chodorow 1978a, quoted in Friedman 1988, p. 41):

> Between women love is contemplative; caresses are intended less to gain possession of the other than gradually to re-create the self through her; separateness is abolished, there is no struggle, no victory, no defeat; in exact reciprocity each is at once subject and object, sovereign and slave; duality becomes mutuality. (de Beauvoir 1949, p. 27)

Because we have been keen to understand the lesbian subject as somehow a case history, we have read *her,* not the textuality of the photograph. Given Stein's interest in the whole notion of the modern self, it is feasible to see her using her own image in a dramatic reconstruction of autobiography, via portrait.

In this way, too, we may read Virginia Woolf and Vita Sackville-West's play with the idea of narcissism in *Orlando*, even the delighted cry of 'twins' by the woman who came upon Sylvia Townsend-Warner and Valentine Ackland in bed.[5] What we may have here is a parodic treatment by Beaton, Stein and Toklas of the idea of the idea of the Lesbian, a pictorial discussion ensuing between written text/theory of lesbians, and the visual embodiment.

Inter-media Dialogue: Visualisation of Literary Texts

Something similar happens when a lesbian autobiographical text is translated to a visual medium, as with dramatisation of *Portrait of a Marriage* and of *Oranges Are Not the Only Fruit*. The visual is treated as if it is unproblematic, and has simply replicated a literary truth, with little sense of the several parallel contextualisations which may jostle for supremacy in both the writing and the reading: of the original literary work and its author, of the dramatist, and of the social circumstance of the drama (when it appeared and for what audience), all of which informed a theory of lesbian Lives, which is either oblique or blatant.

Vita Sackville-West's autobiography and biography (it is both, because of Nigel Nicolson's interventions) was dramatised for TV in 1990. The Life, therefore, underwent a further transformation, which was not at Nicolson's chagrined hands,[6] though he had 'implored [the producer] to give the public some idea of their happiness before and after the brief Violet affair'. The producer, he says, 'thought it irrelevant ... Her version was not so much the portrait of a marriage as the portrait of an affair' (Sackville-West 1973, p. 3).

None the less, the dramatisation was *about* marriage 'brought into focus through perversity' (Harding 1994, p. 120). The transmission coincided with public expression of Tory party/New Right ideas about divorce which was being blamed for lawlessness (Merck 1993, p. 114), and in the period immediately after the introduction of Section 28 (Wilson 1990). The TV drama, and reviews of it, thus operated as a corrective to possibly dangerous ideas, and levelled the potential of lesbianism as radical, having it sit alongside and within marriage.

Sackville-West, in the TV drama, was visually depicted in unthreatening ways, her sporadic masculinisation being countered by her return to feminised appearance, and subsequently to the marital home. The idea of the Lesbian as a temporary aberration is thus enforced by the TV version, despite Nicolson's misgivings; and Sackville-West's own Life is several times immersed in a paintpot of differently motivated hues.

The period context was all, too, in the adaptation, by Jeanette Winterson, of her autobiographical *Oranges Are Not the Only Fruit*, also in 1990. It appeared at a time when there was particular hostility expressed to fundamentalist religion (a fatwah had been declared on the novelist Salman Rushdie in 1989), and the focus was on 'the power of extremist ideologies to corrupt family relationships … here it is Christianity that is "deviant"' (Marshment and Hallam 1994, p. 149). As such, lesbianism was rendered marginally more acceptable by its internal comparison to greater oddness. Reviews of the TV drama suggested that the Winterson family's 'fundamental religious beliefs make the Ayatollah Khomeini … seem a model of polite tolerance' (*Evening Standard*, 22 January 1990).

In this sense, then, the dramatisation does not radically develop the auto/biographical material in its visualisation of lesbians, beyond responding to an immediate imperative of gaining acceptability in a New Right milieu. Marriage and family, whilst probed by the visual, remain culturally embedded and are only moderately shaken by the lesbian action.

The Subtle State of Amorous Desire: Contradictory Visualisation

There has been much more effective dialogue between text and visualisation in other Life sites, less obviously or explicitly lesbian in their subject. 'Within gay culture, much of the conflict between what is experienced and what can be expressed can be identified as the "subtle state of amorous desire" that Roland Barthes called *langueur*' (Cooper 1996, p. 21, citing Barthes 1990, p. 155). In visual terms, *langueur* has been present, *inter alia* in portraiture of feminists. There is a tension between revealed and expressed, and pleasure in that tension, between what is seems to be happening visually and what our mind tells us is possible.

Feminists are often depicted as being axiomatically lesbian, and their appearance may bear this out. 'Everybody thinks they know all there is to know about Andrea Dworkin. You may not have read her books, you may never have heard her speak, but the popular imagination has her fixed: the fat, miserable feminist in denim dungarees … ' (Viner 1997). She is 'the epitome of everything a militant feminist should be, from the bulging dungarees, through the face like a beef Madras' (*Sunday Telegraph*, 29 November 1992). In a cartoon with this piece Dworkin is depicted in said dungarees next to a tree with a snake in it, she chops off its head: she is an undesirable Eve, castrating the snake; icono-graphically lesbian in her breaking up of paradise, even though (because) she subverts the image of the Fall.

The pictures and the way she is visualised by the text both point to her sexuality being deviant; yet she may not be a lesbian, and her inter-viewers express surprise at her voice 'unexpectedly soft, urgent, moving even' (*Guardian*, 9 April 1986), 'soft, gentle and low' (*The Times*, 18 May 1988). The surprise is shared by the ideal reader who views in both articles a photograph of Dworkin in her dungarees. Mention is made of a long-term male partner. There is, then, a teasing, a tension between the written (the aural within it) and the visual. There is a playing with the (anti-) desire that Dworkin might be, must be, a lesbian, and the alter-native indicators that she might not be, a male partner, a soft voice.

Restructuring the Lesbian Gaze

> This raises the question of whether/how far one can distinguish an overtly lesbian gaze, that self-consciously desires the represented woman, from a narcissistic one that identifies with the represented woman as an object of a presumed-to-be-male desire? (Lewis and Rolley 1996, p. 181)

Lesbian artists, like Romaine Brooks and others of the later twentieth century, have sought to portray lesbian lives in ways which give the lesbian subject some control and which restructure the lesbian gaze, formulating new ways in which to conceptualise lesbian auto/biography.

Two examples of reconfiguration may suffice in the work of Sally Potter and of Sadie Lee. Potter's film *Orlando* (1994), based on Virginia Woolf's biography (1928) of Vita Sackville-West, visualises the lesbian as both an object of desire and in some command of her situation. Orlando frequently turns to the camera, with direct gaze and address. S/he is an object of desire (for example of the Queen, Elizabeth I, punningly played by Quentin Crisp), becomes her own object of pleasure when she looks at herself in the mirror (Walker 1994, p. 36, gives a Freudian/Lacanian reading of this scene), and transforms into a later twentieth-century woman, by self-birth. 'Birth' is the title of the final section of the film. Potter uses the lesbian auto/biographical text (both the object of the biography and the subject of it) to transform or query ideas about lesbian self-expression and autonomy. The film jokingly questions notions of sexuality within a Life, one that is being written by someone else, who has authorial and directorial control, and yet over which the subject has power. Ideas of self-will within a determining structure, present within Woolf's work, are translated by Potter to a visual field.

A further example of development of the lesbian auto/biographical gaze is within the paintings of Sadie Lee, who describes herself as an artist who is a lesbian. Her painting *Erect* (1991), is a self-portrait with her partner. The title is punning, on male turgidity and also, by reference to the Latin roots of the word, to ideas of setting upright, (self-) direction. The women are seated, directly facing the observer, their postures mirroring each other, each holding the other with one arm across, with their other arm on their lap. Their gazes are straight at the viewer, compelling and holding eye contact. Sadie Lee challenges ideas about the lesbian and as such has self-consciously related to heterosexualised positions within visual art: she writes of the male tradition of female portraiture as having a 'perfecting technique' which

> turns the woman into a fantasy figure and instead of being a representation of a real person she becomes exaggerated and moulded into an ideal form by the spectator …
>
> The women (sometimes nude) in my paintings differ from nudes by male artists in that they are aware of their sexuality. In fact, their sexuality is so evident that their awareness of it gives them a challenging, threatening presence not shown in most traditional paintings of women. (1996, p. 122)

Lee consciously transforms traditions: her portrait *La Butch en Chemise* (1992), for example, translates by its title and subject-matter Picasso's *La Femme en Chemise*, with wordplay drawing attention to the restriction around the butch/femme opposition contrived within other-definitions of lesbian sexuality. The lesbian in the portrait, herself a fantasy-figure for the artist who had seen her from afar, 'looked like a predator but she still retained an air of vulnerability' (p. 123). Her gaze and posture encapsulates this: she is part defiant, and yet her eyes are not directly confrontational (unlike in the women in *Erect*), and one arm protectively crosses her body.

Sadie Lee plays with the idea of auto/biography, weaving her own fantasy of the woman into the portrait itself, and of herself into her own self-portrait. Artistically formulated traditions in representing lesbians, paired or alone, are accordingly alluded to and the stereotypes are redrawn to include the lesbian viewer in reading the work. Arrangement and control are thus given to both the portrait subject, and the larger lesbian subject outside the work, who is adumbrated by the lesbian gaze being made possible.

Writing Ahead and Behind: Futuring the Lesbian Eye

Carolyn Heilbrun has suggested that there are four ways to write a woman's life, namely autobiography, fiction, biography and texts in which a woman unconsciously writes her own life in advance of living it (1989, p. 14). In visual terms, lesbian lives can also be written in this way, with '"subjunctive images" – photographs hurled toward the future cast ahead of us as visual guideposts to what we hope to become' (Grover 1991, p. 185, using Raymond Williams's term).

Within the postmodern, these images often carry elements of the past with them. As with most art, the creator is actually commenting on what has gone before, amending assumptions about 'reality': for a postmodern artist, this transformation may be consciously invoking the past in order to parody or cast doubt upon its relevance as an absolute message of truth. Artists portraying lesbian lives in the later twentieth century accordingly invert or challenge previous ideas of Lives. Some such techniques are knowingly reclaiming, such as Jill Posener's photographic sequence on Lesbian Sex in Public Places (1988), an assertiveness exercise after Section 28 showing lesbians embracing in public sites around London (1991, pp. 204–9); or parodies of Raphael's *Three Graces* by Tee Corinne (1991, p. 226) or by Della Grace (a name-punning reference to her own portrait; rep. *Guardian Weekend*, 22 July 1995, p. 16).

Other work cross-references to textual models of the lesbian, so Mumtaz Karimjee's *In Seach of an Image* (1991) plays with racist constructions of lesbians. She quotes alongside her photographs of what appears to be an Eastern veiled woman texts about a Moslem Harem being 'a great school' for lesbian love (1991, pp. 30–3; citing Kabbani 1988, p. 53). The woman eventually turns, to reveal she is Western. 'The piece is a direct challenge to cultures that have historically sought to blame the Other for the "habit" of homosexuality' (Gupta 1996, p. 174).

Such works operate as parodic postmodern, elbowing inside heterosexual confines. They are effective if we are in the know, able to recognise references to previous artistic constraints. Other images seek to future lesbian auto/biographical identity, write ahead visual lives.

Photography by Della Grace and by Tessa Boffin, and by Sally Potter in film, represents the next step in lesbian utopics. The artists play with ideas of artificiality embedded in the postmodern itself, within a *fin de siècle* decadence and within lesbian chic and Queer theory. Elaine Showalter (1990) has alerted us to the fact that the decadent aesthetic rejects all that is 'natural' in favour of the artificial. At this end-of-century, lesbian chic has been acceptable to heterosexuals because it is blatantly artificial, unthreatening to the hegemony because it is seen to be game-play, posturing within the confines of gender-norm, flirting with subversion only to retreat. These artists work within that aesthetic to investigate role-play and fantasy, reinvent them as threatening rather than simply fun.

Della Grace's self-portrait with a beard appeared on the front page of *Guardian Weekend* (22 July 1995). It shows the photographer in three-quarter length, gazing out at the viewer. She is wearing a T-shirt, revealing a tattoo on her arm, and she is holding the remote control of her camera, so in effect staring at herself in the lens. Her beard is real, grown because she stopped plucking, as she tells the interviewer (Orr 1995, pp. 12–16). The self-portrait appears to play with ideas of self-reference, narcissism, yet it is serious: '"I've grown my beard in protest". During a recent discussion about lesbian visibility ... she argued that the media's images of lesbians had created an anti-butch backlash' (p. 16).[7]

Similarly, the work of Tessa Boffin has sought to challenge notions of lesbian self. Her photographic sequence *The Knight's Move* (1991) 'pillaged the past for images from which to reinvent an identity and articulate desire' (Smyth 1996, p. 109). It depicts lesbians in a variety of dress, including medieval knight in armour and eighteenth-century courtier. 'Real' lesbians from history appear in photographs in bushes in a cemetery, over which a memorial stone angel presides; and in written references when characters hold up signs listing lesbian names. Boffin opens her piece by quoting Stuart Hall: 'it is worth remembering that all discourse is "placed", and the heart has its reasons' (1990, p. 223; p. 49):

> My starting point for *The Knight's Move* was the intense frustration I feel when people prioritise reality – everyday experience, 'real' sex and so on – over and above fantasies ...
>
> If we persist in prioritising reality – actual historical role models at the expense of fantasy figures – we leave our sense of selves and our imagery wanting, and certain questions unasked. For example, who

mobilises our desires and fantasies, given that they cut across the fragile boundaries of sexual identity and gender; and which archetypes do our desires attach themselves to? Are these dramatis personae the same as the real life historical role models? Somewhere within this tension, this gap between reality and fantasy, we model ourselves on tattered old photographs and hazy daydreams. (1991, pp. 49, 50)

Boffin raises questions, therefore, about the whole way in which a lesbian life is configured, by whom and for what motive. Her visualisation challenges the idea of ownership within time and space, creating new possibilities within a textual dismemberment of theory.

Her work is given reference by other writers interested in lesbian identity and its formation. The cover of Annamaria Jagose's *Lesbian Utopics* (1994) uses one of Boffin's photographs, *The Angel*, from this sequence. This shows the lesbian reappropriation of each other's visual images to reinforce the importance of joint ownership, especially as the book is precisely on that subject of lesbian cultural space. In a similar way, Sally Potter's *Orlando* plays with notions of fantasy and reality, in line with Woolf's original excursions, with cross-reference to images such as that of Boffin. In the written biography, Orlando's life spans several centuries, during which s/he transforms from seventeenth-century courtier to eighteenth-century bewigged woman to nineteenth-century romantic hero in Brontë mode, then twentieth-century New Woman. This was drawn from Vita Sackville-West's own family portraiture (Woolf, 1975/80, vol. III, pp. 434, 442, 510, 558) and her own self-fashioning based on historical personages, her personal preference for 'mannish' clothing. The visual images Potter employs in her film draw upon this 'internal' and semi-private (Woolf and Sackville-West) heritage, and also upon contemporary, and public, material. Interestingly, given Tessa Boffin's span of lesbian images, from medieval to modern, Potter's Orlando wears similar attire, across the same time-frame. Boffin's sequence ends with *You All Come Together*, with Knave, Knight, Casanova, Lady-in-waiting grouped in the cemetery around the Angel (Jagose's cover) with uplifted arm. And Potter's film ends with a fantasy sequence, involving an angel rising above the scene, having transmogrified across several centuries from the bow of Elizabeth I's boat, as a singing castrato. The roles are played by the actor/singer Jimmy Somerville, again, like Quentin Crisp, in cross-reference to the actor's own sexuality and part-play.

Parts and characters merge and remerge across time. Potter uses the novel (and the film) as 'a celebration of impermanence': 'The film ends on a similar metaphysical note to the book, with Orlando caught somewhere between heaven and earth, in a place of ecstatic communion with the present' (Potter 1994, p. xiv). As in Woolf's biography, at the end past, present and fantasy merge in the film when Orlando's daughter takes the hand-held camera and the scene becomes her shaky viewpoint. This is a piece of additional appropriation which takes the text to the film's time-present, like Woolf had done in 1928, and which gives a female line of ownership: 'In these sequences we find no difficulty in moving between cinematic languages: from naturalism, to arch cinematic illusion to undisguised, hand held camera image. Orlando has ceded to her daughter a command in equal measure of all language' (Walker 1994, p. 38).

Sally Potter's use of images relates to sequences such as Tessa Boffin's, either consciously (it is interesting that they coincide so much) or with knowledge of the context of lesbian auto/biographical visualisation. Like Virginia Woolf in her modernist literary biography, and Vita Sackville-West as autobiographer and subject, both Potter and Boffin use fantasy as a means to interrogate sexual realities. All these artists create, with their cross-reference to traditions of self-writing, a series of 'visual guideposts' ahead. It is as if, autobiographically writing in advance, Vita Sackville-West's own title, *No Signposts in the Sea* (1961) has been transformed into a positive set of visualised lesbian markers.

Conclusions

A review of an autobiography by Katrin Fitzherbert highlights the issues around women's Lives more generally. She had been brought up in Germany by a Nazi father, whom she loved, and an English mother who, after the Second World War, divorced and moved with her child to England. Thereafter, the child's Germanness had been denied:

> she had to grapple with uneasy notions of identity that most of us can complacently take for granted ... History, for her, has not been a river bearing her along, but a floodtide pulling her apart in its cross-currents.

On the one hand, her autonomy is asserted by the reviewer: 'She became a woman who, unlike so many of her peers, learned to look at her life and name it'; on the other, rights to author-ship are denied: her 'early life was extraordinary, perhaps too extraordinary for her plain pen'. (Gerrard 1998, p. 28)

The authority of the subject is thus questioned, and her turbulence is set against a posited serenity in women's general identity. This belies the often difficult negotiation of selfhood (via others, within and without herself) expressed within many life narratives.

For lesbians, there may be particular pressures affecting this other-referentialisation or self-fragmentation; and these seem to have been manifested in different ways over the twentieth century, as lesbians engaged in different, personally and historically contingent, relationships with conceptualisations of self:

> Charged with history, representational imprints, and self-representational politics, 'I's' are consolidated, naturalized, centralized or

> marginalized ... For subject peoples, slaves and ex-slaves, subalterns, homosexuals, women, such membership [of the community of the fully human, through positioning oneself as a white male bourgeois autobiographer] is psychologically and politically expedient and potent. (Smith 1991, p. 187)

Various techniques to self-ownership appear to be on offer, including such mimicry of male textual politics, or, alternatively, separatism,[1] or (as Benstock 1988) proposing fragmentation as an alternative to male traditions of autobiographical unity, though this may itself reproduce oppression.[2] All such techniques have been observed of lesbians in the twentieth century, as they mediate between received and self-generated ideas.

The idea of mediation between determining ideas and experiential, again, may suggest an inevitability to language of thrall. Lesbians, in this conception, cannot merely be, but accrete layers of interpretative substance: a thing to be understood becomes, by process of explanation, a simultaneous equation of self plus explanation to equal meaning and reality. Lesbian in this sense is a hefty portmanteau word. Questioned at the airport whether she packed her luggage herself, and whether she left it unattended, raises for the lesbian many and various answers. Historically reconfiguring reasons for these, possibly disparate, replies, depends upon knowledge of choice contingencies, social circumstances. It may be possible to revisit moments in personal formation, where testimony exists, to recognise factors contributing to the construction of lesbian eidolon – a spectre or an idealised figure, one and the same in different lights, perhaps, or one and several. Relationships between 'me' and 'them' may shift and determining and self-discourse cross and merge and separate, define by difference: the lesbian may be a pebble in the cultural shoe, or the heterosexual may be the grit in the lesbian machine, as relativity, mutuality, cultural dominance and liberation are effected.

If 'Decolonialisation never takes place unnoticed' (Fanon 1967, cited in Smith 1991, p. 187), it might be expected to be seen and to have an impact on lesbian auto/biography. Yet proposing this assumes that lesbians experience a sense of being objectified, of thingness, caused by sexuality, around which they might organise a Life. Even if they do, formation of this may not be directly in the form of auto/biography, and self-expression may not be possible evenly, and in all forms, at all times. Historical circumstances surrounding auto/biography may not allow all forms of expressive language to be available at any given time;

or, conversely, individual epiphanies may be of non-change, when individuals recognise a rootedness of self, against the thrust of discourses of discontinuity. Identity, in other words, may be more stable than theories of the self (especially within the modern and post-modern) may imply; and this, as well or instead of oppression, may explain the relative dearth of lesbian autobiographies across the century: '"Time Passed" ... and nothing whatever happened'.[3]

There has, perhaps, been a dubious liberation within Queer politics for the lesbian autobiographer. On one hand, notions of the Queer posit individualism within diversity, and challenge Enlightenment principles of progress, and this may facilitate confidence in selfhood. On the other, Queer also infers uncertainty, potentially antonymic to lesbian expressions of fixity, personal integrity and identity (if momentary) stillness. Alternatively, again, Queer may have had an effect beyond the written, possibly in stabilising the lesbian reader, who may recognise still points within the lesbian text.

The relationship between readers and text (lesbian Life or life) is potentially resettled, then, within the politics of the postmodern, into a lesbian-conducive state. Though this may not have been the imperative, the mêlée within and around later twentieth-century ideas of the self may have afforded lesbian space beyond the mimetic, in the construction of reading community. Changes may be detected over the course of the century, as one set of expectations of the text are supplanted, or supplemented, (potentially) by another, the modernist by the postmodern. Whereas the former may have sought to make sense, even within multipersoned narrative, of the discontinuity of self, the postmodern may have staged the possibilities of non-sense. Earlier ideas of the lesbian reading 'community' for auto/biography may have depended upon assumptions of identification between reader and subject. That reciprocation may have shifted in the later century, so that lesbians reading a text may construct a variety of meanings, from what is said, what is inferred, or what is unstated. Engagement may be personal, contingent upon personal interpretation by readers freed from notions of mimesis and one-to-one referentiality. Accordingly, self-reference may be within and beyond the text; and a lesbian reader may write aspects of self by her response to the Life.

In asking the question, therefore, about whether there is a separate genre of lesbian auto/biography, perhaps the fragmentation of the genre itself, under pressure of theories of self, allows there to be a continually separating literary form, across the century. Relativities shift. The text and its writer may be constant, and the reader change, both historically and within the experience of a given text. The unsettled reader may arrive at self-recognition and thence self-write. Perhaps, then, the question is a different one, not of the text but of the reader outside, not Is there a Lesbian in this Life, but is there a Life in this Lesbian?

Notes

Frontispiece

1. 'Cow Lick' is my own, previously unpublished, poem.

Preface

1. 'Auto/biography' is used for autobiography and/or biography. This is not to suggest that the genres are identical in their theories of self but to avoid repeating 'both autobiography and biography' each time. The conjunction is also intended to draw attention to possibility of similarities/differences, not to answer the question of distinctions but to raise it as an issue. When a distinction *is* being made, the separate words autobiography and biography are used.

Introduction

1. For example, in popular culture, Griffin 1993a, Gibbs, 1994; in film, Wilton 1995; in writing, Griffin 1993b; in fiction, Zimmerman 1992a.
2. 'In this country American means white. Everyone else has to hyphenate' (Toni Morrison, *Guardian*, 29 January 1992).
3. 'Aspersion': calumny, slander; sprinkling with holy water (Roman Catholic) (*Chamber's English Dictionary* 1990). Like 'hagiography' (a biography of a saint; a biography which over-praises its subject), the potential double meaning is appealing when applied to individual lives who may attract approval or criticism, blessing or damnation.
4. 'To regard one's own life as an exemplary case-study is modest because it assumes the determining importance of the writer's social environment; it is also potentially arrogant in claiming a universal status for particular forms of subjection' (Montefiore 1994, p. 58).
5. For example, DuPlessis 1990; Walkerdine 1990; Miller 1991; Stanley 1992; Hallett 1998.

6. Judith Brown wrote of Sister Benedetta Carlini, a Renaissance nun charged by her church with lesbianism: 'Though refracted through the perception of other participants ... the clerics, who wrote down what they heard or thought they heard, and Bartolomea [her lover], who told them what happened or what she thought would implicate her the least – the voice and longings of Benedetta Carlini can still be heard' (Brown 1984, p. 277).
7. See Finlayson 1986; Masters 1991; Castle 1996; Cockin 1998.

Chapter 1

1. The writer Vita Sackville-West was married to Harold Nicolson, a diplomat. Since she used her unmarried name throughout her career, I refer to her in this way. Violet Keppel is called by that name before she was married, and Trefusis afterwards. It is telling that Sackville-West used her married initials in the book's flyleaf here.
2. For example, Faderman 1981; Lister 1988; Castle 1993; Liddington 1994; Aughterson 1995; Ballaster 1995; McCormick 1997.
3. The idea of 'poor imitation' seems to run through the configuration of lesbian identity. Jeffrey Weeks, for example, described *fin de siècle* Paris and Berlin: 'A lesbian sub-culture of sorts did exist, but was a pale version of the male' (1977, p. 87). He continues with this judgement in his later writing, asserting that 'by the end of the nineteenth century a recognisable "modern" male homosexual identity was beginning to emerge, but it would be another generation before female homosexuality reached a corresponding level of articulacy ... the lesbian subculture was minimal in comparison with the male ...'. Of Weeks (1977) it has been observed: 'One of the saddest consequences of combined lesbian and gay history written from a gay male perspective is that the male experience is likely to be seen, as in history generally, as the norm, with lesbian experience as a deviant or inferior version' (Auchmuty *et al.* 1992, p. 96).
4. Charles Darwin (1809–1882) in *On the Origin of Species* (1859), had postulated the idea that present-day forms had evolved from simpler ancestral types by natural selection. Ideas of typology-species had originated with Plato and Aristotle, whereby the species represents some ideal form, in which individual variation is merely imperfect expression (the exception that proves the rule). Morphological-species definition is observational of resemblance (similarity of a group of individuals separated from other groups by morphological, structural, variation). The 'pale copy' concept (note 3) suggests a typological approach. What may have been claimed as morphological techniques, frequently reveal a typological investment, just as constructionism and essentialism cross over.
5. Havelock Ellis's *Studies in the Psychology of Sex* was considered to be 'lewd and obscene' in a legal case in 1897, after which Ellis refused to publish further volumes of his study in England until the 1930s (Weeks 1981, p. 142).
6. In the trial of George Kedger for sodomy (1742), a speaker in his defence stated: 'I have always found the speaker to be a very civil man, and I believe he loved a girl too well to be concerned in other affairs'

(McCormick 1997, pp. 77–8). Civility (as opposed to baseness, primitivity) and heterosexual action are thus used as proofs against the likelihood of homosexuality.

7. 'Performative' language makes things happen, causes, creates; see also Chapter 2, note 2.

8. In Charlotte Brontë's *Jane Eyre* (1847), for example, Bertha Rochester is a woman feared for her 'madness' and she is represented as animal and as sexual: 'In the deep shade, at the farther end of the room, a figure ran backwards and forwards: what it was, whether beast or human being, one could not, at first sight, tell ... like some strange wild animal: but it was all covered in clothing, and a quantity of dark, grizzled hair, wild as a man, hid its head and face' (p. 321). *Jane Eyre* was published in the same year that Dr Thomas Savage, an American missionary in western Africa, first described gorillas, believing them at first to be members of a tribe of hairy women (*The American Heritage Dictionary of the English Language*, 1992).

Elsewhere in Brontë's novel, the working class (exemplified by Jane Eyre as governess) is discussed by upper-class characters: 'I noticed her; I am a judge of physiognomy, and in hers I see all the faults of her class', 'I will tell you in your private ear ...', 'I have just one word to say of the whole tribe; they are a nuisance' (p. 206). The idea of the subhuman, the unutterableness of its habits, forms a parallel commentary to the construction of lesbianism in this, and the later, period.

9. John Carey does not relate his ideas to lesbianism, or homosexuality more generally, though they may be applied: 'I would suggest, then, that the principle around which modernist literature and culture fashioned themselves was the exclusion of the masses, the defeat of their power, the removal of their literacy, the denial of their humanity ... The metaphor of the mass serves the purpose of individual self-assertion because it turns other people into a conglomerate. It denies them the individuality which we ascribe to ourselves and to the people we know. Being essentially unknowable, the mass acquires definition through the imposition of imagined attributes' (Carey 1992, p. 21).

10. The language of fire, in positive (warmth) and negative (destructive) form, is frequently associated with lesbian passion: see pp. 71–2, 91, 140.

11. This was one of a number of pieces of legislation which increased womens' rights within, or after, marriage. The 1878 Act gave magistrates the powers to grant separation orders (including the custody of children under ten) and maintenance to a wife who was separated on the basis of assault by her husband (see Weeks 1981, pp. 66–7, 180).

12. Lydia Maria Child's influence on perpetuating the language (and sense) of self-subordination can be seen in Harriet Jacobs's *Incidents in the Life of a Slave Girl* (1861). This was edited by Child, and Jacobs 'so doggedly followed the model of domestic fiction that for a long time it was assumed that her editor ... had written the book' (Fox-Genovese 1988, p. 75). Charlotte Forten Grimké, an early twentieth-century black woman, also read Child (along with Shakespeare, English Romantic poets and other white writers) to prepare her own writing (Braxton 1988, p. 255). Other patterns of analogy between slave and lesbian narratives are discussed on pp. 143, 207.

13. Octavia Hill referred to Florence Nightingale, who was used by parents as an 'Awful Example' of the perils of emancipation. Writing to one of her own sisters, on 19 December 1858, just after Nightingale's return from the Crimea, Hill reports that an acquaintance 'has been offered the secretary-ship of the Children's Hospital; but her father and mother say that no daughter ought to leave home except to be married, or to earn a living: witness Florence Nightingale, who has returned a mere wreck. Why! If ever there was an example fit to stir up heroism it might be hers!' (Hill 1956, pp. 38–9).

14. Wyndham Lewis had contempt for women, and 'the jigging, laughing and crying, yapping and baaing, average Negro': 'He persistently characterises the female in terms of repellently soft or fluid textures and consistencies' (Carey 1992, p. 185), and identifies the masses with this femininity, in contrast to the sharpness of the intellectual, white maleness.

15. Corridors, a space of transition between rooms, are themselves heterosex-ualised in twentieth-century literary tropism. Lesbians invade such spaces (see pp. 95, 112–13). As such, they are, though occupying no-man's-lands between places, nevertheless inhabiting (invading) crucial crossing places.

16. That this was read in English feminist circles is indicated in its advertise-ment, for example, in *The Suffragette* (22 November 1912, p. 88), along with Cicely Hamilton's *Marriage as a Trade* (1909) and Gertrude Colmore's *Suffragette Sally* (1911) (Morley with Stanley 1988, pp. 90–1).

17. Such ideas, associated with 'divine order' in society, had been expressed by the influential Lydia Maria Child (see note 12) who wrote about the sepa-ration of male and female spheres: 'The more women become rational companions, partners in business and in thought, as well as in affection and amusement, the more highly men will appreciate home' (Letter, January 1843).

18. The Contagious Diseases Acts, passed in the 1860s to impose compulsory medical examination and regulation on working-class women suspected of being prostitutes, had been highly controversial (see Sigsworth and Wyke 1972, p. 77).

19. Similar ideas had been earlier expressed by Marie Corelli, among others: 'in England, women – those of the upper classes at any rate – are not to-day married, but bought for a price' (*Lady's Realm*, April 1897, quoted in Calder 1976, p. 167).

20. The Carpenter Collection, in Sheffield City Archives, includes correspon-dence between lesbians and Edward Carpenter, an English sexologist. Liz Stanley (1992a, p. 237, note 19) uses only the initials of the letter-writers, since 'these personal letters [were] clearly not intended for other eyes'. None the less, confidentiality has frequently been broken, so I have decided to use names, to avoid resilencing these women by (virtual) anonymity.

21. 'Recesses of the mind' was a phrase used by Virginia Woolf to explore rela-tionships between women (see p. 70–1).

22. Such an idea of usurpation is repeated in the later twentieth century, with the language of lesbian motherhood and relation of lesbians with divinity (see pp. 116–17).

23.   Lovat Dickson (1975) in his writing on Radclyffe Hall, describes Una Troubridge's marital problems with her husband, Admiral Troubridge, as if she had emasculated the nation: 'He insinuates that lesbianism was somehow responsible for England's naval problems in World War I, when searching for a reason for Admiral Troubridge's failure to pursue the German fleet. Had his sex life been in order, the admiral ... would have followed orders' (Marcus 1990, p. 175).

Chapter 2

1.   Reginald Rowe wrote a Foreword to Moberly Bell's biography of Octavia Hill (1942). This concludes: 'I maintain that the story of Octavia Hill should be known to the rising generation of every school ... to the greatness of our country the lives of its noblest men and women are the essential contributory leaven' (p. xiii). Throughout, he praises Hill's lifegiving capacity: she 'has sown seeds from which so much has grown and is still growing' (p. ix). Her triumph, in Rowe's terms was in humanising slum-dwellers, transforming the 'pig-like occupants into decent folk' (p. x).

2.   'Performative' refers to a kind of statement that performs with language the deed to which it refers. J.H. Miller (1991, p. 139) uses the example of a cheque which has no value as a piece of paper, the signing of which transforms it into the value inscribed on it. Originating in the ideas of Austin (1962), speech-act theory challenges the assumption that writing or speech consists solely of true or false statements. 'Constative' statements, which do report truly, or with attempt at truth, are contrasted to 'performatives', which are verbal actions rather than statements. For Derrida, the performative 'produces or transforms a situation' (1982, p. 322). This takes a percolutory view of language: an utterance has an effect on actions. This may be a different effect from that intended by the speaker's interlocutionary act.

3.   See Plummer 1981; Tiefer 1987; Kitzinger 1995, p. 138.

4.   *Jouissance/jouir*: 'Barthes himself declares the choice between pleasure and the more ravaging term, to be precarious, revocable, the discourse incomplete' (Richard Howard, Notes, in Barthes 1973). 'Pleasure is a state, of course, bliss/jouissance an action.'
      We can place the phrase in an arena of male-appropriation (both linguistic and in usage). *Jouir*: to enjoy, applied as a proprietorial sexual verb, man to woman, in Barthes' sense of (male) reader to (female) text. It has a nuance of possession, tenure (Harrap's *New Shorter French and English Dictionary*, London: Harrap, 1975): 'Avoir la jouissance/de certains droits/de ses biens; Maison à vendre avec jouissance immédiate; Jouissance de passage. Jouisseur: sensualist.' The term can be applied to a desire for the taking of a partially prohibited space or thing, aroused by the unsettling thrill of lesbian presence: Maison à vendre avec jouissance – peut-être?

5.   'She led the way for women in entertainment to start bringing down role stereotypes which then threw up questions about how people perceived gender-swapping and sexuality', Rose Collis, Review of Sara Maitland,

Vesta Tilley (London: Virago, 1986) in *City Limits*, 1–8 May 1986, Fawcett Library.

6. This suggests a sense of celibacy, and of the non-sexual, a common feature of lesbian representation.

7. Throughout *The Well of Loneliness*, hands feature in each erotic encounter (1928, pp. 14, 15, 26, 31, 182). Significantly, references are often combined with loss of words: 'Stephen bent down and kissed Mary's hands very humbly, for now she could find no words any more ... and that night they were not divided' (p. 316). Language of humility and of division, again, are common features of lesbian (self-) expression.

8. See Horner and Zlosnik 1998, Chapter 1, for discussion of the 'Disembodied Spirit' and the Gothic imagination, a study I read after I had written this piece, and which echoes my own thoughts.

9. The links between Enoch Powell's speeches and lesbian lives is discussed on pp. 61, 130–1.

10. See Horner and Zlosnik 1998, Chapter 5, for a discussion of 'foreignness' and du Maurier's fiction.

11. Andrea Dworkin has reclaimed the female earth: 'I love, cherish and respect women in my mind, in my heart, and in my soul. This love of women is the soil in which my life is rooted. It is the soil of our common life together. My life grows out of this soil. In any other soil, I would die. In whatever ways I am strong, I am strong because of the power and passion of this nurturant love' (Speech at Lesbian Pride, 28 June 1975, Central Park, New York City; published in *Our Blood*, 1976, Chapter 7). For discussion of the representation of Dworkin, see pp. 188–9.

12. See Curb and Manahan 1985; Jeffreys 1985; Raymond 1986; Auchmuty 1989; Johnson 1989; Card 1995, Chapter 5.

13. 'separated from you, but nevertheless haunted by you day and night, the caressing blue sea so unlike the unbridled grey waves of Polperro ... The nights of music and ineffable longing for you – I used to stand at the open window, between the music and the garden. And in the garden were irises which cast very black shadows, and sometimes I would catch my breath: *surely* that was a figure in a leopard-skin that darted out into the dappled moonlight ...' (14 July 1919, Sackville-West 1992, p. 151). Many of the lesbian images of self and other are contained in this letter of longing, see pp. 64–74.

14. In an interview, Irigaray expressed a view of homosexuality as arrested development: 'she feels that homosexuals somehow miss out on the possibilities of a more mystical union, a more developed stage of love. "If I am so far along a path, it does not stop," she explains. "I am walking along, I am a little child, and self-love should come here and homosexuality should come here," she gestures with her hands, "and the relationship with a different other should come here. But if I decided to stop at homosexuality, I would never know the following stages"' (Wallace 1998, p. 19).

15. Similar ideas of death and rebirth/self-birth are expressed by later twentieth-century lesbians (see pp. 140).

Chapter 3

1. Stein's titles suggest this fluidity of self and other: *The Autobiography of Alice B. Toklas* (1933) and *Everybody's Autobiography* (1937).

2. Woolf enjoyed Maurois's study of Disraeli, though she found Maurois himself disappointing when they met (2 April 1927, 25 May 1928, in 1975/90, vol. III, pp. 417, 501).

3. Virginia Woolf sought to reunify female (and lesbian) selves across time in the writing of *Orlando*, a biography of Sackville-West which draws on Anne Clifford as a model, herself disinherited from her northern family home and living in Knole, Kent, which Sackville-West sought to inherit (Hallett 1995). 'I might have been the ghost of Lady Anne Clifford', wrote Sackville-West. (16 May 1928, 1992, p. 196).

4. Lesbianism is frequently associated with ideas of 'sophistication' or lack of it; see pp. 87, 160, 162, 205, 208.

5. The references to hands, stride and gaze echo both Havelock Ellis (see p. 25) and descriptions of Elizabeth Bowen (see pp. 158, 171).

6. Cockin 1998, p. 216, wrongly claims that no obituary mentions Atwood.

7. *The Times*, 13 December 1952 (FL), listed those present at the funeral of Cicely Hamilton: Duchess of Atholl, Viscountess Rhondda, Lady Studd, Ashley Dukes (President of the Dramatist Club), Mrs Eliz. Abbott [author of another memoir of Hamilton, *WFL Bulletin* 9 January 1953, Fawcett Library], Miss Charlotte Marsh, Miss Goulden Bach (Suffragette Fellowship), Miss Marian Lawson, Miss A.M. Pierotti (NUW Teachers) with Miss B. M. Pearson and Miss R. Middleton, Miss Florence Barry (St Joan's Society and Political Alliance), Miss Theodora Bosanquet, Mr Frederick Sharp, Mr C.M. Trelawny Irving, Mr and Mrs Ruthuen Evans and Miss M. Reeves (Women's Freedom League).

8. Whitelaw (1990 p. 246) gives a different reference for this source, but the text appears to be the same.

9. *Morning Post*, 31 May 1916: 'A requiem mass for Mrs George Batten was held at the high altar in Westminster Cathedral at noon yesterday ... Amongst those present were the French Ambassador, the Marchioness of Anglesey, the Dowager Countess of Clarendon, Lady Frances Bourke, Lady Young, Lord Cecil Manners, Lady Arbuthnot, Mr and Mrs Austin Harris, Miss Radclyffe Hall ...' (Cline 1997, p. 131).

    The *Lady*, 10 June 1916: 'Her daughter Mrs Austin Harris was there with her husband and her tall young daughter Miss Honey Harris, and Mrs Batten's sisters Lady Clarendon, Mrs George Marjoribanks and Miss Hatch were all present as well as her nieces Mrs Burroughs and Miss Whitbread, and others I saw there were Miss Marguerite Radclyffe-Hall (who was one of her greatest friends), Admiral and Mrs Troubridge etc. ...' (Cline 1997, p. 131).

Chapter 4

1. Such an idea is implicit in Lilian Barker's mention of a girl's education as an activity of which parents should not feel ashamed (p. 94); and is more

explicit in Vita Sackville-West's reassuring letter to her husband about her previous relationship with Violet Trefusis and any potential one with Virginia Woolf: 'there is no muddle at all, anywhere! I keep on telling you so. PADLOCK! ...' (17 August 1926, Sackville-West 1992, p. 158).

2. Dogs feature frequently in lesbian iconography, throughout the century. 'For what else do women come into the world but to be good wives? ... Poor profitless, forlorn creatures they are, when they live single and get to be old; unless they are rich enough to keep up an establishment, with a parcel of dogs and cats and parrots' (Geraldine Jewsbury, *The Half Sisters*, 1848, cited in Oram 1989, p. 103). Photographs of du Maurier (discussed p. 181), of Edith Somerville (p. 207), of ordained lesbians (*Guardian*, 26 January 1998, p. 8) and a story about Ethel Smyth, on a walking tour of Cornwall in 1886 'with two friends and their retriever "Hurry"' (*Scilly-up-to-Date*, February/March 1992, Fawcett Library), as well as portraits by Romaine Brooks (discussed pp. 182–3) all represent lesbians in this way.

3. This story was subeditorially fixed on the page just above 'Family Notices'.

4. This appeared below an 'unconnected' photograph captioned 'One-night stand' of stockinged legs wearing designer shoes with a condom on each, proceeds of the sale of which were to go to the Terrence Higgins Trust for Aids research.

5. The military was exempted from the 1967 Sexual Offences Act, and those serving in the services faced prison sentences for homosexual acts. Homosexuality was decriminalised under the 1994 Criminal Justice Act, but lesbians and gay men still face discharge, irrespective of their service record.

6. Though the fact that it affected gay men precludes inclusion of the debate around the move to equalise the age of sexual consent, in June/July 1998, it is interesting to note that the main (stated) basis of opposition was in order to protect young men from corruption; that this was a phase they were going through; that they should learn the benefit of family life. On the same day (22 July 1998) that the House of Lords rejected the Bill, the government announced it was to establish a group for family and parenting. When the Bill received its second approval in the House of Commons in January/February 1999, it had a subsection added, to prohibit sexual relations of any kind between figures in authority (primarily teachers, social workers) and those under the age of 18 years.

7. The idea of heat, common in lesbian language of desire/destruction, is suggested, too, in the use of 'flame' for same-sex desire (see Vicinus 1984); and in reference to 'the leaping fires of my high school and college girl-friend crushes' (quoted in Curb and Manahan 1985, p. xxiv).

Chapter 5

1. The same phrase was used by Vita Sackville-West and Violet Trefusis to describe their own feelings (p. 58).

2. Peter Pan was also mentioned, of herself, in this context, by Violet Trefusis (Jullian and Phillips, 1976, p. 195).

3. Recently, in a second-hand bookshop, I came across a photograph of Edith Somerville, from *The Tatler, Sporting and Country House Supplement* (26 November 1913). She is in hunting gear, with a whip, surrounded by hounds. It is headlined 'Diana and the "Dogs", The Only Lady MFH in Ireland', and shows 'Miss E. Somerville, "Master" of the West Carbery Hounds ... a charming snapshot of ... the popular "master" ... In collaboration with her cousin "Martin Ross" (Miss Violet Martin ...) she has written many delightful books ... She is to be congratulated for giving excellent sport in such rough country as the picturesque west coast of Cork.'

4. A review of *Oranges Are Not the Only Fruit* referred to Jeanette Winterson as the 1990s Salman Rushdie (see Hinds 1995).

5. The Labour government's 'Supporting Families' Green Paper (launched 4 November 1998) also joins reference to single parents with lesbian motherhood.

6. Black women writers, too, on occasion, use such metaphors: for example, Toni Morrison's 'Rootedness: the ancestor as foundation' (1984) and Alice Walker's *In Search of Our Mother's Gardens* (1984). Perhaps this reflects/inverts observations made of black autobiographies, where the self is on the move, in transit, 'in a long, historic march toward Canaan' (Stephen Butterfield, *Black Autobiography in America*, Amherst: University of Massachusetts Press, 1974, p. 2, cited in Friedman 1988, p. 43).

Chapter 6

1. This is my own, previously unpublished, poem. Quotations are from a Ghanaian song, *A Formidable Foe*, on mosquitoes; a statement by the writer Alice Thomas Ellis (*Desert Island Discs*, BBC Radio 4, 3 April 1998); and Janet Flanner on herself (Castle 1993, p. 188).

2. Stanton is referring to Margaret, Duchess of Newcastle, who wrote of her own reasons for composing an autobiography: 'why hath this Lady writ her own life? ... I write for my own sake, not theirs; neither did I intend this piece for to delight, but to divulge; not to please the fancy but to tell the truth lest after-ages should mistake ... I was daughter to ... second wife to ... (1892, pp. 309–10).

3. Harriet Jacobs wrote: 'I was born a slave; but I never knew it till six years of happy childhood had passed away' (1861, p. 3). Fox-Genovese suggests that it was a common claim not to have identified one's condition, of race or slave, until around six or seven years of age. She cites Zora Neale Hurston, 'Ah was wid dem white chillun so much till Ah didn't know Ah wuzn't white till Ah was round six years old' (1937, 1978, p. 21, in Fox-Genovese 1988, pp. 75, 85). My own self-recognition, in retrospect, came at a similar age (see Hallett 1998).

4. For example, Collis 1994; Ainley 1995; Groocock 1995; Markowe 1996.

5. In Carol Ann Duffy's poem 'Recognition' (1987, pp. 24–5), a mature woman struggles with her own identity, and, metaphorically, 'goes to pieces' in a shop. Like de Beauvoir's woman, she has felt the coming of

age, and she looks at herself, as at a stranger, in a cold mirror: insight through non-recognition.

6. Manning (1987) quotes Adrienne Rich's poem to/of Willa Cather (pp. 168–9) and George Sand (p. 234), setting up her own means of escaping oblivion, via other women's words.

7. This has a similar effect to that in the treatment of Andrea Dworkin, see pp. 188–9.

8. Again, the association of lesbian with the unsophisticated is made, this time linked with the idea of 'simple colonial folk'.

9. The simple-minded women of Kent are the unsophisticated in Glendinning's *Vita* (pp. 348–9).

10. See Sackville-West 1961, Wittig 1975.

11. 'Square pegs fit into round holes if we change their entire shape or force them in. This alteration or forcing changes the nature, the very essence of the peg ... I have learned to love being a square peg in a square hole ...' (Heather Savage in Healey and Mason 1994, p. 59).

12. The dissonance within the title (woman/John) is discussed on p. 182.

Chapter 7

1. Authenticity is doubted within the visualised of modernity, see p. 106.

2. This was a view which Boffin exploited when she used photography to document fantasy, see p. 192–3.

3. 'Lipstick' as a prefix suggests inauthenticity, and also redeemability, since the lesbian state may be temporary.

4. Photographs by Eve Arnold of a lesbian wedding suggest, perhaps, a similar counterdiscourse (Arnold and Morath 1996, No. 30).

5. Sackville-West wrote to Woolf, on receipt of the published *Orlando*: 'you have invented a new form of Narcissism, – I confess, – I am in love with Orlando – this is a complication I had not foreseen ...' (11 October 1928, in Sackville-West 1985, p. 289). Townsend Warner and Ackland were found together: 'Seeing us sitting up in my bed Mrs Wray exclaimed affectionately "twins!"' (11 November 1930, in Harman 1995, p. 74).

6. 'The task [of writing the screenplay] was given to an elderly novelist, Penelope Mortimer, the mother-in-law of one of the producers' (Sackville-West 1973, p. 3).

7. The article was subeditorially arranged opposite an advertisement for cider, which showed a four-part portrait, spliced together: a lizard as the top of the head, human eyes behind tinted glasses, a cat's mouth with whiskers, and a neck and shoulders with a jacket and bowtie (*Guardian Weekend*, 22 July 1995, p. 17).

Conclusions

1. 'Only women can give to each other a new sense of self. That identity we have to develop with reference to ourselves, and not in relation to men ... Our energies must flow towards our sisters, not backward towards our oppressors ...' (Echols 1989, p. 216).

2.   'If oppression is to be defined in terms of loss of autonomy by the oppressed, as well as a fragmentation or alienation within the psyche of the oppressed, then a theory which insists upon the inevitable fragmentation of the subject appears to reproduce and valorize the very oppression that must be overcome' (Butler 1990, p. 327).

3.   Virginia Woolf parodies her own 'Time Passes' section of *To the Lighthouse* (1927) in *Orlando* (1928, p. 94).

Bibliography

Abelove, H. (1993) 'A letter from Freud', in Henry Abelove, Michele Aina Barale and David Halperin (eds), *The Lesbian and Gay Studies Reader* (New York: Routledge) pp. 381–93.

Ackland, V. (1949, rep. 1985) *For Sylvia: An Honest Account* (London: Chatto & Windus).

Ainley, R. (1995) *What Is She Like? Lesbian Identities from the 1950s to the 1990s* (London: Cassell).

Allen, S.M. (1925) *The Pioneer Policewoman* (London: Chatto & Windus).

Alpers, A. (1980, rep. 1982) *The Life of Katherine Mansfield* (Oxford: Oxford University Press).

The American Heritage Dictionary of the English Language (3rd edn, 1992) (Boston, MA: Houghton Mifflin and Co.).

Arnold, E. and Morath, I. (1996) *Women to Women* (Tokyo: Magnum Photos).

Auchmuty, R. (1989) 'By their friends shall we know them: the lives and networks of some women in North Lambeth, 1880–1940', in Lesbian History Group, *Not A Passing Phase, Reclaiming Lesbians in History 1840–1985* (London: The Women's Press) pp. 77–98.

—— (1992) *A World of Girls* (London: The Women's Press).

Auchmuty, R., Jeffreys, S. and Miller, E. (1992) 'Lesbian history and gay studies: keeping a feminist perspective', *Women's History Review*, 1, 1, 89–108.

Aughterson, K. (ed.) (1995) *Renaissance Woman: A Sourcebook, Constructions of Femininity in England* (London & New York: Routledge).

Austin, J.L. (1962, re-ed. 1975) *How to Do Things with Words*, 2nd edn, ed. Marina Sbisa and J.O. Urmson (Cambridge, MA: Harvard University Press).

Baker, M. (1985) *Our Three Selves, A Life of Radclyffe Hall* (London: Hamish Hamilton).

Ballaster, R. (1995) '"The Vices of Old Rome Revived": Representations of female same-sex desire in seventeenth and eighteenth century England', in Suzanne Raitt (ed.), *Volcanoes and Pearl Divers, Essays in Lesbian Feminist Studies* (London: Onlywomen Press) pp. 13–36.

Banks-Smith, N. (1996) 'Enid Blyton: my life with Noddy and Big Ears', *Guardian*, 17 December 1996, p. 9.

Barthes, R. (1968, trans. 1977) 'The death of the author', in *Image, Music, Text* (London: Flamingo) pp. 142–8.

—— (1970, rep. 1990) *S/Z*, trans. Richard Miller (Oxford: Blackwell).

—— (1973, rep. 1975) *The Pleasure of the Text*, trans. Richard Miller (New York: Hill and Wang).

—— (1981) *Camera Lucida* (London: Jonathan Cape).

—— (1990) *A Lover's Discourse: Fragments*, trans. R. Howard (London: Penguin Books).

Bartky, S.L. (1988) 'Foucault, femininity and the modernization of patriarchal power', in Irene Diamond and Lee Quinby (eds), *Feminism and Foucault: Reflections on Resistance* (Boston, MA: Northeastern University Press).

Bartlett, N. (1994) 'Troublesome visibilities: reviewing Queer strategies in contemporary theory and culture', unpublished paper, St Martin's College, London, April 1994 (cited in Smyth 1996, p. 109).

Barzun, J. (1939) 'Truth in biography: Berlioz', *University Review: A Journal of the University of Kansas, 5*, 80.

Battaille, G., (1962, rep. 1986) *Eroticism: Death and Sensuality*, trans. Mary Dalwood (San Francisco, CA: City Light Books).

Becker, H.S. and Horowitz, I.L. (1972) 'Radical politics and sociological research: observations on methodology and ideology', *American Journal of Sociology, 78*, 48–66.

Bell, E.M. (1942, rep. 1946) *Octavia Hill, A Biography* (London: Constable & Co.).

Bell, Q. (1972) *Virginia Woolf* (New York: Harcourt, Brace).

Benson, E.F. (1932) *Charlotte Brontë* (London: Longmans Green).

Benstock, S. (1987, rep. 1994) *Women of the Left Bank, Paris 1900–1940* (London: Virago).

—— (1988) 'Authorizing the autobiographical', in Shari Benstock (ed.), *The Private Self, Theory and Practice of Women's Autobiographical Writings* (Chapel Hill, NC & London: University of North Carolina Press) pp. 10–34.

—— (1990) 'Expatriate Sapphic modernism: entering literary history', in Karla Jay and Joanne Glasgow (eds), *Lesbian Texts and Contexts: Radical Revisions* (London: Onlywomen Press, 1992) pp. 183–203.

Berry, P. and Bostridge, M. (1995) *Vera Brittain: A Life* (London: Chatto & Windus).

Bertens, H. (1995) *The Idea of the Postmodern* (London & New York: Routledge).

Birken, L. (1988) *Consuming Desire: Sexual Science and the Emergence of a Culture of Abundance, 1871–1914* (Ithaca, NY: Cornell University Press).

Blackburn, R. (1980) 'In search of the Black Female Self: African-American Women's Autobiographies and ethnicity', in Estelle C. Jelinek (ed.), *Women's Autobiography: Essays in Criticism* (Bloomington, IN: Indiana University Press) pp. 133–48.

Bloch, I. (1908) *The Sexual Life of Our Time in Its Relations to Modern Civilization* (New York: Allied Book Company).

Boddy, G. (1988) *Katherine Mansfield, The Woman and the Writer* (Harmondsworth: Penguin Books).

Boffin, T. (1991) 'The Knight's Move', in Tessa Boffin and Jean Fraser (eds), *Stolen Glances, Lesbians Take Photographs* (London: Pandora) pp. 42–50.

Bowen, E. (1971) Review of *Katherine Mansfield: The Memoirs of L.M.* (London: Michael Joseph), *Sunday Times*, 4 July 1971 (Fawcett Library).

Brabazon, J. (1988) *Dorothy L. Sayers* (London: Gollancz).

Braxton, J.M. (1988) 'Charlotte Forten Grimké and the search for a public voice', in Shari Benstock (ed.), *The Private Self, Theory and Practice of Women's Autobiographical Writings* (Chapel Hill, NC & London: University of North Carolina Press) pp. 254–71.

Brimstone, L. (1991) 'Towards a new cartography: Radclyffe Hall, Virginia Woolf and the working of common land', in Elaine Hobby and Chris White (eds), *What Lesbians Do In Books* (London: The Women's Press) pp. 86–107.

Bristow, J. (1997) *Sexuality* (London & New York: Routledge).

Brittain, V. (1935, rep. 1985) *Testament of a Generation: the Journalism of Vera Brittain and Winifred Holtby* (London: Virago).

—— (1940, rep. 1980) *Testament of Friendship* (London: Fontana/ Virago).

Brodzki, B. (1988), 'Mother, displacement and language in the Autobiographies of Nathalie Sarrante and Christa Wolff', in Bella Brodzki and Celeste Schenck (eds), *Life/Lines, Theorizing Women's Autobiography* (Ithaca, NY & London: Cornell University Press) pp. 243–59.

Brontë, C. (1847, rep. 1976) *Jane Eyre* (Harmondsworth: Penguin Books).

Brooks, R. (1997) 'So Big Ears and Mr. Plod were stooges of the state regime ... ', *Observer*, 2 March 1997, p. 10.

Brossard, N. (1988) *The Ariel Letter*, trans. Marlene Wildeman (Toronto: The Women's Press).

Broster, L.R., and Vines, H.W.C. (eds) (1938) *The Adrenal Cortex and Intersexuality* (London: Chapman and Hall).

Browett, E. (ed.) (1979) *The King's High School, Warwick, 1879–1979, A Portrait* (Kineton: The Roundwood Press).

Brown, J.C. (1984, rep. 1985) 'Lesbian sexuality in Renaissance Italy: the case of Sister Benedetta Carlini', in Estelle B. Freedman, Barbara C. Gelpi, Susan L. Johnson and Kathleen M. Weston (eds), *The Lesbian Issue, Essays from Signs* (Chicago, IL & London: University of Chicago Press) pp. 271–8.

—— (1986) *Immodest Acts: Life of a Lesbian Nun in Renaissance Italy* (Oxford: Oxford University Press).

Brown, L.S. (1995) 'Lesbian identities: concepts and issues', in Anthony R. D'Augelli and Charlotte J. Patterson (eds), *Lesbian, Gay and Bisexual Identities Over the Lifespan, Psychological Perspectives* (Oxford & New York: Oxford University Press) pp. 3–23.

Buikema, R. and Smelik, A. (1993) *Women's Studies and Culture, A Feminist Introduction* (London & New Jersey: Zed Books).

Butler, J. (1990) *Gender Trouble: Feminism and the Subversion of Identity* (New York & London: Routledge).

—— (1991) 'Imitation and gender subordination', in Diana Fuss (ed.), *Inside/Out: Lesbian Theories, Gay Theories* (New York & London: Routledge) pp. 13–31.

—— (1993a) *Bodies That Matter: On the Discursive Elements of 'Sex'* (London & New York: Routledge).

—— (1993b) 'Critically queer', *Gay & Lesbian Quarterly, 1, 1,* 17–32.

Butler, K. (1997) 'Speed freak', review of Kate Summerscale, *The Queen of Whale Cay: The Eccentric Story of 'Joe' Carstairs, Fastest Woman on Water* (1997) (London: Fourth Estate), *Pink Paper*, 25 July 1997, p. 17.

Butler, M. (1998) 'Simplicity', review of David Nokes, *Jane Austen: A Life* (1997) (London: Fourth Estate), *London Review of Books*, 5 March 1998, pp. 3–6.

Bygrave, S. (1996) *Romantic Writings* (London: The Open University).

Calder, J. (1976) *Women and Marriage in Victorian Fiction* (London: Thames & Hudson).

Card, C. (1995) 'Lesbian friendships: separations and continua', in Claudia Card (ed.), *Lesbian Choices* (New York: Columbia University Press) pp. 83–105.

Cardus, N. (1967) 'Mistress of music', *Guardian*, 11 October 1967 (Fawcett Library).

Carey, H.R. (1928) 'This two-headed monster – the family', *Harpers Magazine*, January 1928, pp. 162–71.

Carey, J. (1992) *The Intellectuals and The Masses, Pride and Prejudice Among the Literary Intelligentsia 1880–1939* (London & Boston, MA: Faber and Faber).

Carlston, E.G. (1997) '"A finer differentiation", female homosexuality and the American medical community 1926–1940', in Vernon A. Rosario (ed.), *Science and Homosexualities* (London & New York: Routledge) pp. 177–96.

Carpenter, E. (1908) *The Intermediate Sex: A Study of Some Transitional Types of Men and Women* (London: Sonnenschein).

—— and Bax, D. (1921) Prefaces to Edith Ellis, *The New Horizon in Love and Life* (London: A.&C. Black).

Carter, A. (1979) *The Sadeian Woman: An Exercise in Cultural History* (London: Virago).

—— (1980) 'The Language of Sisterhood', in *The State of the Language* (London: Virago).

Carter, J. (1997) 'Normality, whiteness, authorship: evolutionary sexology and the primitive pervert' in Vernon A. Rosario (ed.), *Science and Homosexualities* (London & New York: Routledge) pp. 155–76.

Casdagli, P. (1995) 'The whole nine yards', in Suzanne Raitt (ed.), *Volcanoes and Pearl Divers, Essays in Lesbian Feminist Studies* (London: Onlywomen Press) pp. 263–88.

Cass, V.C. (1979) 'Homosexual identity formation: a theoretical model', *Journal of Homosexuality*, 4, 219–36.

Castle, T. (1993) *The Apparitional Lesbian: Female Homosexuality and Modern Culture* (New York: Columbia University Press).

—— (1993, rep. 1997) 'Sylvia Townsend Warner and the counterplot of lesbian fiction', in Robyn R. Warhol and Diane Price Herndl (eds), *Feminisms, An Anthology of Literary Theory and Criticism* (Basingstoke: Macmillan) pp. 532–54.

—— (1995) *The Female Thermometer, Eighteenth Century Culture and the Invention of the Uncanny* (Oxford & New York: Oxford University Press).

—— (1996) *Noel Coward and Radclyffe Hall, Kindred Spirits* (New York: Columbia University Press).

—— (1998) 'If everybody had a Wadley', review of Kate Summerscale, *The Queen of Whale Cay: The Eccentric Story of 'Joe' Carstairs, Fastest Woman on Water* (1997) (London: Fourth Estate), *London Review of Books*, 5 March 1998, pp. 10–12.

Chalon, J. (1979) *Portrait of a Seductress: The World of Natalie Barney*, trans. Carol Barko (New York: Crown).

Chambers English Dictionary (1990) (Edinburgh, New York, Toronto: W.&R. Chambers Ltd).

Chideckel, M. (1935) *Female Sex Perversion: the Sexually Aberrated Woman as She Is* (New York: Eugenics Publishing Co.).

Child, L.M. (1843) Letter 34, January 1843, in *Letters from New York, I* (New York: Walter Teller).

Chisholm, A. (1979) *Nancy Cunard* (London: Sidgwick & Jackson).

Chodorow, N. (1978) *The Reproduction of Mothering: Psychoanalysis and the Sociology of Gender* (Berkeley, CA: University of California Press).

Cicero, M.T. (ed.) (1992) *Essays on Friendship and Old Age*, trans. Cyrus R. Edmunds (New York: Translation Publishing Co.).

Cixous, H. (1981) 'Castration or Decapitation', *Signs*, 7, 1 (Autumn) 36–55.

Clark, V. (1996) 'Passions roused as Trollope's torrid tale becomes a real-village affair', *Observer*, 15 December 1996, p. 9.

Cline, S. (1997) *Radclyffe Hall, A Woman Called John* (London: John Murray).

CLIT Collective (1974) 'CLIT Statement No. 2' reprinted in Sarah Lucia-Hoagland and Julia Penelope (eds), *For Lesbians Only: A Separatist Anthology* (London: Onlywomen Press).

Cockin, K. (1998) *Edith Craig (1869–1947) Dramatic Lives* (London & Washington DC: Cassell).

Colette (1932) *The Pure and the Impure*, trans. Herma Briffault (New York: Farrar, Straus & Giroux).

Colmore, G. (1913, rep. 1988) *The Life of Emily Davison*, rep. in Ann Morley with Liz Stanley, *The Life and Death of Emily Wilding Davison* (London: The Women's Press).

Collis, M. (1968) *Somerville and Ross, A Biography* (London: Faber and Faber).

Collis, R. (1994) *Portraits to the Wall, Historic Lesbian Lives Unveiled* (London: Cassell).

—— (1997) *A Trouser-Wearing Character, The Life and Times of Nancy Spain* (London: Cassell).

Colquhoun, M. (1980) *A Woman in the House* (London: Scan Books).

Connor, S. (1997) 'The modern auditory I', in Roy Porter (ed.), *Rewriting the Self, Histories from the Renaissance to the Present* (London & New York: Routledge) pp. 203–23.

Cook, B.W. (1979) '"Women alone stir my imagination": lesbianism and the cultural tradition', *Signs*, 4, 718–39.

Cooper, E. (1996) 'Queer spectacles', in Peter Horne and Reina Lewis (eds), *Outlooks, Lesbian and Gay Sexualities and Visual Cultures* (London & New York: Routledge) pp. 13–27.

Corinne, T. (1991) 'Portraits', in Tessa Boffin and Jean Fraser (eds), *Stolen Glances, Lesbians Take Photographs* (London: Pandora) pp. 223–8.

Craig, P. (1986) *Elizabeth Bowen* (Harmondsworth: Penguin Books).

Cruikshank, M. (1986) 'A note on May Sarton', in Monika Kehoe (ed.), *Historical, Literary and Erotic Aspects of Lesbianism* (New York & London: Harrington Park Press) pp. 153–5.

Culler, J. (1983) *Barthes* (Glasgow: Fontana).

Cullingford, E. (1993) *Gender and History in Yeats' Love Poetry* (Cambridge: Cambridge University Press).

Curb, R. and Manahan, N. (1985, rep. 1993) *Lesbian Nuns, Breaking Silence* (London: The Women's Press).

D'Emilio, J. (1992) 'Capitalism and gay identity', in John D'Emilio (ed.), *Making Trouble: Essays on Gay History, Politics and the University* (New York: Routledge).

Dane, C. (1917, rep. 1966) *Regiment of Women* (London: Heinemann).

Darwin, C. (1859) *On the Origin of Species by Means of Natural Selection, or the Preservation of Favoured Races in the Struggle for Life* (London: John Murray).

—— (1871) *The Descent of Man, and Selection in Relation to Sex*, 2 volumes (London: John Murray).

Davidson, B. (1978) *Africa in Modern History: The Search for a New Society* (London: Allen Lane).

De Acosta, M. (1928) *Until the Day Break* (New York: Longmans).

—— (1960) *Here Lies the Heart* (London: Andre Deutsch).

de Beauvoir, S. (1949) *The Second Sex* (Harmondsworth: Penguin Books).

—— (1972) *The Coming of Age*, trans. Patrick O'Brian (New York: Warner).

Dekker, R. and van de Pol, L. (1989) *The Tradition of Female Transvestism in Early Modern Europe* (London: Macmillan).

de Lauretis, T. (1994) *The Practice of Love: Lesbian Sexuality and Perverse Desire* (Bloomington & Indianapolis: Indiana University Press).

Dellamora, R. (1996) 'Absent bodies/absent subjects: *the political unconscious of postmodernism'*, in Peter Horne and Reina Lewis (eds), *Outlooks, Lesbian and Gay Sexualities and Visual Cultures* (London & New York: Routledge) pp. 28–47.

Delman, R. (1980) 'Afterword' to Vera Brittain (1940, rep. 1980) *Testament of Friendship* (London: Fontana/Virago).

DeLombard, J. (1998) 'Drawing from the Well', review of Sally Cline, *Radclyffe Hall: A Woman Called John* (1997) (London: John Murray) *Guardian Weekly*, 1 March 1998.

de Man, P. (1979) 'Autobiography as De-Facement', *Modern Language Notes, 94*, pp. 919–30.

Derrida, J. (1976) *Of Grammatolgy*, trans. G.C. Spivak (Baltimore, MD: Johns Hopkins University Press).

—— (1982) *Margins of Philosophy*, trans. Alan Bass (Brighton: Harvester Press).

—— (1983) *On Deconstruction: Theory and Criticism After Structuralism* (London: Routledge Kegan Paul).

DeSalvo, L.A. (1982) 'Lighting the cave: the relationship between Vita Sackville-West and Virginia Woolf', *Signs, 8*, 195–214.

Deutsch, H. (1933) 'Homosexuality in women', *International Journal of Psycho-Analysis, 14*, 34–56.

—— (1944) *The Psychology of Women* (New York: Grune & Stratton).

Dexter, B. (1983) 'Literary Paris is given life', review of Noel Riley Fitch (1983) *Sylvia Beach and the Lost Generation: A History of Literary Paris in the 20s and 30s* (New York: Norton), *San Diego Union*, 10 July 1983, p. 14.

Diamond, E. (1990/91) 'Realism and hysteria: notes towards a feminist mimesis', *Discourse, 13, 1*, 59–92.

—— (1995) 'The shudder of catharsis in twentieth-century performance', in Andrew Parker and Eve Kosofsky Sedgwick (eds), *Performativity and Performance* (New York & London: Routledge) pp. 152–73.

Dickinson, R.L. and Beam, L. (1934) *The Single Woman: A Medical Study in Sex Education* (London: Williams & Norgate).

Dickson, L. (1975) *Radclyffe Hall at the Well of Loneliness: A Sapphic Chronicle* (London: Collins).

Docherty, T. (1996) *Alterities, Criticism, History, Representation* (Oxford: Clarendon Press).

Dollimore, J. (1986) 'The dominant and the deviant: a violent dialectic', *Critical Quarterly, 28*, 179–92.

—— (1991, rep. 1995) *Sexual Dissidence: Augustine to Wilde, Freud to Foucault* (Oxford: Clarendon Press).

Donoghue, E. (1993, rep.1994) *Passions Between Women: British Lesbian Culture 1668–1801* (London: Scarlet Press).

—— (ed.), (1997) *What Sappho Would Have Said, Four Centuries of Love Poems Between Women* (London: Hamish Hamilton).

Duffy, C.A. (1987, rep. 1992) *Selling Manhattan* (London: Anvil Press).

du Maurier, A. (1966) *Old Maids Remember* (London: Peter Davis).

du Maurier, D. (1938, rep. 1992) *Rebecca* (London: Arrow).

Duncan, A. (1998) Interview with Anna Friel, *Radio Times*, 14–20 March 1998, pp. 14–16.

DuPlessis, R.B. (1990) *The Pink Guitar: Writing as Feminist Practice* (London: Routledge).

Durham, M. (1991) *Sex and Politics: The Family and Morality in the Thatcher Years* (London: Macmillan).

During, S. (1993, rep. 1994) 'Introduction', in Simon During (ed.), *The Cultural Studies Reader* (London & New York: Routledge) pp. 1–25.

Eakin, P.J. (1985) *Fictions in Autobiography: Studies in the Art of Self: Invention* (Princeton, NJ: Princeton University Press).

Echols, A. (1989) *Daring to Be Bad: Radical Feminism in America 1967–1975* (Minneapolis, MN: University of Minnesota Press).

Elliott, B. and Wallace, J.-A. (1994) *Women Artists and Writers, Modernist (Im)positionings* (London & New York: Routledge).

Ellis, D. (ed.) (1993) *Imitating Art, Essays in Biography* (London & Boulder, CO: Pluto Press).

Ellis, E. (1921) *The New Horizon in Love and Life* (London: A.&C. Black).

—— (1924) *Stories and Essays I* (New York: Free Spirit Press).

Ellis, H. (1895) 'Sexual inversion in women', *Alienist and Neurologist, 16*, 141–58.

—— (1904) *A Study of British Genius* (London: Hurst & Blackett).

—— ([1897]1910, rep. 1936) *Studies in the Psychology of Sex*, 4 volumes (New York: Random House).

—— (1931) 'Introduction', in R.L. Dickinson and L. Beam, *A Thousand Marriages: A Medical Study in Sex Adjustment* (Baltimore, MD: Williams & Wilkins).

—— (1940) *My Life* (London: Heinemann).

Ettorre, E. (1980) *Lesbians, Women and Society* (London: Routledge).

Evans, M. (1993) 'Masculine and feminine biography', in David Ellis (ed.), *Imitating Art, Essays in Biography* (London & Boulder, CO: Pluto Press) pp. 108–23.

Faderman, L. (1981, rep. 1985) *Surpassing the Love of Men: Romantic Friendship and Love Between Women from the Renaissance to the Present* (London: The Women's Press).

—— (1985) *Scotch Verdict* (London: Quartet).

—— (1986) 'Love between women in 1928: why progressivism is not always progress', in Monika Kehoe (ed.), *History, Literature and Erotic Aspects of Lesbianism* (New York & London: Harrington Plc. Press) pp. 23–42.

Fanon, F. (1967) *The Wretched of the Earth*, trans. Constance Farrington (Harmondsworth: Penguin Books).

Feinstein, H. (1998) 'Tie me up, tie me down', *Guardian*, 13 March 1998, pp. 2–3.

Felski, R. (1989, rep. 1998) 'On confession', in Sidonie Smith and Julia Watson (eds), *Women, Autobiography, Theory* (Wisconsin, WI & London: University of Wisconsin Press) pp. 83–95.

Ferguson, A. (1981) 'Patriarchy, sexual identity and the sexual revolution', *Signs, 14, 1* (Autumn), 159–72.

Finlayson, I. (1986) *The Sixth Continent: A Literary History of Romney Marsh* (New York: Atheneum).

Findlater, R. (1975) *Lilian Baylis, The Lady of the Old Vic* (London: Allen Lane).

Fitch, N.R. (1983) *Sylvia Beach and the Lost Generation: A History of Literary Paris in the 20s and 30s* (New York: Norton).

—— (1990) 'The elusive "seamless whole": a biographer treats (or fails to treat) lesbianism', in Karla Jay and Joanne Glasgow (eds), *Lesbian Texts and Contexts: Radical Revisions* (London: Onlywomen Press, 1992) pp. 59–69.

Florence, P. (1995) 'Portrait of a production', in Tamsin Wilton (ed.), *Immortal, Invisible: Lesbians and the Moving Image* (London & New York: Routledge) pp. 115–30.

Forster, M. (1993, rep. 1994) *Daphne du Maurier* (London: Arrow).

Foster, J. (1958, rep. 1985) *Sex-Variant Women in Literature* (Florida: The Naiad Press).

Foucault, M. (1972) 'What is an author?', in Donald Bouchard (ed.), *Language, Counter-Memory, Practice* (Oxford: Blackwell, 1977) pp. 113–38.

—— (1977) *Language, Counter-Memory, Practice: Selected Essays and Interviews*, ed. D.F. Bouchard (Oxford: Blackwel).

—— (1978) *The History of Sexuality, Volume 1: An Introduction*, trans. Robert Hurley (New York: Random House).

—— (1985) *The History of Sexuality, Volume 2: The Use of Pleasure*, trans. Robert Hurley (New York: Random House).

—— (1986) *The History of Sexuality, Volume 3: The Care of the Self*, trans. Robert Hurley (New York: Random House).

—— (1993, rep. 1994) 'Space, power, knowledge', in Simon During (ed.), *The Cultural Studies Reader* (London & New York: Routledge) pp. 161–9.

Fox-Genovese, E. (1988) 'My statue, my self: autobiographical writings of Afro-American women', in Shari Benstock (ed.), *The Private Self, Theory and Practice of Women's Autobiographical Writings* (Chapel Hill, NC & London: University of North Carolina Press) pp. 63–89.

Frandenburg, L. and Freccero, C. (eds) (1996) *Premodern Sexualities* (London & New York: Routledge).

Fraser, R. (1988) *Charlotte Brontë* (London: Methuen).

Freely, M. (1994) 'Mirroring the difference', Review of Diana Souhami, *Greta and Cecil* (1994, rep. 1996) (London: Flamingo), *Observer Review*, 2 October 1994, p. 20.

Freud, S. (1905) *Three Essays on the Theory of Sexuality*, rep. *Standard Edition*, vol. 7 (London: Hogarth Press).

—— (1914) 'On narcissism', rep. *Standard Edition*, Vol. 14. (London: Hogarth Press).

—— (1926) 'The quest of lay analysis, Part 4', rep. *Standard Edition*, Vol. 20 (London: Hogarth Press).

—— (1953–73) *The Standard Edition of the Complete Psychological Works of Sigmund Freud*, 24 volumes, trans. James Strachey *et al.* (London: Hogarth Press).

Friedman, S.S. (1987) 'Creativity and the childbirth metaphor', *Feminist Studies,* *13,* 49–82.

—— (1988) 'Women's autobiographical selves: theory and practice', in Shari Benstock (ed.), *The Private Self, Theory and Practice of Women's Autobiographical Writings* (Chapel Hill, NC & London: University of North Carolina Press) pp. 34–62.

Frye, M. (1983) *The Politics of Reality: Essays in Feminist Theory* (New York: Crossing Press).

Fuseli, H. (1801, rep. 1831) 'On the present state of art, and the causes which check its progress' and 'Aphorisms on art', in J. Knowles, *The Life and Writings of Henry Fuseli* (London) pp. 40–52, 98–146.

Fuss, D. (1989) *Essentially Speaking: Feminism, Nature and Difference* (New York: Routledge).

—— (ed.) (1991) *Inside/Out: Lesbian Theories, Gay Theories* (London: Routledge) .

Gagnon, J. (1977) *Human Sexualities* (Glenview, IL: Scott, Foresman & Co.).

Gagnon, J. and Simon, W. (1973) *Sexual Conduct: The Social Sources of Human Sexuality* (New York: Aldine de Gruyter).

Gallichan, W. (1927) *Sexual Apathy and Coldness in Women* (London: T. Werner Laurie).

Gerrard, N. (1998) 'A happy childhood recalling in anguish', review of Katrin Fitzherbert, *True to Both My Selves* (London: Virago 1998), *Guardian Weekly,* 18 January 1998, p. 28.

Gibbs, L. (ed.) (1994) *Daring to Dissent, Lesbian Culture from Margin to Mainstream* (London: Cassell).

Gibson, M. (1997) 'Clitoral corruption: body metaphors and American doctors' constructions of female homosexuality 1870–1900', in Vernon A. Rosario (ed.), *Science and Homosexualities* (New York & London: Routledge) pp. 108–32.

Gilbert, S. and Gubar, S. (1979) *The Madwoman in the Attic* (New Haven, CT: Yale University Press).

—— (1989) *No Man's Land: The Place of the Woman Writer in the Twentieth Century,* Volume 2: *SexChanges* (New Haven, CT: Yale University Press).

Gill, B. (1972) *Tallulah* (New York: Holt, Rinehart & Winston).

Gilmore, L. (1994) *Autobiographics, A Feminist Theory of Women's Self-Representation* (Ithaca, NY & London: Cornell University Press).

Glasgow, J. (1992) 'What's a nice lesbian like you doing in the Church of Torquemada? Radclyffe Hall and Other Catholic Converts', in Karla Jay and Joanne Glasgow (eds), *Lesbian Texts and Contexts: Radical Revisions* (London: Onlywomen Press).

Glendinning, V. (1977, rep. 1993) *Elizabeth Bowen, Portrait of a Writer* (London: Phoenix).

—— (1983) 'On the mystery of marriage and the glamorous ambiguities of Vita', Interview, *Sunday Times,* 25 September 1983 (Fawcett Library).

—— (1983, rep. 1984) *Vita, the Life of V. Sackville-West* (London: Penguin Books).

Gombrich, E.H. (1960, rep. 1980) *Art and Illusion: A Study in the Psychology of Pictorial Representation* (Oxford: Oxford University Press).

—— (1967, rep. 1979) 'In search of cultural history', in *Ideals and Idols: Essays on Values in History and Art* (Oxford: Phaidon) pp. 24–59.

—— (1968) 'Style', in David L. Sills (ed.), *International Encyclopaedia of the Social Sciences, 15,* pp. 352–60.

—— (1974, rep. 1979) 'The logic of Vanity Fair: alternatives to historicism in the study of fashions, style and taste', in *Ideals and Idols: Essays on Values in History and Art* (Oxford: Phaidon) pp. 60–92.

Gonsiorek, J.C. (1995) 'Gay male identities: concepts and issues', in Anthony R. D'Augelli and Charlotte J. Patterson (eds), *Lesbian, Gay and Bisexual Identities Over the Lifespan, Psychological Perspectives* (Oxford & New York: Oxford University Press) pp. 24–47.

Gordon, L. (1984) *Virginia Woolf. A Woman's Life* (Oxford: Oxford University Press).

Gore, E. (1965) *The Better Fight: The Story of Dame Lilian Barker* (London: G. Bles).

Graham, E. , Hinds, H., Hobby, E. and Wilcox, H. (eds) (1989, rep. 1996) *Her Own Life: Autobiographical Writings by Seventeenth Century Englishwomen* (London & New York: Routledge).

Gramsci, A. (1985) *Selections from Cultural Writings*, ed. David Forgacs and Geoffrey Nowell-Smith, trans. William Boelhower (London: Lawrence & Wishart).

Greer, G. (1979) *The Obstacle Race: The Fortunes of Women Painters and Their Work* (London: Secker & Warburg).

Griffin, G. (1991) '*The Chinese Garden*, a cautionary tale', in Elaine Hobby and Chris White (eds), *What Lesbians Do in Books* (London: The Women's Press) pp. 134–54.

—— (ed.) (1993a) *Outwrite, Lesbianism and Popular Culture* (London & Boulder, CO: Pluto Press).

—— (1993b) *Heavenly Love? Lesbian Images in Twentieth-Century Women's Writing* (Manchester & New York: Manchester University Press).

Groocock, V. (1995) *Changing Our Lives, Lesbian Passions, Politics, Priorities* (London: Cassell).

Grover, J.Z. (1991) 'Framing the questions: positive imaging and scarcity in lesbian photographs', in Tessa Boffin and Jean Fraser (eds), *Stolen Glances, Lesbians Take Photographs* (London: Pandora Press) pp. 184–96.

Gupta, S. (1996) 'Culture wars: race and queer art', in Peter Horne and Reina Lewis (eds), *Outlooks, Lesbian and Gay Sexualities and Visual Cultures* (London & New York: Routledge) pp. 170–7.

Gusdorf, G. (1980) 'Conditions and limits of autobiography', in James Olney (ed.), *Autobiography: Essays Theoretical and Critical* (Princeton, NJ: Princeton University Press) pp. 28–48.

Hall, R. (1928, rep. 1981) *The Well of Loneliness,* ed. Alison Hennegan (London: Virago).

Hall, S. (1990) 'Cultural identity and diaspora', in J. Rutherford (ed.), *Identity: Community Culture Difference* (London: Lawrence & Wishart).

Hallett, N.A. (1995) 'Anne Clifford as Orlando: Virginia Woolf's feminist historiology and women's biography', *Women's History Review, 4, 4,* 505–24.

—— (1998) 'Reading and writing auto/biography: the displacement of lesbian subtexts', *Women: A Cultural Review, 9, 2,* 158–64.

Hamer, D. (1994) 'Netting the press: playing with Martina', in Diane Hamer and Belinda Budge (eds), *The Good, the Bad and the Gorgeous, Popular Culture's Romance with Lesbianism* (London: Pandora) pp. 57–77.

Hamer, E. (1996) *Britannia's Glory, A History of Twentieth-Century Lesbians* (London: Cassell).

Hamilton, C. (1909) *Marriage as a Trade* (London: Chapman and Hall).

Hanscombe, G. (1991) 'Katherine Mansfield's pear tree', in Elaine Hobby and Chris White (eds), *What Lesbians Do in Books* (London: The Women's Press) pp. 111–33.

Hanscombe, G. and Smyers, V.L. (1987) *Writing for Their Lives, the Modernist Women 1910–1940* (London: The Women's Press).

Harding, E. (1933, rep. 1970) *The Way of All Women: A Psychological Interpretation* (London: Longmans Green & Co.).

Harding, J. (1994) 'Making a drama out of difference: *Portrait of a Marriage*', in Diane Hamer and Belinda Budge (eds), *The Good, the Bad and the Gorgeous, Popular Culture's Romance with Lesbianism* (London: Pandora) pp. 119–31.

Harman, C. (1989) *Sylvia Townsend Warner, A Biography* (London: Chatto & Windus).

Harman, C. (ed.) (1995) *The Diaries of Sylvia Townsend Warner* (London: Virago).

Hart, L. (1994) *Fatal Women, Lesbian Sexuality and the Mark of Aggression* (London: Routledge).

Healey, E. (1978) *Lady Unknown: The Life of Angela Burdett-Coutts* (London: Sidgwick & Jackson).

Healey, E. and Mason, A. (eds) (1994) *Stonewall 25, The Making of the Lesbian and Gay Community in Britain* (London: Virago).

Hebdige, D. (1993) 'From culture to hegemony', in Simon During (ed.), *The Cultural Studies Reader* (London & New York: Routledge) pp. 357–67.

Hegel, G.W.F. (1977) *The Phenomenology of Spirit*, trans. A.V. Miller (Oxford: Clarendon Press).

Heilbrun, C. (1985) 'Women's autobiographical writing: new prose forms', *Prose Studies, 8, 2*, 20–7.

—— (1988) 'Non-autobiographies of "privileged" women: England and America', in Bella Brodzki and Celeste Schenck (eds), *Life/Lines: Theorizing Women's Autobiography* (Ithaca, NY & London: Cornell University Press) pp. 62–76.

—— (1989) *Writing a Woman's Life* (London: The Women's Press).

Hennegan, A. (1986) Introduction, Vita Sackville-West, *Pepita* (1937) (London: Virago).

Hill, W.T. (1956) *Octavia Hill, Pioneer of the National Trust and Housing Reformer* (London: Hutchinson).

Hinds, H. (1995) '*Oranges Are Not the Only Fruit*: reaching audiences other lesbian texts cannot reach', in Tamsin Wilton (ed.), *Immortal, Invisible, Lesbians and the Moving Image* (London & New York: Routledge) pp. 52–69.

Hitchman, J. (1979) *Such a Strange Lady: A Biography of Dorothy L. Sayers* (Sevenoaks: New English Library).

Hobby, E. (1988) *Virtue of Necessity, English Women's Writing, 1646–1688* (London: Virago).

Hobby, E. and White, C. (eds) (1991) *What Lesbians Do in Books* (London: The Women's Press).

Hoogland, R.C. (1994a) 'Perverted knowledge: lesbian sexuality and theoretical practice', *Journal of Gender Studies, 3, 1*, 15–29.

—— (1994b) *Elizabeth Bowen, A Reputation in Writing* (New York & London: New York University Press).

Horner, A. and Zlosnik, S. (1998) *Daphne du Maurier, Writing, Identity and the Gothic Imagination* (Basingstoke: Macmillan).

Hughes, A. (1987) *Politics, Society and Civil War in Warwickshire, 1620–1660* (Cambridge: Cambridge University Press).

Hunt, A. (1935) *Reminiscences* (Shrewsbury: Wilding & Son).

—— (1938) *This is My Life* (London & Glasgow: Blackie).

Hunter, F. (1994) 'Hilda Matheson and the BBC 1926–1940', in Sybil Oldfield, (ed.), *This Working-Day World: Women's Lives and Culture(s) in Britain 1914–45* (London: Taylor & Francis) pp. 171–83.

Hurston, Z.N. (1937, rep. 1978) *Their Eyes Were Watching God* (Urbana, IL: University of Illinois Press).

Hutcheon, L. (1989) *The Politics of Postmodernism* (New York & London: Routledge).

Hutton, L. (1935) *The Single Woman and Her Emotional Problems* (London: Bailiere, Tindall & Cox).

Iremonger, L. (1957) *The Ghosts of Versailles: Miss Moberly and Miss Jourdain and Their Adventure* (London: Faber and Faber).

Irigaray, L. (1977) *Ce Sexe Qui N'en Est Pas Un* (Paris: Editions de Minuit).

—— (1982, trans. 1992) *Elemental Passions*, trans. Joanne Collie and Judith Still (London: The Athlone Press).

—— (1985) *Speculum of the Other Woman*, trans. Gillian C. Gill (Ithaca, NY: Cornell University Press).

Jacob, N. (1940) *Me in War-Time* (London: Hutchinson).

—— (1964) *Me – and the Stags* (London: William Kimber).

Jacobs, H. (1861, rep. 1973) *Incidents in the Life of a Slave Girl, Written by Herself*, ed. Lydia Maria Child (New York: Harcourt Brace Jovanovich).

Jagose, A. (1994) *Lesbian Utopics* (New York & London: Routledge).

Jauss, H.R. (1970) 'Littérature médiévale et théorie des genres', *Poetique*, 1, 1, 91.

Jay, K. (1988) *The Amazon and the Page: Natalie Clifford Barney and Renée Vivien* (Bloomington, IN: Indiana University Press).

Jeffreys, S. (1985) *The Spinster and Her Enemies: Feminism and Sexuality, 1880–1930* (London: Pandora).

—— (1989) 'Does it matter if they did it?', in Lesbian History Group, *Not a Passing Phase, Reclaiming Lesbians in History 1840–1985* (London: The Women's Press) pp. 9–28.

—— (1994) *The Lesbian Heresy: A Feminist Perspective on the Lesbian Sexual Revolution* (London: The Women's Press).

—— (1996) 'The essential lesbian', in Lynne Harne and Elaine Miller (eds), *All The Rage, Reasserting Radical Lesbian Feminism* (London: The Women's Press).

Jelinek, E. (1980) 'Women's autobiography and the male tradition', in Estelle Jelinek (ed.), *Women's Autobiography: Essays in Criticism* (Bloomington, IN: Indiana University Press).

Johnson, P. (1989) '"The best friend whom life has given me": does Winifred Holtby have a place in lesbian history?', in Lesbian History Group, *Not A Passing Phase, Reclaiming Lesbians in History, 1840–1985* (London: The Women's Press) pp. 141–57.

Jones, E. (1927) 'The early development of female sexuality', *International Journal of Psycho-Analysis*, 8, 459–72.

Jowell, R., Witherspoon, S. and Brook, L. with Taylor, B. (eds) (1990) *British Social Attitudes, The Seventh Report* (Aldershot: Gower, Social and Community Planning Research).

Jullian, P. and Phillips, J. (1976) *The Other Woman, A Life of Violet Trefusis* (Boston, MA: Houghton Mifflin Co.).

Kabbani, R. (1988) *Europe's Myth of Orient* (London: Pandora).

Kaplan, C. (1986) *Sea Changes* (London: Virago).

Karimjee, M. (1991) 'In search of an image', in Tessa Boffin and Jean Fraser (eds), *Stolen Glances, Lesbians Take Photographs* (London: Pandora Press) pp. 30–3.

Keith-Cohen, A. (1987) 'Notes on *Time & Tide* and Lady Rhondda' (Fawcett Library).

Kellerman, F. (1978) 'A new key to Virginia Woolf's *Orlando'*, *English Studies, 59*, 138–50.

Kelsall, M. (1993) 'Manderley revisited: *Rebecca* and the English country House', *Proceedings of the British Academy, 82*, 303–15.

Kenealy, A. (1920) *Feminism and Sex Extinction* (London: T. Fisher Unwin).

Kennard, J.E. (1985) 'Ourself behind ourself: a theory for lesbian readers', *Signs, 9, 4* (Summer), 157–68.

Kiernan, J. (1891) 'Psychological aspects of the sexual appetite', *Alienist and Neurologist, 12*, 188–219.

Kimmel, D.C. and Sang, B.E. (1995) 'Lesbians and gay men in midlife', in Anthony R. D'Augelli and Charlotte J. Patterson (eds), *Lesbian, Gay and Bisexual Identities Over the Lifespan, Psychological Perspectives* (Oxford & New York: Oxford University Press) pp. 190–214.

King, F. (1993) *Yesterday Came Suddenly* (London: Constable).

Kitzinger, C. (1987) *The Social Construction of Lesbianism* (London: Sage Publications).

—— (1995) 'Social constructionism: implications for gay and lesbian psychology', in Anthony R. D'Augelli and Charlotte J Patterson (eds), *Lesbian, Gay and Bisexual Identities Over the Lifespan, Psychological Perspectives* (Oxford & New York: Oxford University Press) pp. 136–64.

Klein, Y.M. (1990) 'Myth and community in recent lesbian autobiographical fiction', in Karla Jay and Joanne Glasgow (eds), *Lesbian Texts and Contexts: Radical Revisions* (London: Onlywomen Press, 1992) pp. 330–8.

Knopp, S.E. (1988) 'Sapphism and the subversiveness of *Orlando'*, *P.M.L.A., 103/1*, 24–34.

Krafft-Ebing, R. von (1894) *Psychopathia Sexualis, with Especial Reference to Contrary Sexual Instinct: A Medico-Legal Study*, trans. Charles Gilbert Chaddock (Philadelphia, PA: F.A. Davis) (rep. 1997, London: Velvet Publications).

Kristeva, J. (1982) *Powers of Horror: An Essay in Abjection*, trans. Leon S. Roudiez (New York: Columbia University Press).

—— (1991) *Strangers to Ourselves*, trans. Leon S. Roudiez (New York: Columbia University Press).

L.M. (Ida Baker) (1985) *Katherine Mansfield, The Memories of LM* (London: Virago).

Lacan, J. (1977) *Ecrits: a Selection*, trans. Alan Sheridan (London: Tavistock).

—— (1979, rep. 1981) *The Four Fundamental Concepts of Psychoanalysis*, trans. Alan Sheridan (New York: W.W. Norton and Co.).

Lee, H. (1987) 'Katherine Unveiled', review of Claire Tomalin, *Katherine Mansfield: A Secret Life* (London: Viking 1987), *Observer*, 1 November 1987.

—— (1996, rep. 1997) *Virginia Woolf* (London: Vintage).

Lee, S. (1896) 'National Biography', *Cornhill, NS 24*, p. 265.

—— (1900) 'Statistical account', in Publisher's Note, *Dictionary of National Biography* (Oxford: Oxford University Press, 1975).

—— (1996) 'Lesbian artist?', in Peter Horne and Reina Lewis (eds), *Outlooks, Lesbian and Gay Sexualities and Visual Cultures* (London & New York: Routledge) pp. 120–5.

Lejeune, P. (1971) *L'Autobiographie en France* (Paris: Armand Colin).

—— (1989) *On Autobiography*, ed. Paul John Eakin, trans. Katherine Leary (Minneapolis, MN: University of Minnesota Press).

Lesbian History Group (1989) *Not A Passing Phase: Reclaiming Lesbians in History 1840–1985* (London: The Women's Press).

Lewis, G. (1985) *Somerville and Ross: The World of the Irish RM* (London: Viking).

—— (1988) *Eva Gore-Booth and Esther Roper* (London: Pandora).

Lewis, J. (1994) 'Hippocratic oafs', review of Shirley Roberts, *Sophia Jex-Blake: A Woman Pioneer in Nineteenth-Century Reform* (London: Routledge, 1994) *Times Higher*, 14 January 1994, p. 20.

Lewis, R. and Rolley, K. (1996) 'Ad(dressing) the dyke: lesbian looks and lesbians looking', in Peter Horne and Reina Lewis (eds), *Outlooks, Lesbian and Gay Sexualities and Visual Cultures* (London & New York: Routledge) pp. 178–90.

Lewis, W. (1926) 'Family and feminism', in *The Art of Being Ruled* (London: Chatto & Windus).

Lichtenstein, P.M. (1921) 'The "fairy" and his lady lover', *Medical Review of Reviews, 27*, 369–74.

Liddington, J. (1994) *Presenting the Past: Anne Lister of Halifax (1791–1840)* (Hebden Bridge: Pennine Press).

Lister, A. (1988) *I Know My Own Heart, The Diaries of Anne Lister (1791–1840)* , ed. Helena Whitbread (London: Virago).

Lock, J. (1979) *The British Policewoman: Her Story* (London: Robert Hale).

Lowry, E. (1998) 'Pull up now yourself', review of Margaret Scott (ed.), *The Katherine Mansfield Notebooks* (Canterbury, NZ: Lincoln University Press 1998), *Times Literary Supplement*, 4 September 1998, pp. 3–4.

Lutyens, E. (1972) *A Goldfish Bowl* (London: Cassell).

Lyotard, J.F. (1989) *The Lyotard Reader*, ed. Andrew Benjamin (Oxford: Blackwell).

Mackworth, C. (1987) *Ends of the World* (Manchester: Carcanet).

Maitland, S. (1986) *Vesta Tilley* (London: Virago)

Manning, R. (1987) *A Corridor of Mirrors* (London: The Women's Press).

Manvell, R. (1968) *Ellen Terry* (London: Heinemann).

Marcus, J. (1990) 'The Woolf and The Well', in Karla Jay and Joanne Glasgow (eds), *Lesbian Texts and Contexts: Radical Revisions* (New York & London: New York University Press) pp. 164–79.

Marcus, L. (1994) *Auto/biographical Discourses: Theory, Criticism and Practice* (Manchester & New York: Manchester University Press).

Margaret, Duchess of Newcastle (1892) 'A true relation of my birth, breeding and life', in Mark Antony Lover (ed.), *The Lives of William Cavendish, Duke of Newcastle and of His Wife, Margaret, Duchess of Newcastle* (London: John Russell).

Markowe, L.A. (1996) *Redefining the Self, Coming Out as Lesbian* (Cambridge: Polity Press).

Marshment, M. and Hallam, J. (1994) 'From string of knots to orange box: lesbianism on prime time', in Diane Hamer and Belinda Budge (eds), *The*

Good, the Bad and the Gorgeous, Popular Culture's Romance with Lesbianism (London: Pandora) pp. 142–65.

Martin, B. (1988) 'Lesbian identity and autobiographical difference(s)', in Bella Brodzki and Celeste Schenck (eds), *Life/Lines: Theorizing Women's Autobiography* (Ithaca, NY & London: Cornell University Press) pp. 77–103.

Mason, M.G. and Greed, C.H. (eds) (1979) *Journeys: Autobiographical Writings by Women* (Boston, MA: G.K. Hall).

Masters, B. (1991) *E.F. Benson* (London: Chatto & Windus).

Mattelart, A., Delcourt, X. and Mattelart, M. (1993) 'International image markets', in Simon During (ed.), *The Cultural Studies Reader* (London & New York: Routledge) pp. 421–37.

Maurice, C.E. (ed.) (1913) *Life of Octavia Hill, as Told in her Letters* (London: Macmillan).

Maurois, A. (1924) *Ariel: A Shelley Romance*, trans. Ella d'Arcy (London: Bodley Head).

Mazzini, G. (1844/58, trans. 1907) *The Duties of Man* (New York: Doubleday).

McCormick, I. (ed.) (1997) *Secret Sexualities: a Sourcebook of Seventeenth and Eighteenth Century Writing* (London & New York: Routledge).

McIntosh, M. (1968) 'The homosexual role', *Social Problems, 16(2)*, 182–92 (rep. 1981) Kenneth Plummer (ed.), *The Making of the Modern Homosexual* (London: Hutchinson) pp. 30–49.

McKay, N.Y. (1988) 'Race, gender and cultural context in Zora Neale Hurston's *Dust Tracks on a Road*', in Bella Brodzki and Celeste Schenck (eds), *Life/Lines, Theorizing Women's Autobiography* (Ithaca, NY & London: Cornell University Press), pp. 175–88.

Meagher, J.F.W. (1929) 'Homosexuality: its psychobiological and psychopathological significance', *Urologic and Cutaneous Review, 33*, 505–18.

Meese, E. (1990) 'Theorizing lesbian: writing – a love letter', in Karla Jay and Joanne Glasgow (eds), *Lesbian Texts and Contexts* (New York & London: New York University Press) pp. 70–87.

Melville, J. (1987) *Ellen and Edy: a Biography of Ellen Terry and her Daughter Edith Craig 1847–1947* (London: Pandora).

Merck, M. (1991) '"Transforming the suit": a century of lesbian self-portraits', in Tessa Boffin and Jean Fraser (eds), *Stolen Glances, Lesbians Take Photographs* (London: Pandora) pp. 22–9.

—— (1993) *Perversions: Deviant Readings* (London: Virago).

Merritt, S. (1998) 'Inverted Dogmas', review of Diana Souhami, *The Trials of Radclyffe Hall* (London: Weidenfield & Nicolson, 1988) *Guardian Weekly*, 23 August 1998, p. 28.

Messud, C. (1992) 'The body politic', *Guardian 2*, 26 August 1992.

Miller, E. (1989) 'Through all changes and through all chances: the relationship of Ellen Nussey and Charlotte Brontë', in Lesbian History Group, *Not A Passing Phase* (London: The Women's Press) pp. 29–54.

Miller, J.H. (1991) *Tropes, Parables, Performatives: Essays on Twentieth Century Literature* (Durham, NC: Duke University Press).

Miller, L. (1998) 'John, Ladye and Una', review of Diana Souhami, *The Trials of Radclyffe Hall* (London: Weidenfeld & Nicolson 1998), *Times Literary Supplement*, 14 August 1998.

Miller, N. (1995) *Out of the Past, Gay and Lesbian History from 1869 to the Present* (New York & London: Vintage).

Miller, N.K. (1988) *Subject to Change: Reading Feminist Writing* (New York: Columbia University Press).

—— (1991) *Getting Personal: Feminist Occasions and Other Autobiographical Acts* (New York: Routledge).

Moi, T. (1985, rep. 1995) *Sexual/ Textual Politics: Feminist Literary Theory* (London & New York: Routledge).

Montefiore, J. (1987) *Feminism and Poetry, Language, Experience, Identity in Women's Writing* (London & New York: Pandora).

—— (1993) 'Sylvia Townsend Warner: authority and the biographer's moral sense', in David Ellis (ed.), *Imitating Art, Essays in Biography* (London & Boulder, CO: Pluto Press) pp. 124–48.

—— (1994) 'Case-histories versus the "undeliberate dream": men and women writing the self in the 1930s', in Gabriele Griffin (ed.), *Difference in View: Women and Modernism* (London: Taylor & Francis) pp. 56–74.

—— (1996) *Men and Women Writers of the 1930s, the Dangerous Flood of History* (London & New York: Routledge).

—— (1998) 'Jealousy in Conneticut', review of Susanna Pinney (ed.), *I'll Stand By You, Selected letters of Sylvia Townsend Warner and Valentine Ackland* (London: Pimlico Paperbacks 1998), *Times Literary Supplement*, 3 July 1998, p. 10.

Montgomery-Massingberd, H. (1991) 'Beyond the Irish RM, Somerville and Ross, those devoted spinster cousins', *Daily Telegraph*, 15 June 1991 (Fawcett Library).

Morley, A. with Stanley, L. (1988) *The Life and Death of Emily Wilding Davison* (with Gertrude Colmore's *The Life of Emily Davison*) (London: The Women's Press).

Morrison, T. (1984, rep. 1990) 'Rootedness: the ancestor as foundation', in Dennis Walder (ed.), *Literature in the Modern World, Critical Essays and Documents* (Oxford: Oxford University Press).

Mulford, W. (1988) *This Narrow Place* (London: Pandora).

Mullan, B. (1987) *The Enid Blyton Story* (Twickenham: Boxtree).

Munt, S. (ed.) (1992) *New Lesbian Criticism: Literary and Cultural Readings* (Hemel Hempstead: Harvester Wheatsheaf).

Naffine, N. (1987) *Female Crime: The Construction of Women in Criminology* (Boston, MA: Allen & Unwin).

Nalbantian, S. (1994, rep. 1997) *Aesthetic Autobiography, From Life to Art in Marcel Proust, James Joyce, Virginia Woolf and Anais Nin* (London: Macmillan).

Nead, L. (1998) 'The naked and the damned', *Times Higher*, 10 April 1998, p. 15.

Neild, S. and Pearson, R. (1992) *Women Like Us* (London: The Women's Press).

Neill, E. (1997) 'Jobbery, snobbery, robbery', review of David Nokes, *Jane Austen: A Life* (London: Fourth Estate 1997), *Times Higher*, 21 November 1997, p. 27.

Newton, E. (1984) 'The mythic mannish lesbian: Radclyffe Hall and the new woman', *Signs, 9, 4* (Summer) 557–75.

O'Brien, M. (1981) *The Politics of Reproduction* (London: Routledge).

O'Connor, N. and Ryan, J. (1993) *Wild Desires and Mistaken Identities, Lesbianism and Psychoanalysis* (London: Virago).

Olney, J. (1972) *Metaphors of Self: The Meaning of Autobiography* (Princeton, NJ: Princeton University Press).

Olney, J. (ed.) (1980) *Autobiography: Essays Theoretical and Critical* (Princeton, NJ: Princeton University Press).

Omosupe, E. (1991) 'Black/lesbian/bulldagger', *differences, 3, 2*, 101–11.

Oosterhuis, H. (1997) 'Richard von Krafft-Ebing's "Step-Children of Nature": psychiatry and the meaning of homosexual identity', in Vernon A. Rosario, (ed.), *Science and Homosexualities* (New York & London: Routledge) pp. 67–88.

Oram, A. (1989) ' "Embittered, sexless or homosexual": attacks on spinster teachers 1918–1939', in Lesbian History Group, *Not A Passing Phase* (London: The Women's Press) pp. 99–118.

Orr, D. (1995) 'Say Grace', *Guardian Weekend*, 22 July 1995, pp. 12–16.

Pankhurst, C. (1913) *The Great Scourge and How to End It* (London: E. Pankhurst).

——— (1931, rep. 1977) *The Suffragette Movement* (London: Virago).

Parker, A. and Sedgwick, E.K. (eds) (1995) *Performativity and Performance* (London & New York: Routledge).

Patmore, D. (1971) '"Passionate friends", interview with Natalie Barney', *Observer Supplement*, 5 September 1971 (Fawcett Library).

Pfeffer, N. (1985) 'The hidden pathology of the male reproductive system', in Hilary Hormans (ed.), *The Sexual Politics of Reproduction* (London: Gower) pp. 25–39.

Plaza, M. (1978) '"Phallomorphic Power" and the Psychology of "Woman"', *Ideology and Consciousness, 4*, pp. 4–36.

Plummer, K. (1981) *The Making of the Modern Homosexual* (London: Hutchinson).

Ponse, B. (1978) *Identities in the Lesbian World: The Social Construction of Self* (Westport, CT: Greenwood Press).

Porter, R. (ed.) (1997) Introduction, *Rewriting the Self, Histories from the Renaissance to the Present* (London & New York: Routledge) pp. 1–14.

Posener, J. (1991) 'Dirty girls' guide to London', in Tessa Boffin and Jean Fraser (eds), *Stolen Glances, Lesbians Take Photographs* (London: Pandora Press) pp. 204–7.

Potter, S. (1994) *Orlando (Script to the Film)* (London & Boston, MA: Faber and Faber).

Powell, K. (1990) Article on Octavia Hill, *Daily Telegraph*, 20 January 1990 (Fawcett Library).

Probyn, E. (1996) *Outside Belongings* (London & New York: Routledge).

Raban, J. (1987) *For Love and Money* (New York & London: Routledge).

Ragland-Sullivan, E. (1986) *Jacques Lacan and the Philosophy of Psychoanalysis* (Urbana, IL: University of Illinois Press).

Raitt, S. (1993, rep. 1997) *Vita and Virginia, The Work and Friendship of V. Sackville-West and Virginia Woolf* (Oxford: Clarendon).

——— (ed.) (1995) Introduction, *Volcanoes and Pearl Divers, Essays in Lesbian Feminist Studies* (London: Onlywomen Press) pp. vii–xvii.

Raymond, E. (1948) *In the Steps of the Brontës* (London: Rich & Cowan).

Raymond, J. (1986) *A Passion for Friends: Toward a Philosophy of Female Affection* (London: The Women's Press).

Rich, A. (1979, rep. 1980) *On Lies, Secrets and Silences, Selected Prose 1966–1978* (London: Virago).

——— (1980) 'Compulsory heterosexuality and lesbian existence', *Signs, 5, 4*, 631–60.

Richardson, D. (1981) 'Lesbian identities', in J. Hart and D. Richardson (eds), *The Theory and Practice of Homosexuality* (London: Routledge & Kegan Paul) pp. 111–24.

Rimbaud, A. (1871, rep. 1972) Letter to Paul Demeny, 15 May 1871, in *Œuvres Complètes* (Paris: Gallimard, Pleiade).

Rivers, J.E. (1980) *Proust and the Art of Love: The Aesthetics of Sexuality in the Life, Times and Art of Marcel Proust* (New York: Columbia University Press).

Roberts, C. (1952) *One Year of Life* (London: Gollancz).

Roberts, S. (1994) *Sophia Jex-Blake: a Woman Pioneer in Nineteenth Century Reform* (London: Routledge).

Robins, E. (1980) *The Convert*, ed. and introduction Jane Marcus (London: The Women's Press).

Robson, R. (1992) *Lesbian (Out)law: Survival Under the Rule of Law* (Ithaca, NY: Firebrand Books).

Roget's Thesaurus of English Words and Phrases (1994) (London: Longman).

Rolley, K. (1990) 'Cutting a dash: the dress of Radclyffe Hall and Una Troubridge', *Feminist Review, 35*, 54–66.

Roof, J. (1991) *A Lure of Knowledge: Lesbian Sexuality and Theory* (New York: Columbia University Press).

Roper, E. (ed.) (1934) *The Prison Letters of Countess Markievicz* (London: Longman).

Rosanoff, A.J. (1929) 'Human sexuality, normal and abnormal, from a psychiatric standpoint', *Urologic and Cutaneous Review, 33*, 523–30.

Rosario, V.A. (1997) ' Homosexual bio-histories: genetic nostalgias and the quest for paternity' in his *Science and Homosexualities* (London & New York: Routledge) pp. 1–25.

Rose, J. (1991, rep. 1992) *The Haunting of Sylvia Plath* (London: Virago).

Rose, M.B. (1986) 'Gender, genre and history. Seventeenth century Englishwomen and the art of autobiography', in Mary Beth Rose (ed.), *Women in the Middle Ages and the Renaissance* (Syracuse, N.Y.: Syracuse University Press) pp. 245–78.

Rowbotham, S. (1973a) *Woman's Consciousness, Man's World* (London: Penguin Books).

—— (1973b) *Hidden From History: Three Hundred Years of Women's Oppression and the Fight Against It* (London: Pluto Press).

Rubin, G. (1993) 'Thinking sex: notes for a radical theory of the politics of sexuality', in Henry Abelove, Michele Aina Barate and David M. Halperin (eds), *The Lesbian and Gay Studies Reader* (New York: Routledge).

Ruehl, S. (1982) 'Inverts and experts: Radclyffe Hall and the lesbian identity', in Rosalind Brunt and Caroline Rowan (eds), *Feminism, Culture and Politics* (London: Lawrence & Wishart) pp. 15–35.

—— (1991) 'Developing identities', in Tessa Boffin and Jean Fraser (eds), *Stolen Glances, Lesbians Take Photographs* (London: Pandora) pp. 34–41.

Rule, J. (1975) *Lesbian Images* (Garden City, NJ: Doubleday and Co.).

Rybczinski, W. (1986) *Home: A Short History of the Idea* (New York: Viking Penguin).

Sackville-West, V. (1922, rep. 1994) *Knole and the Sackvilles* (London: The National Trust).

—— (ed.) (1923) *The Diary of Lady Anne Clifford* (London: Heinemann).

—— (1924, rep. 1974) *Challenge* (London: Virago).

—— (1926) *The Land* (London: Heinemann).

—— (1930, rep. 1983) *The Edwardians* (London: Virago).

—— (1937, rep. 1986) *Pepita* (London: Virago).

—— (1938) *Solitude* (London: Hogarth Press).

—— (1961) *No Signposts in the Sea* (London: Michael Joseph).

—— (1973, rep. 1997) *Portrait of a Marriage*, ed. Nigel Nicolson (London: Phoenix).

—— (1985) *The Letters of Vita Sackville West to Virginia Woolf*, ed. Louise DeSalvo and Mitchell A. Leaska (New York: William Morrow & Co.).

—— (1992, rep. 1993) *Vita & Harold, The Letters of Vita Sackville-West & Harold Nicolson 1910–1962*, ed. Nigel Nicolson (London: Phoenix).

Said, E.W. (1978) *Orientalism* (London: Routledge & Kegan Paul).

—— (1993, rep. 1994) *Culture and Imperialism* (London: Vintage).

St John, C. (1935) *Christine Murrell, M.D.* (London: Williams & Norgate).

Sarton, M. (1969, rep. 1995) *I Knew a Phoenix, Sketches for an Autobiography* (London: The Women's Press).

—— (1976, rep. 1996) *A World of Light, Portraits and Celebrations* (London: The Women's Press).

—— (1997) *Selected Letters 1916–1954*, ed. Susan Sherman (London: The Women's Press).

Savin-Williams, R.C. (1995) 'Lesbian, gay male and bisexual adolescents', in Anthony R. D'Augelli and Charlotte J. Patterson (eds), *Lesbian, Gay and Bisexual Identities Over the Lifespan, Psychological Perspectives* (Oxford & New York: Oxford University Press) pp. 165–89.

Schlack, B.A. (1979) *Continuing Presences, Virginia Woolf's Use of Literary Allusion* (University Park, PA & London: Pennsylvania State University Press).

Schreiner, O. (1911) *Woman and Labour* (London: T. Fisher Unwin).

Schwarz, J. (1986) *Radical Feminists of Heterodoxy* (Lebanon, NH: New Victoria Publishers).

Sedgwick, E.K. (1985) *Between Men: English Literature and Male Homosocial Desire* (New York: Columbia University Press).

—— (1986) *The Coherence of Gothic Conventions* (London & New York: Methuen).

—— (1990) *Epistemology of the Closet* (Berkeley, CA: University of California Press).

—— (1994) *Tendencies* (London: Routledge).

Shepherd, S. and Wallis, M. (1989) 'Introduction', *Coming on Strong: Gay Politics and Culture* (London: Unwin Hyman).

Shorter, C. (1905) *Charlotte Brontë and Her Sisters* (London: Hodder).

Showalter, E. (1990) *Sexual Anarchy: Gender and Culture at the Fin-de-Siècle* (New York: Viking).

Sibley, D. (1995) *Geographies of Exclusion* (London: Routledge).

Sigsworth, E.M. and Wyke, T.J. (1972) 'A study in Victorian prostitution and venereal disease', in Martha Vicinus (ed.), *Suffer and Be Still* (Bloomington, IN & London: Indiana University Press) pp. 62–80.

Sischy, I. (1989) 'White and black', *New Yorker*, 13 November 1989, pp. 124–46.

Smith, A.M. (1991) 'Which one's the pretender? Section 28 and lesbian representation', in Tessa Boffin and Jean Fraser (eds), *Stolen Glances, Lesbians Take Photographs* (London: Pandora) pp. 128–39.

—— (1994) *New Right Discourse on Race and Sexuality, Britain 1968–1990* (Cambridge: Cambridge University Press).

Smith, S. (1991) 'The autobiographical manifesto: identities, temporalities, politics', in Shirley Neuman (ed.), *Autobiography and Questions of Gender* (London: Frank Cass) pp. 186–212.

Smyth, C. (1996) 'Dyke! Fag! Centurion! Whore! *An Appreciation of Tessa Boffin'*, in Peter Horne and Reina Lewis (eds), *Outlooks, Lesbian and Gay Sexualities and Visual Cultures* (London & New York: Routledge) pp. 109–12.

Soja, E. (1993) 'History: geography: modernity', in Simon During (ed.), *The Cultural Studies Reader* (London & New York: Routledge) pp. 135–50.

Sommerville, P. (1992) 'Homelessness and the meaning of home: rooflessness or rootedness?', *International Journal of Urban and Regional Research, 16*, 528–39.

Sontag, S. (1977, rep. 1984) *On Photography* (Harmondsworth: Penguin Books).

Souhami, D. (1988, rep. 1989) *Gluck: her Biography* (London: Pandora).

—— (1991, rep. 1993) *Gertrude and Alice* (London: Pandora).

—— (1994, rep. 1996) *Greta and Cecil* (London: Flamingo).

—— (1996, rep. 1997) *Mrs Keppel and her Daughter* (London: Flamingo).

Spain, N. (1949) *Poison for Teacher* (London: Hutchinson).

—— (1952) *Out Damned Tot* (London: Hutchinson).

Spalding, F. (1989) *Stevie Smith, A Biography* (New York & London: Norton).

Spitzka, E.C. (1888) 'The Whitechapel murders: their medico-legal and historical aspects', *Journal of Nervous and Mental Disorders, 13*, 765–78.

Spivak, G.C. (1988) 'Can the subaltern speak?', in Cary Nelson and Lawrence Grossberg (eds), *Marxism and the Interpretation of Culture* (New York: New York Literary Forum) pp. 271–313.

—— (1990) *The Post-Colonial Critic: Interviews, Statements, Dialogues* (London: Routledge).

Sprigge, E. (1973) *The Life of Ivy Compton-Burnett* (London: Gollancz).

Sprinker, M. (1980) 'Fictions of the self: the end of autobiography', in James Olney (ed.), *Autobiography: Essays Theoretical and Critical* (Princeton, NJ: Princeton University Press) pp. 321–44.

Spurling, H. (1974, rep. 1995) *Ivy, The Life of I. Compton-Burnett* (London: Richard Cohen Books).

—— (1990) review of Gillian Darley, *Octavia Hill: A Life* (London: Constable), *Guardian*?, Unlabelled (FL).

Stanley, L. (1991) 'Feminist auto/biography and feminist epistemology', in Jane Aaron and Sylvia Walby (eds), *Out of the Margins: Women's Studies in the Nineties* (London, New York, Philadelphia: The Falmer Press) pp. 204–19.

—— (1992a) *The Auto/biographical I, The Theory and Practice of Feminist Auto/biography* (Manchester & New York: Manchester University Press).

—— (1992b) 'Romantic friendship? some issues in researching lesbian history and biography', *Women's History Review, 1, 2*, 193–216.

Stanton, D.C. (1984) 'Autogynography: is the subject different?', in Domna C. Stanton (ed.), *The Female Autograph* (New York: New York Literary Forum) pp. 5–21.

Stein, E. (ed.) (1990) *Forms of Desire: Sexual Orientation and the Special Constructionist Controversy* (New York: Routledge).

Stein, G. (1933) *The Autobiography of Alice B. Toklas* (Harmondsworth: Penguin Books).

—— (1937, rep. 1971) *Everybody's Autobiography* (New York: Cooper Square).

Steinem, G. (1981) Speech to National Women's Political Caucus, Albuquerque, New Mexico (July 1981), in *The Columbia Dictionary of Quotations* (Columbia University Press).

Stendhal, R. (1995) *Gertrude Stein, in Words and Pictures* (London: Thames & Hudson).

Stimpson, C.R. (1977) 'The mind, the body and Gertrude Stein', *Critical Inquiry, 3, 3* (Spring) 489–506.

—— (1981) 'Zero degree deviancy: the lesbian novel in English', *Critical Inquiry, 8*, 363–79.

—— (1984) 'The female sociograph: the theater of Virginia Woolf's letters', in Domna C. Stanton (ed.), *The Female Autograph* (New York: New York Literary Forum) pp. 193–203.

—— (1990) 'Afterword: lesbian studies in the 1990s', in Karla Jay and Joanne Glasgow (eds), *Lesbian Texts and Contexts: Radical Revisions* (New York & London: New York University Press) pp. 377–82.

Stocks, M. (1949) *Eleanor Rathbone* (London: Gollancz).

Stoler, L.A. (1995) *Race and the Education of Desire: Foucault's History of Sexuality and the Colonial Order of Things* (Durham, NC: Duke University Press).

Stopes, M. (1918) *Married Love: A New Contribution to the Solution of Sex Difficulties* (London: A.C. Fifield).

—— (1928, rep. 1953) *Enduring Passion. Further New Contributions to the Solution of Sex Difficulties, Being the Continuation of Married Love* (London: G.P. Putnam's Sons).

Stott, C. (1969) Interview with Maureen Duffy, *Guardian*, 30 January 1969 (Fawcett Library).

Stott, M. (1978) *Organisation Women: The Story of the National Union of Townswomens' Guilds* (London: Heinemann).

Summerscale, K. (1997) *The Queen of Whale Cay, The Eccentric Story of 'Joe' Carstairs, Fastest Woman on Water* (London: Fourth Estate).

Symonds, J.A. (1928, rep. 1984) *Sexual Inversion* (New York: Bell).

Talmey, B.S. (1904, rep. 1910) *Woman: A Treatise on the Normal Pathological Emotions of Feminine Love* (New York: Practitioners Publishing Co.).

Tiefer, L. (1987) 'Social constructionism and the study of homosexuality', in P. Shaver and C. Hendrick (eds), *Sex and Gender* (London: Sage).

Tilly, L.A. and Scott, J.W. (1978) *Women, Work and Family* (New York: Rinehart & Winston).

Todd, M. (1918) *The Life of Sophia Jex-Blake* (London: Macmillan).

Toklas, A.B. (1963, rep. 1989) *What is Remembered, an Autobiography* (Harmondsworth: Penguin Books).

Tomalin, C. (1987, rep. 1988) *Katherine Mansfield, a Secret Life* (New York: St. Martin's Press).

Trautmann, J. (1973) *The Jessamy Brides: The Friendship of Virginia Woolf and V. Sackville-West* (University Park, PA: Pennsylvania State University Studies No. 36).

Trefusis, V. (1952) *Don't Look Round* (London: Hutchinson).

—— (1989, rep. 1991) *Violet to Vita, The Letters of Violet Trefusis to Vita Sackville-West, 1910–21*, ed. Mitchell A. Leaska and John Phillips (London: Mandarin).

Turner, J. (1994) 'Preacher woman', *Guardian Weekend*, 18 June 1994, pp. 18–25.

Uglow, J. (1993) 'Unsolved crimes of the heart', review of Barbara Reynolds, *Dorothy L. Sayers: Her Life and Soul* (London: Hodder 1993) *Independent on Sunday*, 21 March 1993, p. 30.

Valentine, G. (1998) '"Sticks and stones may break my bones": a personal geography of harassment', *Antipode, 30, 4*, 305–32.

Vallance, E. (1982) *Women in the House: Study of Women MPs* (London: The Athlone Press).

Vicinus, M. (1984) 'Distance and desire: English boarding school friendships', *Signs, 9, 4* (Summer) 600–22.

—— (1985) *Independent Women. Work and Community for Single Women 1850–1920* (London: Virago).

Viner, K. (1997) 'The bigger picture', *Guardian*, 30 September 1997, pp. 4–5.

Wallace, J. (1998) 'The feminine mystique', *Times Higher*, 18 September 1998, p. 19.

Walker, A. (1984) *In Search of Our Mothers' Gardens: Womanist Prose* (London: The Women's Press).

Walker, C.F. (1994) 'Sally Potter', in *Ecstasy, Ecstasy, Ecstasy. She Said. Women's Art in Britain; a Partial View* (Manchester: Cornerhouse) pp. 32–8.

Walkerdine, V. (1990) *Schoolgirl Fictions* (London & New York: Verso).

Walter, N. (1995) 'The passionate governess', review of Margaret Smith (ed.), *The Letters of Charlotte Bronte, Volume 1, 1829–1847* (Oxford: Oxford University Press 1995,) *Guardian*, 21 July 1995, p. 7.

—— (1996) 'Life comes breaking in', review of Hermione Lee, *Virginia Woolf* (London: Chatto 1996) *The Guardian*, 12 September 1996, p. 18.

—— (1997) 'Not divided', review of Sally Cline, *Radclyffe Hall: A Woman Called John* (London: John Murray, 1997) *Guardian*, 10 July 1997, pp. 14–15.

Warland, B. (ed.), (1991) *Inversions: Writings by Dykes, Queers and Lesbians* (London: Open Letters).

Warner, M. (1993) Introduction in Michael Warner (ed.), *Fear of a Queer Planet: Queer Politics and Social Theory* (Minneapolis, MN: University of Minnesota Press).

Weeks, J. (1977) *Coming Out: Homosexual Politics in Britain From the Nineteenth Century to the Present* (London: Quartet).

—— (1981, rep. 1997) *Sex, Politics and Society, the Regulation of Sexuality Since 1800*, 2nd edn (London & New York: Longman).

—— (1995) *Invented Moralities: Sexual Values in An Age of Uncertainty* (London: Polity Press).

Weiss, A. (1995) *Paris was a Woman* (London: Pandora).

Weissberg, L. (1996) 'Gothic spaces and the political aesthetics of Toni Morrison's *Beloved*', in Victor Sage and Allan Lloyd Smith (eds), *Modern Gothic, A Reader* (Manchester & New York: Manchester University Press) pp. 104–20.

West-Burnham, J. (1994) '"Twinned pairs of eternal opposites": the opposing selves of Vita Sackville-West', in Gabriele Griffin (ed.), *Difference in View: Women and Modernism* (London: Taylor & Francis) pp. 37–47.

White, C. (1991) '"She was not really man at all": the lesbian practice and politics of Edith Ellis', in Elaine Hobby and Chris White (eds), *What Lesbians Do in Books* (London: The Women's Press) pp. 68–85.

Whitelaw, L. (1990) *The Life and Rebellious Times of Cicely Hamilton, Actress, Writer, Suffragist* (London: The Women's Press).

—— (1995) 'Making of our lives a study: reading and writing lesbian biography', in Suzanne Raitt (ed.), *Volcanoes and Pearl Divers, Essays in Lesbian Feminist Studies* (London: Onlywomen Press), pp. 103–22.

Wilkinson, S. and Kitzinger, C. (1994) 'The social construction of heterosexuality', *Journal of Gender Studies 3, 3,* 305–14.

Wilson, A. (1992) 'Lorde and the African-American tradition', in Sally Munt (ed.), *New Lesbian Criticism: Literary and Cultural Readings* (Hemel Hempstead: Harvester Wheatsheaf).

Wilson, E. (1980) *Only Halfway to Paradise: Women in Post-War Britain: 1945–68* (London: Tavistock).

—— (1990) 'Borderlines', *New Statesman,* 2 November 1990.

Wilton, T. (ed.) (1990) *Immortal, Invisible, Lesbians and the Moving Image* (London & New York: Routledge).

—— (1995) *Lesbian Studies: Setting an Agenda* (London & New York: Routledge).

Wineapple, B. (1989) *Genêt: A Biography of Janet Flanner* (New York: Ticknor & Fields).

—— (1996, rep. 1997) *Sister Brother, Gertrude and Leo Stein* (London: Bloomsbury).

Winterson, J. (1985) *Oranges Are Not the Only Fruit* (London: Pandora).

—— (1990) *Oranges Are Not the Only Fruit – The Script* (London: Pandora).

Wittig, M. (1975, rep. 1986) *The Lesbian Body* (Boston, MA: Beacon Press).

—— (1992) *The Straight Mind and Other Essays* (London: Harvester Wheatsheaf).

Wolbarst, A.L. (1931) 'Sexual perversions: their medical and social implications', *Medical Journal and Record, 134,* 5–9, 62–5.

Wolfe, W.B. (1935, rep. 1946) *A Woman's Best Years* (Garden City, NY: Garden City Publications).

Wollstonecraft, M. (1792, rep. 1989) *Vindication of the Rights of Women,* in Janet Todd and Marilyn Butler (eds), *The Works,* 7 volumes (London: William Pickering).

Wood, C. (1995) *State of a Queer Nation, a Critique of Gay and lesbian Politics in 1990s Britain* (London: Cassell).

Woodward, K. (1988) 'Simone de Beauvoir: ageing and its discontents', in Shari Benstock (ed.), *The Private Self, Theory and Practice of Women's Autobiographical Writings* (Chapel Hill, NC & London: University of North Carolina Press) pp. 90–113.

Woolf, L. (1970) *The Journey Not the Arrival Matters: an Autobiography of the Years 1939–69* (London: Hogarth Press).

Woolf, V. (1925, rep. 1979) *Mrs Dalloway* (London: Granada).

—— (1927, rep. 1992) *To the Lighthouse* (London, Vintage).

—— (1928, rep. 1992) *Orlando* (London: Vintage).

—— (1929, rep. 1931) *A Room of One's Own* (London: Hogarth Press).

—— (1940) *Roger Fry: A Biography* (New York: Harcourt Brace).

—— (1966/67) 'The new biography', in *Collected Essays, Volume 4* (London: Hogarth Press) pp. 229–35.

—— (1975/80, rep. 1994) *The Letters of Virginia Woolf,* ed. Nigel Nicolson and Joanne Trautmann, 6 volumes (London: Hogarth Press).

—— (1977/84) *The Diary of Virginia Woolf,* ed. Anne Olivier Bell and Andrew McNeillie, 5 volumes (London: Hogarth Press).

Zaretsky, E. (1976) *Capitalism, the Family and Personal Life* (London & Boulder, CO: Pluto Press).

Zimmerman, B. (1986, rep. 1993) 'What has never been: an overview of lesbian feminist literary criticism', in Elaine Showalter (ed.), *The New Feminist Criticism, Essays on Women, Literature and Theory* (London: Virago), pp. 200–24.

—— (1992a) *The Safe Sea of Women, Lesbian Fiction 1969–1989* (London: Onlywomen Press).

—— (1992b) 'Lesbians like this and that: some notes on lesbian criticism for the nineties', in Sally Munt (ed.), *New Lesbian Criticism, Literary and Cultural Readings* (Hemel Hempstead: Harvester Wheatsheaf) pp. 1–16.

Index

Abbott, Elizabeth:
  and Cicely Hamilton 101, 205
Ackland, Valentine:
  on sexuality 63–4
  and Sylvia Townsend Warner 21,
    133, 139, 162, 187
Aids:
  and obituaries 169, 170
  advertisements 206
  and see Lesbian: Body
Allen, Mary:
  antagonism to 55
  biography 159
  known as Robert 52
  and Margaret Damer Dawson 18,
    21, 96–7
  life interviews 42
  obituaries 96–7
  and Miss Taggart and circle 16, 18,
    97
Antoinette, Marie:
  as lesbian in *Mrs Dalloway* 57
Atwood, Tony (Clare):
  burial 20
  and Edy Craig and Christopher St
    John 16, 18, 97–8, 135, 166
  obituary mention 97, 205
Austen, Jane:
  biography, reviews of 167
Author:
  death of 9, 144
Auto/biography:
  confession 83–4

and fiction 5, 78
genre 3, 4–5, 75–9, 142–50, 203
and modernism xi, 66, 75–80,
    85–6
and postmodernism xi–xii, 8,
    142–50
scope of study x–xi, 4–5
theories of self 76–9, 80–1, 142–3,
    145, 207
and see Biography, and under indi-
    vidual subject entries
Auto/biography: lesbian:
  duality in 76, 80–5, 86, 151, 165
  genre of xii, 79–103, 145–9,
    156–75, 195–6, 197–8
  reader of 66, 78–9, 92–3, 146, 149,
    197–8
  relation to black and other muted
    groups 9, 48–9, 84, 145,
    148, 196, 207

Balfour, Eve:
  air pilot 17
  companion 18
  Egyptian face 57
  masculine and feminine 51
  obituary 171, 181
  photograph 181
  representation of 129
  style 56
Bankhead, Tallulah:
  biography 157
  friends and circle 16